Beaten Into Violence

Anger, Masculinities, Alcohol, Narcotics

Dean Whittington

authorHOUSE®

AuthorHouse™
1663 Liberty Drive, Suite 200
Bloomington, IN 47403
www.authorhouse.com
Phone: 1-800-839-8640

AuthorHouse™ UK Ltd.
500 Avebury Boulevard
Central Milton Keynes, MK9 2BE
www.authorhouse.co.uk
Phone: 08001974150

First published by AuthorHouse 8/20/2007

ISBN: 978-1-4343-3118-2 (sc)
ISBN: 978-1-4343-3119-9 (hc)

Printed in the United States of America
Bloomington, Indiana

This book is printed on acid-free paper.

Contents

Acknowledgements ix

I. INTRODUCTION 1

    Hidden Lives 1

    White Masculinities 3

    Violence 5

    Drug Misuse 7

    Deptford, London SE8 8

    Orexis/DID 11

    Stereotypes 14

    Shared Care 16

II. RELATIONAL RESEARCH 21

    Resistance 23

    Sustaining Trust 26

    Being Tested 29

    Re-examining the Counselling Technique 32

    Analysis of the emerging patterns 34

    Rationale for a small-scale qualitative study 37

    Research Issues 39

    Organising the Transcripts 45

    Relational Method 50

    Researching Masculinity, Violence and Drug Misuse 54

    Key Texts - Thewelait, Cannetti, Miller, Deleuze and Guattari 56

    Drug Use and Self-medication for Pain 63

    Ontological Security 65

    Pain, Violence and Dissociation 69

    Counter Transference within Research 72

III. FATHERS AND SONS 77

    Billy's family life 78

    Fronts 81

    Masks 84

    The Mask as a Physical Act of Silence 87

Fragmentation 87

The Unspoken Fears of Gary and Simon 90

Violence Enforcing Masculinity 94

The Double bind of empathy and fear 100

Deflection of Violence and the Internalisation of Pain 103

Stings 104

Protective Cocoon 108

Stings in the Memory 112

Self-medication and Masks 114

John's Mask 117

Simon's Mask 119

Gary's Mask 122

IV. FATHERS AND STRATEGIES FOR COPING 125

Historical Forces 126

Return to Oedipus 129

Rejection 132

The Resonance of Rejection - the Reversal of Stings 133

Silence and Wounds 139

"Emotional Arrows" 142

Transecting Historical Events - Death Camp 144

Recoil from Pain 151

Institutional Silence 152

V. MOTHER AND SON 159

It's Hard to Say I Love You 160

Wearing a Mask 161

Flows 163

Emotional Language 165

Camouflaging Shyness 170

The Mask of Shame 173

Crying 175

Gutted/Shame 178

Wounded Mother 180

Anger 182

Heroin 183

Expressions of violence 184

Dissolving Stings...185

VI. RELATIONSHIPS 191

Great Expectations..193

Changing roles...195

Pressure - the Desire for Money 198

The Pressure of Fatherhood 201

Money as a "Flow of Care" 204

Children and Jealousy.. 206

The Pressures Released through Revenge.. 208

Self-medication as an Emotional Insurance Policy.............................213

The Aftermath, Faith Destroyed...216

Strength 218

Making his Bed.. 225

VII. VIOLENCE 229

Truancy, Billy's Emotional Connection with his Mother...................... 229

Correction - the Appliance of the Disciplines................................... 231

The Severance of Empathy 232

Humiliation and Resistance 239

The Reversal of 'Stings' 245

Risk-Taking? 249

Fighting State Violence with Violence: An Escalation 252

The 'Front' of a Hard Man 258

Drug Use: An Alternative to the Culture of Violence 261

Violence as an Expression of Love 263

VIII. BODY UNDER THREAT – 'SHRINKING' 271

Embodied Pain 274

Post-traumatic Stress Disorder.. 279

Being Labelled 290

Being Bullied 292

The Fear of Care... 295

Injecting Confidence.. 297

Flows of Love and Care 300

IX. STRATEGIES OF REVENGE.. 307

The Treasure of Silence... 308

The Descent into Shame...312

Three Strategies of Reversal 315

Images of Respect 329

Criminality as a form of revenge 329

Rob's World 331

Upholding Respect 336

X. CONCLUSION 341

BIBLIOGRAPHY 355

Acknowledgements

I would like to thank Professor Vic Seidler (Goldsmiths College) for his guidance, support and ability to help me reflect upon and learn from this research experience.

I would also like to offer my heartfelt thanks to the Management Committee of Orexis and DiD for providing me with the opportunity to undertake this study, in particular Rev. Jack Lucas, Michael Shiner, Dr. Said Abdi and Christine McInnes for their support and care.

I also wish to thank the many clients who have come to DiD/ Orexis for their bravery in looking for solutions to some fundamental human problems and for their honesty and openness in their quest for some form of inner peace.

I would like to thank the people who took the time to read through this study and provide comments, in particular Jean Atkinson, Tony Freedman and Anita Pilgrim.

For my son, Lyon.

I. INTRODUCTION

Hidden Lives

This research arose from my experiences working with people having drug problems in Deptford, South East London, in the late nineties and early years of this decade. I had become aware that the dominant medical paradigms for "treating" drug and alcohol misuse contained within the Models of Care (2002) and the National Strategy and encoded in "Tackling Drugs to Build a Better Britain" (1998) had an emphasis primarily on top-down solutions. This has caused the voices of drug users to be absent leading to some fundamental errors in trying to resolve the problem.

This research began prior to the election of the Labour Government in 1997 and the implementation of the Government's (1998) Ten Year Plan for drug treatment. This research aims to provide a voice for those men who have been silent. It also aims to provide an insight into the complex issues intertwined and connected with drug use, highlighting how the emotional worlds of these men relate to their drug use. This leads me to conclude that fighting a "drug war" without establishing its causes has created a treatment paradigm that attempts to cure the presenting problem without an analysis of what lies behind it. I was struck by the similarities with Gitta Sereny's (1998) exploration in "Cries Unheard" concerning Mary Bell's actions prior to her murder of two young boys. I gained an insight into how solutions were applied to a presenting problem without analysing the underlying causes; this excerpt outlines one of the major theoretical issues associated with working within an emotional paradigm.

In 1968, neither the Newcastle Social Services, Education or Health authorities, the police, nor most importantly, any of the psychiatrists who examined the eleven year old prior to the trial (and thus eventually the court), knew anything at all about Mary's childhood. This almost total ignorance of the traumas she suffered left a large question mark in my mind about the two court appointed psychiatrists even before I knew of the totality of her troubles. They no doubt for want of a better explanation, labelled her with that catch all diagnosis (considered highly questionable by most specialists when applied to children) of a psychopath. (Sereny 1998, p. 11)

Growing up in a white working class area of Newcastle, Mary Bell experienced considerable trauma within her family, information about which was not analysed prior to her trial. Through the building of trust, Sereny (1998) allows Mary to reveal what had happened to her, attempting to piece together how her family life impacted upon her actions. This was not undertaken to condone her behaviour when two young boys were murdered, but to provide an insight into the types of intervention needed to prevent a recurrence. This struck me as resonating with current drug misuse provisions where the proposed drug treatment is based upon a minimal analysis of the patient's emotional life. This leads to a vast amount of resources aiming at curing a problem which, I will contend, has not been appropriately defined. In order to provide a similar understanding, this research will draw on the emotional worlds of white working class men in Deptford.

The research themes emerged through engaging white working class men from South East London in therapy and building trust with them, and also after undertaking a research project at the Maudsley Hospital in 1996. From my experiences, I realised there was a significant gap in the substance misuse literatures. This provided the impetus to undertake this research in 1996. Initially, I had some ideas about how sexual, physical and emotional abuse constituted precedents of drug misuse, but I was unsure of the connections. It was through the patient work with Vic Seidler that I began to understand the role of emotions in men's lives; what was allowed to flow outwardly and what was held within. Then I began to understand how the flows of connection and disconnection led to chronic substance misuse as a coping strategy for dealing with emotional pain.

In creating a structure for my research and reading, an initial choice had to be made as to the scale of the research and whether to work with Afro-Caribbean, White and Vietnamese men and women. I eventually decided to focus upon white working class masculinities and it was from this decision that the key themes of white masculinities, violence and substance misuse emerged.

White Masculinities

The self-discovery process I underwent mirrored to some extent the problems these men faced in defining their masculinities. They too had taken the notion of white masculinities for granted, with little previous reflection on its meaning. Through listening to them, their identities gradually emerged, and in reflection, I also learnt about myself through this counselling and research process.

In 1996, when I asked them to reflect upon 'masculinity', I remember the querying looks, *"what do you mean?"* I felt cumbersome stating the term, as I had not defined it for myself. Therefore, I refrained from asking the men openly about masculinity, as I needed to reflect on what it meant myself. This research provided a door for the exploration of this concept, and my ideas were shaped through reading as well as by my ongoing work with these men.

As I became more aware of the differing masculinities, I began to realise how deeply embedded these notions were, for others and as well as for myself. Apart from conceptualising the issues surrounding masculinities, another difficulty I faced was in framing the methodological approach, as I realised from the outset that I was embroiled in the research process and was not a detached observer. As the men spoke, I recognised an emotional flow between us creating a different form of interaction in exploring their emotional worlds. I had to think through the type of relationships I was forming within a sociological context, and I drew on the pioneering work in Carol Gilligan's "Mapping the Moral Domain" (1988). This feminist critique of rationality helped me to realise the place of emotions within the social sciences. The sessions I recorded revealed emotional worlds in which the desire to avenge hurts and slights had become paramount in sustaining a 'front of masculinity'.

Another vital text was Jim Gilligan's "Violence" (2000), which drew upon his American experience of masculinities in the prison system, describing how these men upheld a 'front' at great personal cost. I began to see how drug use and violence became forms of sustaining a 'front' and halting intimacy, thereby upholding a code of masculine honour. This led me to the concept of 'fronts'; in this context, a projection of various white masculinities onto the outside world, yet connected to an internal masking or suppression of memories and emotions intrinsically related to love and pain.

Violence

A commonality of themes emerged in the counselling. Violence marked all of these men's lives, initially as childhood recipients, later as adolescent protagonists. It was only after hearing many counselling sessions between 1989 and 1996 that I became confident enough to undertake this research, as I had by then detected a commonality of life experiences. One of the defining connecting themes for the younger white working class men was the levels of violence they had endured as children, primarily wielded by their fathers through physical and verbal acts, creating an emotional and physical after-effect they carried into their adult lives.

The sessions with Gary and Pete especially illuminated how historical and social conditions affect families, and how in particular the after-effects of this violence had a resonant emotional impact upon them. Within this context, institutional violence marks the parameters of everyday existence. I began to explore the effects within an English context after reading Klaus Thewelait (1977, 1978) and Alice Miller (1987) describe the German male experiences in "Male Fantasies Volumes 1 and 2" and "For Your Own Good" respectively. This form of analysis – a juxtaposition of two eras and cultures – allowed me to understand the connections between these differing experiences of violence. I began to comprehend the connections between sadness, emotional pain and anger, and how these become externalised into aggression.

After taping the counselling sessions, a connection arose for me, between the violence inflicted by men and women who work in institutions and its latent impact on the men in this study. What emerged was a lack of empathy in decision-making processes. This was a key concept as this lack of empathy in the execution of orders had a profound effect on the recipients. This minimal conceptualisation of the emotional worlds of the object of command led me to rethink some of the ideas explored in Foucault's "Discipline and Punish" (1977). This became a key text in understanding the process of command as a form of psychological violence. Foucault describes how the state seemingly legitimates certain forms of violence in schools, young offenders' institutions, courts and the police. After reading Thewelait (1977, 1978) and Miller (1987), I began to see the connection between this institutional violence and how it operates as a form of psychological revenge as the effects are passed downwards onto the recipient who is bounded by the command and unable to retaliate. The authors explored the role of command within the German army. It was through reading Thewelait (1977, 1978) that I understood the importance of Cannetti's "Crowds and Power" (1960), which describes how anger is unleashed as a physical and psychological force, conceptualised by Cannetti as the discharge of 'stings'.

Considering the origin of this violence, younger white working class men spoke in detail about their fathers' violence in the family and explored its latent emotional effect. Apart from Phil, they were mostly silent concerning past difficulties in their relationships with their mothers. In terms of this research, I am aware that this reticence either marked a limit of our relationship, because they did not trust me enough to talk about the mother/son bond, or it marked their own perception of the value of the care they received.

Drug Misuse

Through the analysis, I began to explore the relationship between being the victims of violence and drug use. The men in this study were primarily using heroin, methadone and, in one case, amphetamines. Other drugs included crack cocaine, Valium, Temazepam, cannabis and alcohol, which began to be used by the older users along with methadone. This alcohol use had preceded their arrival at Orexis/DiD, a voluntary sector street agency I was developing. All of these men were in shared care support with GPs, meaning we undertook the counselling and practical work, liasing with housing authorities, solicitors and social services, whilst the GPs prescribed methadone and conducted general medical care. This approach had developed from the 'GP Protocols', developed in 1997, outlining expectations of the agency, GPs and clients in their work together.

The younger clients, Gary, Rob, Rod, John, Simon and Billy, presented to the agency with heroin problems in the early 1990s. The first clients arrived as a result of advertising in local newspapers and through word of mouth. From 1990 to 1994 I was a counsellor, development worker and manager of the agency, drawing on counselling techniques to treat a bemused client group.

After they had secured enough money for heroin, crack cocaine was used by all of the Deptford men. Only one man, Damien, used it consistently every day. One other client, Pete, distinguished himself from the heroin users by having an addiction to amphetamines and Valium. I worked with his GP to stabilise his use, trying to see if prescribing amphetamines would work, in the same manner as Methadone. Cannabis appeared in the urine samples but was deemed not to be a problem, reflecting a widespread normalisation in use of the drug in the 1980s and 1990s in the area.

Deptford, London SE8

The men in this study lived in a distinct geographical space defined by its infrastructure. Deptford lies in South East London, opposite the visible affluence of the Isle of Dogs, between the partially regenerated Surrey Quays and Greenwich. Away from the River Thames, Deptford backs onto New Cross, another area with similar problems, where Goldsmith's College is situated. The local football team is Millwall, renowned for their displays of primarily white masculine prowess off the pitch. This connects with issues that arise in this research, as Alex, Simon and John were all active supporters.

In 2007, Deptford was undergoing massive change, with new developments arising near the Thames and the Docklands Light Railway creating an influx of more affluent people. This has meant the gradual displacement of the original occupants with Lewisham Council involved in selling off council properties to property developers in the hope this would transform the area.

Deptford straddles two London boroughs, Lewisham and Greenwich. Until 2002, Deptford was almost entirely made up of public housing. The poverty indicators, based upon "Child Poverty, access, education, employment, income, housing and health" (Holdsworth et al. 2002, p. 9), show two wards in Deptford, Evelyn and Grinling Gibbons, being in the top 10% of deprived wards in England. Historically, Deptford has had a particular class and geographical identity; it is marked by its visible public housing estates, which have declined as employment has withered, creating a downward spiral in self-esteem as the local economic and social infrastructure collapsed. This process is outlined in "Mapping the Tide" (Steele 1993):

> Deptford's Estates have been a problem since they first breached the skyline. In its early years Pepys was a bastion of the respectable white working class: old Dockers in a new town. However as Deptford's reputation sank and housing stock elsewhere in the London Borough of Lewisham increased, the most 'respectable' aspirations became to 'get out of Deptford'. Those who were successful in transferring or buying out of the area left behind a battered community of "don't knows, don't cares and desperates. (Steele 1993, p. 193)

As this quote shows, when I began to work in Deptford in the late 1980s, it was the meeting place of all the problems associated with the term 'inner cities'; it was marked by a declining infrastructure, a shift in population, the new high rise buildings, and the disruption of white working class community networks.

In the early 1970's Deptford was undergoing great changes, especially in the sphere of housing. The physical fabric of the old neighbourhoods had long been deteriorating and the new estates were not a renovation of the old communities but a challenge to them. The rise of containerisation, which killed the inland Docks, had undermined the identities of the riverside areas and caused many young adults to move down-river to deep ports of Essex and Kent. The 'tower blocks' never became vertical spaces of planners' dreams. The decanted populations were dispersed and the notion of community in Deptford all but shattered under the strain. (Steele 1993, p. 213)

This excerpt highlights the fundamental problem in the 'regeneration' of Deptford. This was undertaken with minimal understanding of the psychology of the people who lived there (Steele 1993). It was felt that improving the housing stock could uplift a dispirited working class community. This has proved to be at best an extremely naïve planning view marked the growing numbers of people coming to the drug agency for treatment in the 21st century with chronic drug problems. The agency in effect, one of the busiest in London highlighted the continual institutional failure of Lewisham Council to understand and alleviate the central core problems afflicting the area. These were domestic violence, a euphemism for familial torture and chronic institutional failure amongst the care professions. In particular the key services which were meant to administer care were completely adrift. In particular the problems lay with Lewisham Social Services, the Probation service, the NHS substance use, the council community safety department who were unable to theorise and conceptualise the problems they tasked to solve. This in turn has led to catastrophic mistakes in health, planning, care, policing, education and the judicial system. The question, which arises from this chronic institutional failure, is why was this allowed to happen? A number of government initiatives had been launched to combat the inner city decline after Margaret Thatcher won re-election in 1983, following her observation that something must be done for the 'inner cities'. There was general alarm in the 1980s about a possible move towards an American-style ghetto culture, with 'no go' areas wracked by guns and drugs. Coupled with these images were the riots and disturbances sweeping through the UK in 1981 onwards.

The first quango was the Deptford Enterprise Agency. Then, in the late 1980s and early 90s, there were numerous attempts to stall the decline: The Deptford Task Force, People For Action, Drugs Prevention Initiative, Safer Cities, and, most importantly, Deptford City Challenge. There have also been Estate Action Programmes and Single Regeneration Bids. Millions of pounds have poured into Deptford and New Cross attempting to make it a better place in which to live and work. Whilst the structural appearance has changed, the emotional lives of the people who live there have not received the same detailed attention. Renovating buildings was deemed a solution to the existing psychological problems (Steele 1993). The latest 21st century solution has been to sell off the property nearest to the river in the naïve hope that the new occupants will raise the "standards" of the local population through some form of cultural osmosis. In turn what has happened is that the new residents are trapped within their gated communities unable to intermingle with a resentful local population.

Orexis/DID

DiD evolved from the work undertaken by the Management Committee of the 190 Community Centre in the mid 1980s. The impetus stemmed from their often-direct experience of the heroin problem. The rise of voluntary sector agencies in the 1980s was due to the lack of facilities providing more flexible treatment forms than those being offered by the Statutory Health Agencies. This mirrored the rise of other voluntary agencies in Southwark and Lewisham such as CADA and Brockley Drugline. All these agencies arose from the same anxieties: developed by mothers wanting fast track access treatment for their sons/daughters.

Drugs in Deptford began in 1989, and was funded after a local research report highlighted two key aspects of the drug problem: heroin use by young men in the immediate area, and the high levels of cannabis use (80%) amongst fourteen-year olds on Evelyn Estate (*Deptford Mercury*, May 1989).

Interestingly, drug use at this time was seen as a 'race' issue. This gain marked a complete blind spot by the council. Lewisham Council, through the Race Equality Unit, provided a grant for a counselling project aimed at the local Afro-Caribbean community following the reported use of crack on Milton Court Estate in Deptford. The response was to throw thirty thousand pound with no strategic plan at a problem defined by the media These events set the terms for how the project evolved.

I began to work on the project in 1989, initially as a counsellor and then as the co-ordinator of the project. In advertising the service, it became clear that cannabis use and the provision of counselling were not the main issues facing the community, which also did not just want health education, more lectures from the white middle class on how to live. Through advertising in a local estate paper, the *CO-OP Pepys*, I began to work with the first referrals. The people who came forward were white, wanting support to detoxify from heroin. In meeting this demand, I decided to keep hold of the counselling but also shift from a 'pure' person-centred counselling approach towards liasing with GPs on Methadone reduction programs. The aim at this time was "harm reduction" (Stimson 1990) – stabilising people who were using heroin due to the moral panic about HIV.

In retrospect, this became a major turning point in the evolution of the organisation. It was clear counselling as the sole intervention was not going to be effective if the clients could not access medication. It was also clear to me the provision of methadone by itself was problematic. Unfortunately however the Harm Reduction model although admirable at the time, has now become the norm, as gallons of Methadone are dispensed to a beguiled drug using population within the framework of harm reduction across the UK. This is dispensed along with the provision of key working, undertaken by poorly trained staff, monofocused on the clients' drug use has meant the dynamics which drove him/her to seek support become obfuscated under the guise of harm reduction.

In terms of my approach I began to develop a way of combining both interventions, echoing work that had already been undertaken in the USA.

> Even the most eloquent of supporters of psychotherapy for substance misuse treatment view insight orientated psychotherapy for opiate addiction as useful only in combination with other formal addiction treatment efforts (Khantzian 1985). Psychotherapy as a singular approach for the currently addicted or recently detoxified opiate addict cannot be clinically justified. (Rawson in Ed Washton 1995, p. 60)

This realisation stemmed from my training as a counsellor and community education worker. The latter training had taught me how to be flexible to community needs and not to impose solutions; the former helped me to create a long-term vision for understanding the reasons why people were using drugs.

Stereotypes

This study concentrates on white working class male masculinities arising from the large numbers of white men attending treatment from 1989 to 1996. Subsequently, we developed other services for Afro-Caribbean, Vietnamese, Somali and Cantonese communities, as well as for women and young people. We also became involved in piloting the Adult and Youth Arrest Referral Schemes for the Home Office and latterly the Metropolitan Police. Initially a champion of this type of intervention after seeing the incarceration of a whole generation, disillusion gradually set in as it dawned on all involved that at best is was a superficial intervention and at worst positively dangerous.

Towards the end of its life the focus of the agency shifted to accommodate the new arrivals entering the area although keeping hold of the large numbers of white men and women.

These men were in treatment from 1994 to 1996, when these sessions were recorded. They were not chosen randomly and are drawn from the men who engaged with me in the counselling and treatment process. None of these men had ever had counselling prior to their entry into treatment at DiD/Orexis. They were not specifically chosen for the study. Their engagement with the research process occurred after I asked them if I could tape their counselling sessions. Everyone with whom I was currently working eventually agreed; this provided the selection process.

In terms of biographical details, the younger group who took part in this study were mostly born in South East London. The older group moved into Deptford because of the drug culture and through the connections they had made through prison and crime. I had wrestled with introducing some of their biographical details, feeling that they had exposed enough of themselves within the sessions. I feel unease in revealing any more details of these men's lives. I am also aware of the parameters laid down by the British Association of Counselling and Psychotherapy's Confidentiality Policy and the "Relations with and Responsibilities towards Research Participants" of the BSA (1996).

> Sociologists have a responsibility to ensure that the physical, social and psychological well being of the research participants is not adversely affected by the research. They should strive to protect the rights of those they study, their interests, sensitivities and privacy, while recognising the difficulty of balancing potentially conflicting interests. (BSA Statement on Ethical Practice and Research 1996, p.2)

Within this framework, all of the names and identifying areas related in the sessions have been changed in order to preserve anonymity. Trust is crucial for the therapy to take place. If this were lost, then I felt the men would retreat into silence, having been hurt once again by an institution they had trusted. This was a careful line I had to tread in undertaking this research: to reveal the emotional worlds of these men whilst at the same time ensuring they were not humiliated any further. I recognised the power relationship that existed and had to carefully think through how this impacted upon our relationship, therefore I allowed these men to dictate how their sessions unfolded. This marked the limits of the research.

The younger men who defined themselves as white were a mixture of second generation Irish or English working class. All the men were in their late twenties when these sessions took place. All used primarily heroin and latterly crack.

Their friendships had developed through school, locality, gang membership, detention centres and the drug culture.

In all cases, apart from Damien, their parents had been married for a number of years. Their fathers had worked in the locality, principally in jobs attached to the Docks. They all lived in council housing. At the time the sessions were recorded, none of the men had worked and were living off benefits and the proceeds of crime ranging from burglary and shoplifting to the use of force to gain money, by which they were generating a self-reported income of between £200 and £1800 per week.

The physical appearance of these men would not especially mark them out as chronic drug users, as they did not appear as dishevelled, acned or emaciated. These men dressed in a smart casual manner, in Calvin Klein Jeans, French Connection/Hilfiger jumpers, Ben Sherman shirts and Reebok/Nike trainers. They take a certain pride in their appearance, contrasting directly with the junkie stereotype. As it was clearly put to me: *"you can't go shoplifting looking like a tramp; it looks too obvious"* (Damien).

The older men were drawn to Deptford through the drug culture and through knowing people in the area from spells in prison. There was also another aspect to their arrival in this part of London: flight from their hometowns due to threats of violence. They were primarily drawn from the hippie culture of the late sixties/early seventies, with two of the men fitting this particular stereotype.

Shared Care

All of the men except Pete were on a methadone program. Prior to the agency being established, this had been administered by local GPs without any other form of support; this had produced a number of problems. Prescriptions provided by the GPs were sold for between £10-£15 per 100mls, creating a thriving black market, attracting a large number of drug users to Deptford such as Alan, Ross and Bri. As a result, few GPs were willing to work with this client group, fearing their demands. Those GPs who were working with drug-using patients were overwhelmed. The other GPs simply referred their patients to the statutory services, leading to long waiting lists and creating a bottleneck for those awaiting treatment.

The role of DiD/Orexis became twofold: to try and create a structure with the prescribing GPs and then to work with the non-prescribing GPs to create a better defined structure. The counselling program we offered required the creation of a time and space for clients to sit down and explore the many facets of their lives. In retrospect, this became crucial for establishing trust between the GPs, the clients and us.

As we discovered, this was not an easy process, since men attending the agency were not used to verbalising their feelings and their experiences. By developing an initial compromise, we attempted to see if the men and women attending would engage with therapy. Following a framework gleaned from the Department of Health guidelines (Banks and Waller 1988), we asked the clients what methadone dosage would they wish to stabilise on, again drawing on the person centred approach. This worked with nearly everyone opting for between 30-50 mls of Methadone per day, along with weekly urine testing. The principal rationale for people attending treatment at this point was a desire for respite from the continual physical demands of sustaining a habit, committing crimes, waiting for dealers, police arrest and incarceration. In 1990-92 people were sceptical of the counselling, echoing the counselling experiences of Paul Lockley in "Working with Drug Users", (Lockley 1995):

> Another attitude, especially among male drug users, is that of not involving anyone else in their affairs, and this applies mostly to those who are not users themselves and who represent authority-which includes all counsellors. (Lockley 1995, p. 131)

The challenge for DiD/Orexis was to work with clients to create a structure so that they could turn up on time, sit down and participate in counselling and to put constraints on their drug use, marking a shift away from technical clinical interventions to a "client centred" (Lockley 1995, p. 132) approach, which was new for 1989 and even more novel in 2007.

My method of developing a rapport emerged from asking the clients about their families, their health and other topics such as sport. With the men, football became the main focus of conversation and I began, as an example, to rekindle my interest. On reflection, this convergence of interest helped to create a good working relationship, shifting the emphasis from drug use to looking at the wider social world. They were highly resistant to counselling, as Lockley (1995) highlights, having a strong notion that attending Orexis/DiD and revealing their emotional lives was akin to admitting to a mental health problem. I remember Jim, another local user, referring to us as "fraggle rock", a derogatory term for the Mental Health prison wing in HMP Brixton. However, it was the only tool I possessed and in my training I had seen how it could work. This was a slow process, but as the agency became established, clients began to talk amongst themselves, thereby lowering their scepticism, as marked by Lockley (1995): "Thus the relationship the counsellor has may be with individual clients, but it can also be one with the subculture as a whole" (Lockley 1995, p. 133). This quote illuminates how potential users of the service weigh their perceptions of treatment services.

The people who took part in this study had known of me since 1989. Between 1990 and 1997, I believe I personally had seen just over six hundred people for counselling, initially having twenty-five clients a week. The overwhelming presenting issue was heroin, although crack use began to figure prominently as a second drug of choice in the early 90s. During this time, I estimated I had conducted more than four thousand individual counselling sessions. The majority of these came when the project began to get a greater influx of people, from 1991 onwards. In 2003, the agency saw between 160 and 200 people per week. Gradually my role became managerial and I saw less of the clients which led me to reappraise my position as I preferred working with people rather than working with paper.

To create a safe environment, we had to negotiate boundaries. These were established through creating appointments, thereby ensuring a need for punctuality. We also aimed for clean urine samples, and to get the clients to sit down and talk for an hour. These became the key outcomes for measuring success. Within these parameters, my training as a 'person-centred counsellor' provided a framework for introducing counselling. I could see how the development of empathic values could be utilised by allowing these men to develop ways of expressing themselves. They needed to feel safe within the conditions that we had established within the agency. This allowed us to draw GPs into working with this client group. For example, at the end of the counselling session, we wrote a letter to the relevant

GP and handed it to the client so they had control over the process. The letter provided an outline of the negotiated medication level and brief details on how the client was progressing. This negotiation became a three-way process between the client, the GP and the counsellor. This was a further means of establishing a structure in clients' lives, and was very different to the methods used in local statutory drug services, which were based on a model of treatment focusing more on clinical interventions such as titration, harm reduction and key working. This intervention marked a shift away from being person-centred, ensuring minimal patient control over their detox, with support offered within a medical framework where the primary focus is on 'harm reduction' (Banks and Waller 1988). Here, the client can access a residential unit for the purposes of therapy if the local community care budget has enough resources.

This study shows that therapy with white working class men can take place within the Deptford community once their initial 'resistances' are understood. This has the benefit of the men taking their knowledge back into their communities and creating new forms of relationships based upon their self-knowledge, helping them to understand their own motivations and identities and thereby being in a better position to understand the men and women around them.

II. RELATIONAL RESEARCH

This chapter illustrates how my counselling and sociological background shaped my reading, showing the decisions I made in the course of this research. My aim was to bring elements of the two disciplines together, using texts associated with the 'relational method' of Gilligan et al. (1988) and the counselling theory of Carl Rogers (1967), and latterly the existential work of Irving Yalom (1989).

My educational background as a counsellor, community worker, sociologist and historian influenced the methodological focus of this study. I was influenced in particular by 'person-centred therapy', thereby developing an empathic and congruent relationship with these men, creating the "core conditions", highlighted in this quote from Rogers (1967):

> Effective therapy can occur within a relationship between therapist and client in which the latter perceives the former as being accepting, empathic and congruent. (Rogers 1967, p. 144)

I wanted to link this approach to my sociological background. I began to see how emerging patterns unfolding in the sessions were interlinking with the power relationships within families, and through these men's recollections, how institutions and historical events impacted on an emotional, as well as a physical level. I believed I was gaining an understanding of why these themes were emerging. One of the initial key texts I drew on was Paul Willis's "Learning to Labour" (1978).

Through undertaking an observational study in a school, Paul Willis's (1978) study analysed how young white working class adolescents/young men moved into working class jobs. He interviewed and researched a group of young white males he termed, "the lads", detailing how they perceived the world around them, revealing their 'resistances', based upon a disruption and subversion of a perceived middle class, effeminate value system the school was inculcating, ironically, through coercion. Through dress and manner, the "lads" resisted these values as the culture they were creating became grounded in a desire to enter the male world of their fathers and older brothers. I began to understand how their behaviour involved their desire to overcome and take revenge upon the "discipline" of the school. At the same time, their actions reaffirmed traditional masculine values, based upon aggression and conflict. Willis (1978) shows how it also prepared them for the industrial world they were on the verge of entering, at a time when those jobs still existed.

The community work training I undertook at Moray House in Edinburgh helped me to analyse how these white working class masculinities impacted on the wider environment. I drew upon this in establishing Orexis/DiD, gaining the conceptual tools of empowerment and growth of individuals and communities. I could also locate the social acts of the users within a wider social environment, and I began to see them as victims as well as perpetrators of emotional and physical violence.

My Modern History studies led me to reflect on the historical pressures affecting men in the present, and in particular the after-affects of conflict and the social upheavals of the 20th Century. This became essential in the therapy as it allowed me to place events, thereby making cultural connections for clients and creating a congruency, if not an initial personal understanding of their experiences. This interest in history also helped me to think through the notion of Post-traumatic Stress Disorder. In particular, after reading Sassoon's "The Complete Memoirs of George Sherston" (1972) and "Forgotten Voices of the Great War" by Max Arthur (2002), I began to picture how the after-effects of war impacted psychologically on the men who fought. Both books became crucial in confirming the difficulties English men have had historically in relating their experiences to non-combatants. My starting point in this research concerned the after-effects of the Second World War, which arose in the sessions with Gary and Pete.

I was able to draw upon my own personal resources in growing up in similar working class environments, and therefore having some of the same cultural references. In trying to think through how this impacted upon the research, I believe it led me to have an intuitive understanding of the issues surrounding these white working class masculinities described in the sessions. I was able to reflect on these through my education, counselling supervision and with my supervisor, Vic Seidler, who was key in this process of self-reflection. However, it was chiefly through growing up in similar environments, knowing friends who were having trouble at home, others who moved into the drug culture, and some who moved into crime that I was able to piece together an understanding of the social environment surrounding me as a child, through adolescence and into adulthood.

Resistance

The culture I was experiencing at Drugs In Deptford/ Orexis – the 'resistances' – resonated with Willis's (1978)

23

research. However, through the numerous counselling sessions, I began to see how these were constructed as 'psychological resistances' to the recollection of memory. This is where my research differs from Willis (1978), as the therapeutic work allowed me to gain an understanding of the psychological patterns of 'resistance'. This is why the counselling technique became so useful, as it allowed movement beyond the behavioural "front", connecting to emotional worlds beyond. However, in undertaking a study within this paradigm, I had to make some choices. In substance misuse counselling literature there appears to be an over-emphasis upon technique, and little analysis of effect, other than what is scientifically demonstrable by outside researchers (Ball and Ross 1991; Burgess et al. 1990; Calsyn et al. 1990; Joe et al. 1991; Khantzian 1995; Longwell et al. 1978; Ramer 1971; Renner 1984; Weben 1986; Woody et al. 1983,1987; Yancovitz 1991), rather than hearing the counsellors describing their experiences themselves.

Other issues arose for me, with the prevailing emphasis on cognitive models, particularly the emphasis on reasoning, used extensively in relapse prevention (Young 1995). The primary aim of the cognitive models is to create change without necessarily analysing why they have formed.

> Cognitive models have become so well entrenched in the psychological and human sciences that we are often blind to the philosophical assumptions about reason and emotions upon which they rest. (Seidler 1994, p. 27)

The cognitive model, drawing on this critique from Vic Seidler (1994), has its emphasis on changing thought patterns, but tends to ignore how relationships are formed and subsequently sustained over a period of time. This marks a difference in my research, as I concentrated on how the process of trust and empathic connection through the expression of emotions was sustained. Two of the key texts that helped me to think through the mechanisms of therapeutic relationships work were Irving Yalom's "Loves Executioner" (1989) and Alice Miller's "Paths of Life" (1999), both of which explore how relationships are maintained as well as exploring the emotional processes of therapy.

This approach was not without its detractors within the substance misuse field. The early literature of drug misuse highlights how the problems of heroin use accrue from continued drug consumption. Therefore, the drug is the problem that requires intervention and the underlying issues are secondary. Another prevailing concept emerging from our staff supervision meetings was a quasi Marxist notion that drug misuse is a reaction to poverty. Concerning the latter point, Orexis/DiD grew out of a Deptford welfare rights unit where my colleagues supported clients' housing and welfare rights; it was they who initiated the counselling project, recognising the need for therapeutic support.

In undertaking this therapeutic support, I began to understand how "resistance" intertwined with the 'front' and I began to examine how violence and drug misuse related to these concepts. Through listening to these men, I understood that one form of 'resistance' was to attack – the use of violence described by Willis (1978) – whilst another was to 'shrink' away from connection; to use heroin to blot out emotions (Miller 1987).

This shrinking away from connection was not a form of timidity, as these men appeared physically 'armoured'. The notion of using clothing as a shell arose in a group discussion at DiD/Orexis in 1996 when discussing one man's appearance. I remembered reading Wilhelm Reich's "The Mass Psychology of Fascism" (1946); in discussion with Vic Seidler, he had suggested I read the post-Reichian work of Boadella, "In the Wake of Reich" (1976). This became useful for conceptualising my ideas concerning 'fronts'. Building on this, I also read Erving Goffman's "The Presentation of the Self in Everyday Life" (1959), explored in the chapter on "Fathers and Sons".

The idea of a 'front' projected onto the social world and led me to think about what exists at the 'back of a front'. I began to think of the 'front' as akin to a Rogerian (1967) concept of 'projection'. Rogers perceived this to be linked to the construction of an identity, acting as a form of self-protection.

Sustaining Trust

One of the problems I faced was how to move beyond this 'front'. The answer lay in building and sustaining trust, thereby allowing these men's defences to dissolve. I gained this trust through patience, by being non-judgemental and through setting boundaries, using the techniques derived from Rogerian 'meta communication'. This allowed the clients to find their voice:

> Rather than merely responding directly to the client, the counsellor may make reference to feelings, intentions and understandings that lie behind his or her response. The therapist may offer in a tentative manner, to allow the client every opportunity to disagree with or correct the therapist's understanding of the situation. The style of communicating with the client has a number of

advantages. It conveys the message that the client is in control, it encourages the use of the internal locus of evaluation of the client, and minimises the likelihood of the therapist intruding on the internal processing or "track" (Rennie 1990) being pursued by the client. (Woolfe and Dryden 1996, p. 145)

By letting the client speak and find the confidence to talk about the past, trust began to flourish through the establishment of the 'core conditions' (Rogers 1967). This provided the space for these men to relate their values and beliefs, direct the flow of conversation, and have power within the session. Another aspect of the trust building was in believing what these men were saying about themselves. This provided me with the space to explore their feelings and allowing them to shift their 'projected' defences. I did this without trying to impose my beliefs or challenging their views outright, perhaps forcing them to retreat and say nothing.

One of the aims of counselling is to create 'change'. What I learnt from reflecting on my own counselling experiences as a student was that this did not occur through merely being shown that a 'better way' exists. This alienates the client, who feels as imposition, as described by Rothschild in "Psychotherapy and Substance Misuse" (1995). I had to think of treatment goals and I began to understand what was feasible through listening to the clients. Change did occur – this research provides evidence of one form of change, the building of trust. Clients would not have engaged in this research at the beginning of our relationship.

In sustaining trust, I had to be open to challenge. Clients would often test me on my knowledge of their lifestyles. My most effective technique was to be honest and open when I did not know. This had the effect of empowering these men, as they became almost akin to teachers in allowing me an insight into their worlds. This process I later found had been described in Yalom's "Love's Executioner" (1989). In the chapter "If rape were legal", Yalom speaks openly of learning from his clients, and I felt this resonated with my approach.

I was challenged through a nuanced part of a "meta communication" encoded in a familiar South London phrase, *"Do you know what I mean?"* I remember nodding as images of their words flashed through my mind. When they began to talk, the words created emotions in me as I followed their experiences.

The Rogerian framework provided a set of tools for conducting therapy, but I quickly moved on from Rogerian techniques of 'paraphrasing and mirroring' and silence, as these techniques made these men suspicious. Yalom (1989) describes how he developed his technique through seeing what works rather than following an ideology.

> Indeed the capacity to tolerate uncertainty is a prerequisite for the profession. Though the public may believe that therapists guide patients systematically and surehandedly through predictable stages of therapy to a foreknown goal, such is rarely the case; instead as these stories bear witness, therapists frequently wobble, improvise and grope for direction. The powerful temptation to achieve certainty through embracing an ideological school and a tight therapeutic system is treacherous; such belief may block uncertain and spontaneous encounter necessary for effective therapy. (Yalom 1989, p. 13)

These men wanted to know whether I was 'genuine' or a *'textbook counsellor'*, i.e. someone who was interested in them rather than merely employing a technique of correction. This meant undergoing a test.

Being Tested

One of the therapeutic dilemmas I faced stemmed from having a dual conflicting role, being a person centred counsellor and also the access point for substitute prescribing.

Kaufman and Blaine (1974), quoted in Ward et al. (1992) state: "in methadone maintenance units where counselling or psychotherapy is mandatory, patients think of counselling sessions as a game they have to play to keep up their supply of methadone" (Ward 1992, p. 161). Therefore, in creating the space for counselling with this group, who were not initially motivated, everyone was tested. In terms of technique, this also marked a shift away from the exclusive use of Rogerian 'person-centred counselling' (1967).

I knew it was part of the local culture to be tested – to be stretched to see how gullible you are. It reminded me of school and how we used to 'test' the supply teachers on school procedure. Another aspect of being genuine was their judgement on whether I was a 'weak' man, or whether I could hold my own within this environment. The substitute prescribing issue meant that although the basic tenets of Rogerian counselling – empathy, genuineness and congruence – could be adhered to, there were set boundaries around structure. This entailed challenging people over lateness, taking drugs on top of their script and, when trust flowed, their criminal activities.

Gary told me an apocryphal story highlighting how all newcomers to Deptford are tested. When a new pub landlord arrives, everyone who has been barred by the previous landlord for fighting and stealing would return. After a few months, when they had built a relationship, they would suggest to the landlord he was working too hard and should take time off. When this occurred, a trusted person would run the bar offering everyone free drinks, leading to the pub bankruptcy. Regarding cultural similarities, this story produced a direct memory for me of how my parents had been the near victims of such a scam when we had a pub in North Derbyshire. There were clear resonances for me with this particular story.

Gary explained how newcomers are tested to see how they react to seemingly established trust, and then it is taken advantage of. In establishing Drugs in Deptford/Orexis, I underwent a similar test. I was initially manipulated, and it was a fraught time for everyone involved, trying to establish a structure with the GPs, who were also being tested.

Simon, whose father was involved in testing local landlords, described how he did this to me in 1991.

Simon: *Dean, I'll be honest. I've come here before and told lies, just to get whatever. But I am opening up my heart, and I really feel, and I feel that if I'm lying I'm not to get nowhere and I've got to tell you the truth, so you can help me, you know Dean. I used to lie when I come here. Like I used to paint and work, and things like that. That's a load of, I can't swear, can I?*
Dean: *Do what you want.*
Simon: *It was a load of nonsense, and I used to say to you, and I'd walk in with him and you'd say to me: "Oh you've*

got paint on yer ", and I'd say; "Yeh, I've been helping me old man doing a bit painting". Do you remember, Dean? It was a load of nonsense. I never worked. I used to put paint on me to look, you know, silly things like that. When I used to go for a urine test, I'd be honest, let's see, if it had wee in the water and make out it ain't be pulled, the chain, the urine would still be laying on the water so I would put my thing [urine bottle] in there and as long as it was that colour, you know. I did pull some strokes. I never nicked anything from out here, and that's the God's honest truth. But I pulled some cunning strokes to get out of things".

Simon described how he sabotaged his counselling session by painting his hands, telling me he was working and in a hurry to get back. In reality, he saw talking as a barrier to getting to the doctor on time, so he would always turn up late for the session, demanding his letter, rush off to the doctor and then sell the Methadone to buy drugs.

He was letting me know he was in control, tampering with his urine samples by watering them down. When the results came back, they always detailed the high percentage of water in the sample. A local benefactor challenged me at a local function about my gullibility about how Methadone was being dispensed. Simon and his friend were laughing at the "strokes" they had pulled and she had overheard. She then claimed the moral high ground in telling me how I was not fit to run a project. My reaction was one of a strategy of revenge I confronted Simon about his ruses and then banned him – my revenge strategy. Our relationship at the time this session was recorded was initially precarious. He had returned with his pride intact and tried once again to detox, this time less guardedly. I had gained a currency of respect in the area. In 1989, he decided to see how gullible I was, but four years later a different facet of his life emerged that had been 'masked' by this subterfuge. Again, Lockley (1995) describes a similar test:

> The art of counselling is to maintain the balance between challenging the client usefully in order to make the session more realistic, and allowing the client a measure of denial. Constant lying by the client is an infringement on and disregard of the counsellor as a person. Constant challenging or preoccupation with the truth becomes a game to make the counsellor feel better, and a game the counsellor will not win. Counselling has to allow the client to be themselves and this requires them to discover or rediscover themselves. (Lockley 1995, p. 139)

Resonating with Lockley (1995), I held onto my vision of being able to penetrate beyond the façade, the 'front', in creating an intervention, which was both effective and innovative. Within the process, I had to reflect upon myself and what on type of values I was trying to establish. This took place through team meetings, external supervision and in this research, providing time for reflection. When the clients began to trust me, they began to talk. This was a long and frustrating process. It was not until 1992 that I felt we had made significant headway, three years after starting the agency.

Re-examining the Counselling Technique

The 'client-centred' techniques I had learned were adapted to the client group. Whilst genuineness and empathy were essential, the role of silence, allowing the client to control the silences and breaks in communication, was re-examined. I personally felt it had never worked; feeling that if I just sat there at the beginning of the session and waited for them to talk, it would turn into a game. I felt they needed the counsellor to have some links to their worlds; therefore, the beginning of the session usually centred on cultural references intersecting our lives, or how they were coping on their scripts. This helped to dismantle the barriers between my life and theirs.

Paraphrasing was another technique I had to reappraise. I knew if this were practised too literally, these men would see me as trying to 'be clever' and would walk away, as mimicking was part of the local culture of ridicule. I had to negotiate a cultural obstacle course between the roles of therapist and ordinary human being. Although it was necessary to clarify meanings, this could not be done too often, as I felt they would feel my life was too distant from theirs. Their ability to teach would only stretch so far before they realised that I was a poor student.

Confidentiality became key to sustaining trust. When the clients realised we could keep their secrets, the trust flowed. This was one of the most challenging counselling client groups – white working class men and women in one of the most deprived areas of the UK who lived in a culture that had self-reliance as the key for survival, reputation and self-esteem entangled with organised crime.

Along with confidentiality, being non-judgemental helped the process of trust as clients spoke of acts committed by, as well against them. This also required a patient process of listening and allowing the men and women to talk. Another key component was keeping to boundaries, which are seemingly self-evident, but which were continually tested. This involved not accepting gifts or divulging telephone numbers or addresses and not becoming sexually/socially involved.

Working in this field, I have always felt there was a dividing line between being punitive and over-identifying with the client group. I believe this has become structured in how statutory and voluntary services traditionally operated. On a personal level, I realised that I had to make changes; for example, my social life changed, as I could no longer go to pubs in Deptford or New Cross, because my work and social life criss-crossed when people recognised me and wanted to talk. Limited staff turnover was crucial to this process, and my staying at the agency for a number of years meant that trust developed by me in the early years could be passed on to the new workers. I visualised it as relay baton, which I was able to hand to new people coming into the agency.

Analysis of the emerging patterns

One of the major difficulties I faced with Rogerian counselling (1967) was the silence around any political or social context to his writings. His emphasis was on individuals. Listening and working with these people led me to think about why their problems had arisen. I began to think of the pattern of the sessions and how outside events impacted upon people and had psychological after-effects. Counselling psychology by itself seemingly locates the issues on an individualistic level, as identified in this quote from Giddens' "Modernity and Self Identity" (1991):

> Is therapy only a means of adjusting dissatisfied individuals to a flawed social environment? Is it simply a narrow substitute, in secular vein, for

a deeper range of involvements available in pre-modern settings? There is no denying that therapy can be an indulgence, and can promote narcissistic withdrawal. Most forms of therapy take time and money: therapy is in some degree a cultivated diversion of the privileged. (Giddens 1991, p. 180)

In recognising the validity of Giddens' (1991) critique of the attempt to adjust individuals to a flawed social environment, I became aware of how these men's experiences were critiques of their families' and social institutions' disciplining processes and how these had failed to conceptualise their emotional lives. One of the arguments arising from this research, developed from Arthur's (2002) "Forgotten Voices", an ethnographic study of soldiers who fought in WW1, concerns how men's emotional worlds are bounded by incomprehension.

Corporal Quinnell (9th Battalion, Royal Fusiliers): ...One thing I really noticed was that after being with the young fellows in the Army, we were a race apart from these civilians. You couldn't talk to the civilians about the war, you'd be wasting your time. They hadn't the slightest conception of what the conditions were like and so forth. So after a time you didn't talk about it. (Arthur 2002, p. 133)

This helped me to understand why, for example, drug users often talked about wanting to be supported by other drug users, primarily due to their having a similar set of experiences and understandings. This quote highlights the way in which Corporal Quinnell felt completely alienated from civilians after returning back to the UK; he was unable to relate his experiences and felt trapped within them. The aim at DiD/Orexis was to develop a service where people could be understood, and, although it took time and money, we were providing to men and women who were extremely marginalized a form of support usually reserved for the wealthy.

The supervision sessions were crucial in helping me to understand the 'front' as a performance, rather than taking it as indicative of the whole man. I began to think of the actions that allowed these men to be macho on the 'street', and yet speak to me in a counselling session of their inner worlds. There seemed a mismatch between men who would stab, beat, rob, shoplift, and murder – seemingly without a care – and the men who would break down and cry over bereavements, lost relationships and the terror of being alone. These 'fronts' appeared locked into an image they were unable to transcend. Drug use was helping them to sustain this role/front/projection, but underneath they had little confidence or self-esteem. Most of their daily lives, I perceived, was based on bluster and backed with menace. However, I felt I was connecting to something else – a part of themselves they ordinarily concealed from others for fear of appearing vulnerable and therefore getting hurt – and then I began to notice how often these masculine 'fronts' were used by many men with whom I came into contact.

This research project developed as a response to Paul Willis's "Learning to Labour" (1977) and his study of 12 working class young men. He became involved in a form of participant observation, which gave him access to his research subjects. He then recorded his encounters in the school. The study explored how these young adolescent males experienced the school system, analysing the resistances they developed to learning, which ensured their eventual subordination to dominant interests.

I envisaged my study as a further extension of Willis's (1977) research. The men I worked with had created resistances to emotional pain ensuring that a large part of their adolescence and adult life was spent incarcerated. The obvious difference between Paul Willis and myself was that he was outside the school system having a clear research role. I was a counsellor engaged in helping these men to recover memories subsumed by their drug use. I had a different form of access to these men and gained insights into how they had been shaped and their motivations for their current actions.

I will explain why I chose a small sample, how I came to choose my research subjects, my analysis of the ethnographic data and the challenges I faced in writing up my research.

Rationale for a small-scale qualitative study

In drawing from Trondman and Willis's (2001) definition of ethnography "a family of methods involving direct and sustained social contact with agents, and of richly writing up the encounter, respecting, recording representing at least partly *in its own terms*, the irreducibility of human experience" (Trondman and Willis, 2001, p2) I will show why the study was limited to fourteen men.

My research aim was to illuminate these men's internal worlds. As they described their lives I perceived how their emotional flows of anger and violence had impacted on their social environment and how they had reacted. My methodological framework illustrates how "ethnography and theory should be conjoined to produce a concrete sense of the social as internally sprung and dialectically produced". (Trondman and Willis, 2001, p2). They define ethnographic research as a "critique of over-functionalist, over structuralist and over theorized views and to the positive development of reflexive forms of social theorizing, allowing a voice to those who live their conditions of existence." (Trondman and Willis, 2001 p3). I drew on this form of ethnography to provide a voice for these men and explore why they had been silent. I also drew upon the trust I had built with my male clients in order to help them articulate why they had become embroiled in the drug culture.

These clients attended the agency as self-referrals. They initially came to the Drop In Clinic on a Monday morning where they filled in an initial assessment. They were then placed on a waiting list until a treatment slot became available. The average length of time in 1996 was two weeks. These clients were allocated to the counsellors on a first come first served basis. In 1996 we had six counsellors who had a caseload of 20-25 clients each. We had begun to develop services for other client groups, for example a specialist service for women, another for African Caribbean clients as well as a Vietnamese service. We began to create a distinct service for men and this research helped everyone to understand the rationale for establishing this first innovative service. The agency had engaged with a large number of male clients over the first seven years of its development and there were three male counsellors working with this group.

When clients attended the Drop In Clinic they were asked to fill in a form, detailing their drug use, GP and contact address. We also asked them to provide a urine sample allowing us to verify their drug use. The clients were then allocated at team meetings according to who had treatment slots. After being allocated to a counsellor the client then undertook a more "in depth" assessment. This provided us with an insight into their family, school, work, mental health and prison experiences. This first session involved asking many detailed questions requiring the assessor to draw on their counselling skills to ensure the interview did not become an interrogation.

As a team we met every Thursday to discuss client issues where we began to note patterns to the individual experiences. As I supervised the other counsellors between 1990-1996 I noted similarities in family dynamics when we discussed the white male clients. One of the methods we used in the "in depth assessment" to explore family dynamics was to create family trees. In plotting the relationships between family members we began to see how sons and daughters developed particular coping strategies to cope with familial violence. It was through the group supervision these individual life histories narrated by the counselling team materialised as social phenomena.

Research Issues

In recognising the patterns I began to reflect how I could help a wider public understand drug misuse from our treatment perspective. I first raised the idea with the DiD management committee. They appreciated the energy I was putting into developing the counselling and gave their permission to undertake this research. I then approached Goldsmiths College in 1996 with a proposal aiming to analyse the impact of family dynamics on drug users, drawing on the voices of my clients and their experiences. In my first meeting with my supervisor he asked me to reflect on how men's experiences could be analysed collectively and I was introduced to masculinity as a research topic. In order to proceed with the research, Vic suggested I ask the client's permission to tape the sessions.

Over the seven years since the inception of DiD/Orexis, I had developed trust with the local community. Simon, John, Billy, Gary, Rod and Rob had all been in and out of treatment since the project had begun. I had never asked them if I could tape the sessions and I began to reflect on how I would approach them. I explored the issues with my clinical supervisor and the potential effects on the counselling relationships I had established. My clinical supervisor suggested I talk to my clients about my reasons for undertaking the research to gain their acceptance. I prepared my clients for the research by asking them after their session had finished if they had ever read anything that described their experiences and if they would like to participate in a project, which would be based on their lives. The pre preparation work took place from September until December 1996. Apart from the clients feeling uneasy I also felt some trepidation in exposing my own counselling expertise.

The clients' initial reactions varied from Gary's expression of "yes if it will help others" to an ambivalence expressed by Damien "what's the point?" They all agreed that they would take part when they felt ready. I began the taping process in January 1997, after talking to Bri. I knew from past experiences the research would not evolve if I forced the men to participate. I knew they had all spent time incarcerated and were suspicious of authority figures. They had all been subject to various disciplines where they had been acted upon rather than listened to. It had also taken me a considerable effort to build up trust and I knew it was a fragile relationship, which could be shattered at any moment if they thought I was undermining them or passing on information to the authorities about their lives. I operated within the counselling boundaries concerning threats of violence, child abuse and self-harm. These were made clear at the beginning, but a grey area emerged when they began to talk about fights that had occurred in the past.

In January 1997 I had a caseload of fourteen men attending each week for support. I decided to approach was Bri because he was very open about his life and I knew his criminal activities had ceased. This first taped session provided me with an insight into the issues of trust and influence the dynamics of my research. Ten minutes into the session Bri stated he did not want to talk about certain topics on tape especially as he felt we had already covered them in previous sessions.

My clinical supervisor provided me with invaluable feedback on my counselling technique. I wanted to know if I was "pushing" the client to talk and damaging the trust I had built. The feedback I received from both supervisors was that I needed to be clear about my role. I was first and foremost a counsellor involved in research rather than a researcher involved in counselling. After clarifying my purpose the other sessions took place without this role confusion. Initially I began to tape the older clients and this helped me with my confidence. When I began to talk to the younger clients I was subsequently taken by surprise as using the tape recorder helped to shift the counselling dynamics. These men who had previously found it difficult to articulate their emotions began to speak into the recorder about painful incidents previously unexplored. My last taped session with Damien, who was the most sceptical, illuminated his emotional pain after trying to reconnect with his family.

The taping of the sessions took place during the first eight months of 1997. Initially I presented one transcribed report, along with a copy of the tape, and some written ideas about the themes of the session, at each research supervision review. As I gained confidence in my abilities I began to present two transcripts at each review along with my notes and copies of the tapes. This routine allowed my supervisor to check the contents of my transcribed version whilst listening to the tape. Vic initially suggested I use a computer program to help me highlight the themes but I felt this would hinder the organic analysis of the research. Intuitively I felt it would not help me understand the emotional content of each counselling session. At each supervision review we discussed the contents of the tape and the issues that arose in the sessions. It was during this process of taping and transcribing Vic suggested I begin to read the masculinity literature.

It was through this supervision process that I began to understand the concept of masculinity. When I embarked upon this research process I was ambivalent about the topic having on reflection a minimal understanding of the concept. In order to overcome my initial scepticism Vic suggested I read Jim Gilligan (2000) and Klaus Thewelait (1977, 1978) to help me understand the differing masculinities. The drug misuse literature was embryonic and these books on USA and German masculinities provided me with potential ideas for shaping my research. It was not until I had finished the taping process that I began to understand the issues explored in Gilligan (2000) and Thewelait (1977, 1978).

During the taping process none of the men spoke specifically about their masculinity or what it was it was like to be a man. I felt too awkward to raise it as a topic as I was unsure of what it meant for myself. Discussing the concept in research review meetings was not an easy process and the debates became heated. In the spring of 1998 Vic suggested I needed to undertake more work on myself, meaning I needed to have a clearer understanding of my own motivations and emotions in order to understand others. At the time I was unsure what he meant but in retrospect it has become very clear.

At the end of the eight-month process of taping and writing I had fourteen transcripts and a number of ideas but no systematic template for organising the material. In trying to assemble and write up the data I faced another considerable challenge. This next stage proved to be difficult. I had fourteen individual case studies each having an obvious connection to drug use and family dynamics. One of the methods I used was to try and raise some of my tentative findings with colleagues, friends, family and research peers. It was through this practice that I began to find out about myself.

I began to explore with friends and colleagues the themes that arose in the counselling sessions within the boundaries of confidentiality. The one person apart from Vic who provided particular supportive insights was my sister. Exploring the ideas of a connection between family dynamics and drug misuse with friends was generally met with "So what? Many people have difficult childhoods but they do not become drug users". "Are you saying that all people who are abused use drugs? " "My old man gave me a clip around the ear but it didn't do me any harm". Other community workers questioned me whether the research was an obsession through which I was seeking to impart the causes of all societal problems. I needed to think through the implications of each of these comments. I began to understand I was treading on some very fragile territory. These discussions generally revealed a negative perception of the research, which led to some initial self-doubt. I felt intuitively I was right and this was confirmed when working with other clients over the length of the research. I also explored ideas in 'group supervision' and this provided me with some feedback that helped to shape the research.

I will highlight one example of the personal resistance I faced as it provides an example of the difficulties in exploring these issues with friends. It also highlights how memories and emotions are 'masked'. I explored some of the research themes with a friend who had grown up in Deptford. My friend had already spoken about his father's drinking, his absences and his violence when he returned. I could see a possible connection between his experiences and some of the themes arising in the research. I began by speaking about some of the themes that arose in the research, particularly about the effects of a father's violence on his children and how the clients had masked their childhood memories. He answered that although his father had liked to drink, it was not abuse as he understood it, as it had not affected him. A few months later he invited me to a family gathering, luckily his father was absent. Unexpectedly my friend announced my research theories and his mum instantly reacted by slapping my cheek. The younger brothers then began to talk about other violent incidents, which had previously been masked. I began to reflect on this incident, and noted the similarities in how painful emotions are masked. Other issues arose such as active forgetting, coupled with the repercussions of the denial and the ensuing pain when they re emerge.

This type of research, because of the intensity of the emotions I was exploring, could only be undertaken through cultivating trust. I was fully aware of the sensitivity of the work I was involved in. I had experienced the dangers of the research as I had literally felt the 'sting' from the hand of my friend's mum. The research would necessarily entail visiting the sites of these men's' pain and this affirmed my belief the project could only be undertaken as a small-scale study due to the sensitivity of the emotional lives of these men and the possible repercussions. In drawing on this particular ethnographic method I felt I was not just opening these men up for research purposes but also working to heal them. This also created a different research dynamic. This is why I chose a small research sample.

Organising the Transcripts

Initially I began to organise the transcripts into themes. It became akin to a giant jigsaw puzzle, however what was missing was a dynamic that drew the pieces together. My reading began after the taping had finished. When I finished reading Thewelait's (1977,1978) two volumes on German masculinities I became influenced by his subconscious flow and began write down all the ideas, which materialised. I then began to read the authors who had influenced him, in particular Elias Cannetti (1960) as well as Deleuze and Guattari (1972). It was through this reading and listening to the transcripts I understood there were at least three differing forces acting upon these men, the historical forces, the familial and the institutional forces, although neither was separate or distinct. I visualised them as interconnected dialectical forces. In reading Cannetti (1960) I understood the effects of the 'arrows' and 'stings' and it was through Deleuze and Guattari (1972) I derived the concept of 'flows'. This provided me with a psychological dynamic to help shape the material. As an example the perception of emotions as a 'flow' allowed me to visualise the connections between discharging the violence and its impact upon the recipient. After reading Boadella (1978) I understood how the discharge impacted upon the body and I combined these ideas with Cannetti's 'stings' (1960) to understand the physical pressure of psychological forces. These authors provided me with a template, providing an insight into the forces, which shaped these men. I explored these tentative ideas within clinical supervision, through watching television and through listening to Radio 4's various programs on current events. It was through continuously processing the dynamics and through a gradual self-analysis I became increasingly confident to draw on this theoretical framework. Willis and Trondman (2001) note this process as being part of their definition of an ethnographic method "Even though the final write up need not show every stage, the dialectics of 'surprise' need time and can unfold only over time in relation to the researcher's own 'experience', field and theoretical (Trondman and Willis, 2001 p7).

In attempting to write up the chapters initially I presented them as individual case histories, with the thesis blossoming into fourteen chapters. As I embarked upon this process my supervisor brought to my attention the similarity of the themes emerging in the differing chapters. I realised I was repeating myself and from initial despair I then realised I could draw together the similarities of the differing experiences. This was also a method we had used in 'group supervision' at the agency. The one dominant theme arising in several of these rudimentary chapters was familial violence. This was the basis for the first integrated chapter.

I realised there was overwhelming information arising from the sessions about the differing father/son relationships. In the younger men's cases this relationship was almost wholly based upon being the recipients of violence. Gary, Simon, John and Billy spoke of their fathers' aggression. Bri, Ross, Al and Rob had all spoke previously of the violence they had endured as children but we did not explore this on the taped sessions. Rod. Pete, Wayne, Phil and Alex had all previously spoken of their father's drinking affecting their family. Damien spoke of his mother's drinking problem and how this had affected him in his previous sessions, and as it did not arise on tape, I did not explore it further in the research. These insights provided the basis for the chapter on "Fathers and Sons", the links between familial violence and alcoholism. This was the chapter I presented to the upgrade supervisors.

As I began to work on "Fathers and Sons" I knew Gary and Pete had some understanding of their father's emotional lives. In reading Thewelait (1977, 1978), Miller (1987), Deleuze and Guattari (1972) I began to understand the links between their anger and their suppressed emotions. Vic suggested that I should try to interview family members but I felt it would negate the counselling relationships I had built. This explains why I drew upon the sons' perception of their fathers' alcoholism to try and understand how it had evolved.

The next chapter I wrote analysed the fathers' coping strategies and the effects of the historical epoch, the dynamics of the latter part of the twentieth century. This allowed me to locate these men's emotional responses to how they were treated in their family and their experiences of war and poverty.

In response to the questions that have arisen regarding the validity of this approach my research and counselling experiences had allowed me to build and sustain a form of trust which had allowed me to penetrate beyond the 'front', the presentation to the everyday world of what has been 'masked'. I felt vindicated by my method when the film "Nil by Mouth", (1998) written and directed by Gary Oldman, who spent his formative years in

New Cross, was released. It depicted violent experiences resonating with the issues arising in the counselling sessions. I understood why these men feared articulating their emotions, the connections to the unleashing of their anger and the use of drugs to subsume emotional pain.

The challenge throughout writing this research was when to draw on the research and when to let the men speak for themselves. The theoretical paradigm was based upon innovation and therefore I needed to ensure that this approach had validity when contesting areas that had been scientifically researched.

The counselling sessions had highlighted how these men were victims before they were protagonists and the dialectical connections between being bullied and the explosion of violence. The tapes also revealed the impact of the institutions on these men's psychologies and I began to understand the effects of institutional power and how this had been enacted. The themes of revenge appeared constantly in the sessions and the concept of 'flows' and 'stings' helped me to understand why this was crucial in gaining an understanding on how these men's masculinities had formed. The revenge culture provided local masculine status as a currency of respect. I realised that whilst these men were childhood victims they were adult protagonists and I needed to understand how this had arisen. This led to the on "Violence" and "Strategies of Revenge" where I explored the connections between being the recipient of violence and becoming a protagonist.

The last chapters I wrote were "Relationships and "Bodies under Threat". All of the men apart from Rod had tried to form relationships with women. The themes of loss, not being good enough and explosions of anger arose continuously in the sessions. I explored the dynamics of loss and how this had led to these men to 'self medicate' for their emotional pain. The chapter on "Relationships" portrayed how these men were struggling to emotionally connect with their partners but fearful of the consequences. This resulted in further emotional pain and their return to the drug culture.

In the chapter exploring "Bodies" Rod highlights how he is reliant on others to help him fight back. He does not have the physical power to engage in violence. This highlights the importance of body power in these men's lives. Rod has a sense of shame about his body and as a result he has shrunk away from the world. This lack of confidence has meant that he has been unable to form relationships outside of his family. Rod's narration of the effects of the incidents upon his body and his self esteem has been compounded by the inability of the institutions to understand the latent effects of trauma on a child. I make a link between this inability to conceptualise this trauma and an institutional inability to conceptualise and understand the effects of PTSD. Rod has been unable to verbalise his pain, he can describe it, but not its effects, which he keeps to himself.

Subsequently I have spoken with Gary, Simon, Rob, Rod, Phil and Bri about the research findings. They have all expressed surprise that I have endeavoured over the years to make sense of their lives and they feel a sense of flattery that I found them so interesting, to devote such a large amount of time thinking about them. I hope that if they ever get around to reading the thesis they will not be disappointed.

Relational Method

My relationships with these men changed over time, and I noticed how I was becoming more confident as a counsellor. This led to an easier flow of communication as I began to understand the multi-dimensional nature of these men's lives, rather than accepting the initial 'front'. From the insights they provided, I began to see how crucial were their emotional worlds for understanding their current behaviour patterns. Apart from Willis (1978), Carol Gilligan et al. in "Mapping the Moral Domain" (1988) and "Making Connections" (1990) provided another insight through their work with young women in understanding how emotional worlds impacted upon belief systems. Gilligan et al. (1988, 1990) analysed the concepts of emotional connection and detachment, listening to young women's voices as they revealed their concerns about developing empathic connections around care, justice and truth, whilst also under pressure to conform to patriarchal values, which prized rational, value-free thought.

One of the wider methodological concerns of the research was to highlight how these rational forms of thought were based upon a separation, a detachment, between the object being studied and the observer. Gilligan (1988, 1990) notes how this has become linked to a specific, male psychological viewpoint, reifying this form of thinking that sees its antithesis in the emotional world. Emotions within this paradigm are perceived as being intrusive to the creation of rational knowledge. Vic Seidler's "Unreasonable Men" (1994) draws on this work to challenge the basic assumptions behind these rational forms.

In recognising the emotional life of the body we are challenging a Cartesian dualism and opening up space within our inherited traditions of social theory to recognise that we exist as emotional and spiritual beings as much as mental and physical beings. If we are to recognise the interiority of these different aspects of our experience, we have to break with the reductionisms we inherit. This is to acknowledge that 'rationality' should not simply apply to an independent faculty of reason. It is equally important to recognise the 'rationality' of our emotional lives. (Seidler 1994, p. 25)

With this critique in mind, I read "Mapping the Moral Domain" (1988) and "Making Connections" (1990), and I was struck by the emphasis on empathy and feelings. In their analysis, Gilligan et al. (1988) viewed relationships as crucial to understanding human beings, highlighting their reasons for reconsidering adolescent development.

The ahistorical approach to human events also underlies the fourth reason for reconsideration; namely, the overriding value psychologists have placed upon separation, individuation and autonomy. To see self-sufficiency as the hallmark of maturity conveys a view of adult life that is at odds with the human condition, a view that cannot sustain the kinds of long term commitments and involvements with other people that are necessary for raising and educating a child or for citizenship in a democratic society (see Arendt 1959) The equation of development with separation and of maturity with independence presupposes a radical discontinuity of generations and encourages a view of human experience that is essentially divorced from history and time. (Gilligan 1988, p. xii)

This research follows this paradigm shift. My analysis aims to locate these men within a specific time frame, drawing on historical events and locating them within their neighbourhood. The men in this study are emotionally isolated, which emerged in the sessions as a crucial problem, leading me to question the "development with separation and of maturity with independence". This separation, whilst perceived as a male strength, was at the same time belied by their emotional turmoil and their desire to emotionally connect with others, and by their use of drugs.

Another important aspect of the work of Gilligan et al. (1988) is their theory on how relationships are sustained. These counselling sessions are more than just sociological qualitative interviews; they are snapshots of my relationships with these men, taken at a particular juncture when they felt ready to talk to me with a tape recorder on. This was the result of an ongoing process that allowed these men to access an inner world. Gilligan et al. in "Making Connections" (1990) describes the process of working with the young women:

> In this resonant setting I heard girls speak about storms in relationships, and pleasure in relationships, revealing a knowledge that often was grounded in detailed descriptions of inner psychic worlds - relational worlds through which girls sometimes moved freely and which at other times seemed blocked or walled. Listening for this knowledge, I felt myself entering, to some extent, the underground city of female

adolescence, the place where powerful learning experiences were happening. (Gilligan 1990, p. 14)

The obvious difference is that I was working with adult men, but they similarly allowed me to enter "their inner psychic worlds". However, what they showed me, to continue the imagery, were the dungeons where their emotions languished. They also had walls, and I feel that by no means did they share everything with me. I had been allowed into their lives as someone who could be trusted, but there were still secrets.

The counterpart to the image of the wall is the search for an opening, a way of reaching another person, of finding a place of entry. Yet to open oneself to another person creates great vulnerability, and thus the strength of a girl's desire for relationships also engenders the need for protection from fraudulent relationships and psychic wounding. (Gilligan 1990, p. 21)

This depicts the process of creating and sustaining relationships, the trust building and the manipulation. In the sessions, I often felt as though I was almost literally travelling around a wall, trying to find an opening to make a connection. This would take a considerable time before clients began to show me these other aspects of themselves. What emerged were their desires for self-protection, not to be hurt again, and the desire to inflict violence in order to stop themselves from being hurt. This marked a point of difference with the women studied by Carol Gilligan (1990) and led me to reflect on the costs of sustaining masculinities.

Another key text was Studs Terkel's "American Dreams" (1982). Terkel does not describe his methodological process other than:

> In this book are a hundred American voices, captured by hunch, circumstance and a rough idea. There is not pretence at statistical "truth", nor consensus. There is in the manner of a jazz work, an attempt, of theme and improvisation, to recount dreams, lost and found, and a recognition of possibility. (Terkel 1982, p. 26)

What excited me was his exploration of people's dreams using his "jazz method", and not knowing in advance where he was going. This idea, which was incorporated into my initial research, resonates with Yalom's (1989) description of the therapeutic process of finding a method that works. Terkel's (1982) book is framed as social history, but the interview content struck me emotionally as well as intellectually. I read it when I studied American history, and it had a much greater impact than my readings on the theoretical framings, where the voices of people were often absent. I wanted to emulate this method, but, apart from Willis (1978), it seemed at variance with the methodological texts I was reading in sociology in 1982. In returning to sociology, I wanted to find a way of describing this process in order to locate another form of gendered qualitative methodological research.

Researching Masculinity, Violence and Drug Misuse

The process of sifting through the tapes involved transcribing each 45-minute session. This duration was governed by the length of each tape and the desire not to break the flow of the conversation once the tape was running by turning it over.

The transcribing process involved an organic process of becoming aware of the themes emerging from the tapes, as each one involved five to six hours of listening and writing, playing each tape at least seven times. After this transcription, I wrote a summary of each session highlighting the major themes before presenting the tape to VicSeidler. This formed the basis of our initial supervision sessions where we explored the content with the aim of analysing the emotions arising in each session. Vic initially suggested I use a computer analysis, but I felt that this would thwart my connection to the emotional nuances of the research. Consequently, I embarked upon a program of continuous listening and reflection upon the contents of the tapes.

With the organisation of the material, it was difficult to decide whether to concentrate on individual sessions for each chapter or to try and tie in different sessions where there was an intersection of themes. Following Terkel (1982), these sessions were part of a free-flowing exploration of these men's worlds and my ideas were not specifically organised beforehand, but were part of the organic process of the counselling. Careful listening to the tapes, along with supervision sessions and my own reflections from working with these men, helped me to shape the material. After a considerable period of experimentation, consisting of many initial dead ends, I began to develop my confidence through my reading. Subsequently, I was able to test some of my reflections in the subsequent counselling sessions. This was a dialectical process of discovering notions of "emotional truth", and the men I was working with told me what worked.

Another important aspect to this research was the reflections drawn from my own life. In the course of this research, I felt my own experiences as a man provided me with emotional insights into these men's experiences of events such as relationship loss, birth and bereavement.

I also had the space to reflect on how fortunate I was not to have endured the same experiences, but I also felt uncomfortable when the emotions they revealed resonated with me. Therefore, this research also marked a personal journey for me in relation to my own masculinity, and became part of the congruence of the research, as I was able to see where my life history converged and then significantly diverged from that of the men in this study.

Key Texts - Thewelait, Cannetti, Miller, Deleuze and Guattari

Following the example of Terkel (1982) I began to develop a framework for organising the transcripts, as I wanted the texts to speak for themselves. However, the theoretical gaps in the substance misuse literature and its emphasis on the drug rather than emotions meant that I had to search further afield.

My first decision was to conceptualise men in relation to their 'masculinities'. I knew this intuitively. However, being part of this paradigm made it challenging to think beyond it. A major theoretical shift occurred when I read Klaus Thewelait's "Male Fantasies", Volumes 1 and 2 (1977, 1978). Here, I found an insight into how German masculinities were constructed in the 1920s and I began to see further legitimacy in my ideas drawing sociology and psychology together.

Thewelait, writing in the 1970s, analysed the psychological underpinnings of men who joined the Freikorps, the genesis of the Nazi party, drawing his ideas from a number of sources, including Deleuze and Guattari's "Anti Oedipus" (1972), regarding the 'flows' of desire.

If desire is repressed, it is because every position of desire, no matter how small, is capable of calling into question the established order of a society: not that desire is asocial, on the contrary. But it is explosive; there is no desiring machine capable of being assembled without demolishing entire social sectors. (Deleuze and Guattari 1972, p. 116)

Thewelait (1977, 1978) looks at this repression of desire as a stifling of human potential, drawing on the concepts of flows and dams posited in Deleuze and Guattari's "Anti Oedipus" (1972). All these terms relate to abstract notions of how people communicate – not just with information but also emotions – when words are the carriers.

Dams are described as frozen emotions held within the mind and body. One of the ideas Deleuze and Guattari (1972) analyse is how desire, a notion drawn from Nietzsche (1968), becomes a paramount emotional force. They move away from Nietzsche's "Will to Power" (1968), which they criticise for its implicit emotional coldness, particularly marked by a lack of empathy or ability to be affected, embodied in the following quote:

> ...if pleasure is every increase in power, displeasure
> every feeling of not being able to resist or dominate;
> may we not then posit pleasure and displeasure
> as cardinal facts? (Nietzsche 1968, p. 369)

Instead, they concentrate on 'flows' of emotions that do not require domination, only connection.

> Two words for power exist in French, puissance and pouvoir. In Deleuze and Guattari they are associated with different concepts (although the terminological distinction is not consistently observed). Puissance refers to a range of potential. It has been defined by Deleuze as a "capacity for existence", a capacity to affect or be affected", a capacity to multiply connections that may be realized by a given "body" to varying degree in varying situations. It may be thought of as a scale of intensity or fullness of existence (or a degree on such a scale) analogous to the capacity of a number to be raised to a higher power. It is used in the French translation of Nietzsche' s term will to power. (Massumi, in the Preface to Deleuze and Guattari's "Thousand Plateaus", 1980, p. xvii.)

Deleuze and Guattari (1972) challenged Freudian analysis, with its emphasis on repression of the instinctual drives leading to a civilising process. Deleuze and Guattari (1972) are concerned with how human beings can unleash their potential instead of continuing to be bound by repression. Thewelait's (1977, 1978) analysis, using Deleuze and Guattari (1972), illustrates how army induction and its punishments, coupled with the strict upbringing in German families and the harsh treatment of children and women, creates men who repress their empathic feelings and emotions; thus empathically sterilised, the become involved in state-sanctioned violence.

Thewelait (1977) describes men tightly bound and rigid in their thinking and emotional responses as the literal products of institutional and familial beatings, creating a rigid masculinity, discharging itself through killing the other. I noted he drew his ideas from Cannetti's "Crowds and Power" (1960) and Wilhelm Reich's "Mass Psychology of Fascism" (1946).

I have explored both of these different facets of Thewelait's research within my literature review. In "Character Analysis" (1933), Reich introduced the idea of 'streamings' – energy flowing through the body – in his search for the vitality of life. Reich saw these 'streamings' as having a primarily sexual function, emerging through the (hetero) sexual act. Thewelait develops this argument by seeing streamings as repressed desires rather than a repressed sexual sphere. This extract from Gerda Boyesen (1976), a post-Reichian, provides an account of the term 'streamings', which I feel is akin to Thewelait (1977, 1978). It also conceptualises the idea of 'flows', providing further illumination of the ideas I drew from Deleuze and Guattari (1972).

> If all goes well, the streamings or energy potential of the body should give natural growth and self-realization both psychologically and physically. Such energy should be available as a sort of reservoir to be drawn upon in emotional or emergency situations and also in ecstasy or delight. If a critical situation arises, the organism has to draw from the reservoir the amount of energy needed to cope with the situation; but after this has been abreacted and the danger is over, the energy should be free to **flow** back to the

reservoir and to circulate around the body giving the natural feeling of aliveness and well being.

But if emotional expression is inhibited or stuck and the person is in a permanent situation of emotional provocation, the amount of energy in the reservoir is less because it is being used in the frustrated emotional block. This causes the organism to be exhausted or irritable and the natural feeling of euphoria disappears. But if the body is able to work out nervous energy, biochemical stress products are released into the blood stream and the organism can return to a free energy flow.

Each time the organism is not able to get rid of emotional stress products (adrenaline, lactic acid etc) there will be a build up, an obstacle, for moving energy; and for each layer of restored neurotic defence or armouring there will be a fresh layer hampering the full streaming energy from coming through. (Boyesen in Boadella 1976, p. 83. My emphasis in bold.)

This quote links emotions to the body's biology, drawing on the analogy of 'flows'. It provides an insight into the 'masking' process, linking it directly to the construction of a 'front' and hampering the 'full streaming energy' by restricting its flow.

In his study, Male Fantasies (1977, 1978), Thewelait describes this damming of the flows. He analyses the development of coping mechanisms, the 'front' and how the emotions are released through violence, 'reconnecting' through 'flows of blood'. The above quote provides a background to the physiological and psychological processes accompanying the interactions that take place in daily life. This helped me to create an understanding of the construction of white working class masculine identities in this study.

The ideas I am analysing are akin to those Thewelait explored in "Male Fantasies" (1977, 1978) – the construction of rigid white male identities. However, the men in this study are not just engaged in violence; they have also created strategies for nullifying it, marking a shift in generational coping. Alice Miller's "For Your Own Good" (1987) illuminated these connections, reaching similar conclusions to those of Klaus Thewelait and tracing the similarities in coping mechanisms between various Nazi leaders as well as a mass killer (Peter Kurten) and a heroin user (Christiane F) (Miller 1987).

Miller (1987) portrays the family circumstances of various Nazi leaders such as Hoss, Himmler and Hitler, concentrating on their childhoods. She analyses how the punishment they received, principally at the hands of their fathers, led to a burning sense of anger. This had links to the work that Gitta Sereny (1974, 1995, 1998) had undertaken with Franz Stangl, Albert Speer and Mary Bell. The works of Thewelait (1977, 1978), Reich (1946) and Miller (1987) analysed in particular the German family structure as a source of the patriarchal flow of power, enacted through displays of violence aimed at wives and children. Stangl, the extermination camp commandant, spoke to Sereny (1974) regarding his relationship with his father.

> He put me over his knees and leathered me. He had cut his finger some days before and wore a bandage. He thrashed me so hard, his

cut opened and blood poured out. I heard my mother scream, "Stop it, you are splashing blood all over the clean walls." (Sereny 1974, p. 26)

Alice Miller (1987), quoting from John Toland (1976) draws attention to a similarity of backgrounds between Hitler and Stangl when Hitler related this story to his secretaries:

Enduring
Pain

"Years later he told one of his secretaries that he had read in an adventure novel that it was proof of courage to show no pain. And so I resolved not to make a sound the next time my father whipped me. And when the time came - I can still remember my frightened mother standing outside the door - I silently counted the blows. My mother thought I had gone crazy when I beamed proudly and said, "Father hit me thirty two times! (Miller 1987, p. 156)

Although there is a cultural, temporal and geographical distance involved, these types of family dynamics resonated with my therapeutic experiences. It is interesting to note that although none of the Deptford men had been National Front skinheads, the other younger men who lived outside Deptford had joined various national parties. Miller's (1987) understanding of the emotional repercussions of violence within the family allowed me to conceptualise how emotions become encoded within language and their effect upon the psychological and physical well being of the recipient. She also introduced the ideas of exploding with violence and shrinking from emotional contact, echoing Thewelait (1977,1978), and portraying violence and drug use as particular forms of coping in the late twentieth century. I will explore this concept extensively, marking two particular forms of coping deployed by the men in this study.

Drug Use and Self-medication for Pain

In the process of shrinking, heroin use plays a crucial role. This led me to Khantzian's 'self-medication' hypothesis, described in "Psychotherapy and Substance Abuse" (1995). In the sessions, the theme of family violence emerged constantly. I wanted to understand how this developed and how it affected these men. Khantzian and Murphy (1995) describe how drug use helps to block memories:

> In attempting to adapt to one's emotions and one's environment, the action of the substance and the immersion in the drug subculture could be used to mute, extinguish and avoid a range of feelings and emotions. Rather than settling for more ordinary defensive, neurotic, characterological or other adaptive mechanisms as a way of dealing with distress, substance misusers adopt an extraordinary solution by using a powerful drug. (Khantzian and Murphy, Ed. Washton, 1995, P23)

Murphy and Khantzian (1995) depict how drug users develop strategies for coping with feelings and emotions by using substances to extinguish memories and feelings. Miller (1987), Felicity De Zulueta (1993) and Heinl (2001) explore how emotions become internalised after children have suffered pain: one such strategy is disassociation.

I noted how being a drug user allowed these men to create new identities through masking their emotions, as they were terrified of the transformation this would entail. I shifted from Willis's (1978) analysis of 'lads culture' to looking at the terror behind the 'front'.

Cannetti's "Crowds and Power" (1960) became invaluable in thinking around ideas of pain and humiliation and masculine identity and his symbolic references to explain physical events, particularly the 'stings' of anger, as drawn on by Thewelait (1977,1978), impressed me. These stings are described as an arrow, with the victim being emotionally wounded by the anger. This led me to reconsider some of the articles concerning the body in Boadella's "In the Wake of Reich" (1976). I felt that Boyesen's (1976) notion of the build-up of anger in the biology of the body could be developed further in looking at the relationships between people. In conceptualising these as 'flows', I shifted from a Reichian emphasis on sexual energy to one of a psychic relationship between people. Talk about sex hardly ever arose in the sessions, perhaps either marking a limit or because most of the men expressed no interest. In the course of the reading I was beginning to sift through these various ideas for framing of the research, and the post-Reichian work was useful for visualising the effects of pain. But I also wanted to analyse these Deptford masculinities within a wider social framework, rather than focusing exclusively on the body. Again, drawing on Thewelait (1977, 1978), I began to see 'masculinity' as an act displayed for onlookers. I began to understand how these men could behave on the 'street', then shift when trust was created to explore the difference between the 'fronts' and their relationship to what had been 'masked'.

I began to retrace these 'fronts' and 'masks' back to the worlds of their fathers as described in the counselling sessions. The local culture seemingly promoted a certain type of stoicism in the face of emotional pain. The number of public houses in Deptford, many now closed and transformed into offices or flats, points to their once central role in local men's lives. Indeed, in the sessions, their fathers' alcohol use had emerged as a form of emotional coping.

Ontological Security

In hearing the accounts of so much emotional pain, I felt the need to conceptualise its opposite, to understand one of the elements that had been 'masked'. R.D. Laing in "The Divided Self" (1960) and "The Self and Others" (1961) provides a notion of 'ontological security'. Giddens, in "Modernity and Self Identity" (1991), drawing on Laing (1960, 1961), describes how a person nurtured in a family where love and affection is given gains a sense of wonder at being alive. This empathic dialectic relationship, allows the infant to develop self-confidence through having an emotional anchor. When this bond is ruptured, the infant is left with a sense of dread (Bowlby 1951, 1973). Giddens (1991) described how children are nurtured through the development of an emotional 'cocoon', as the bonds of love and nurturing (food, warmth, play) created between parent and child reaffirms the child's sense of being valued. This idea of a cocoon of love helped me to integrate Cannetti's (1960) notion of 'stings', as representing a break in this flow.

Nancy Chodorow in "Reproduction of Mothering (1978) and Carol Gilligan (1990) provided the connection between these flows of nurture and the relationship between mother and child. Nancy Chodorow (1978) illuminates how she perceives masculinity being forged:

A boy, in order to feel himself adequately masculine, must distinguish and differentiate himself from others in a way a girl needs not - must categorize himself as someone apart. Moreover he defines masculinity negatively as that which is not feminine and/or connected to women, rather than positively. This is another way boys come to deny and repress relation and connection in the process of growing up. (Chodorow 1978, p. 174)

This link between masculinity and denial of the emotions helped me to frame these sessions and conceptualise my relationship with these men. It illuminates why I believe these men found counselling so challenging: because it necessarily implies connection.

The mother and son relationship and its importance in shaping these men's emotional lives was a surprising finding of this study. This is the primary bond these men have created and sustained with another human being with the potential to nurture and care for them. The role of the mother was seen to be crucial in these sessions. Initially, I was drawn to Winnicott (1965), but in listening to these sessions, it became apparent these men's talk was not about the "good enough mother", but principally about their fathers. Winnicott (1965) describes the effects of emotional turmoil in families as being gendered, with men mostly externalising their anger and women generally internalising their anger. This resonated with the notions of explosion and shrinking I had found in Thewelait (1977, 1978) and Miller (1987).

....the psychopathic personality - here we are concerned mainly with fathers, whereas depression chiefly concerns mothers. The psychopathic is an adult who has not recovered from the delinquency of childhood. This delinquency was originally (in the history of the individual) an antisocial tendency in a deprived child. The deprivation at the beginning was real and was perceived as such by the child; it was a loss of something that was good. And I am intending to imply that something happened, after which nothing was the same again. The antisocial tendency therefore represented a compulsion in the child to make external reality mend the original trauma, which of course became forgotten and therefore became unmendable by simple reversal. In the psychopath this compulsion to go on forcing external reality to make good its failure continues...(Winnicott 1965, p. 51)

This theme of trying to force external reality to mend the original trauma is extensively explored in the chapter on "Fathers and Sons", focusing on Gary's father's violence toward his family.

Winnicott (1965), drawing on John Bowlby's (1951) work on separation, highlighted how care 'flows' from mother to child, shifting the medical emphasis on rational technique to locating the importance of the flow of emotional care. Winnicott states that the primacy of the initial bond is key for providing emotional security. However, as Sereny's (1998) work with Mary Bell highlights, if the mother is abusive then this ruptures the emotional anchor, leading to a sense of deficit of care and nurturing. Ultimately, in this case, it led to disastrous consequences for everyone.

...the ordinary mother is not only the expert; she is actually the only one who can know how to act for that particular baby. There is a reason. It is because of her devotion, which is the only motivation that works. (Winnicott 1965, p. 24)

The men in this research consistently spoke of their mother's care, despite the problems that may have existed in this relationship. However, this care could become a site of pain in itself; having a continuous connection to the feminine world seemingly hampered Rod and Phil's masculinities, creating within them feelings of tension. I do not know what feelings these men had towards their mothers when they were the recipients of their fathers' rage. This marked a limit of the research. The emotional connection between family members becomes, through the relational work I undertook with these men, a method of understanding the importance they attach to these bonds.

Winnicott's (1965) analysis, written in the 1960s when gender roles were more firmly demarcated, focuses primarily on the nurturing effect of the mother. The change in the emphasis in the provision of childcare has led to the conceptualisation of 'masculinity' and how it is formed. In "The Reproduction of Mothering" (1978), Chodorow describes masculinity as a reaction that forms as boys learn to separate from their mothers and as they learn about the expectations attached to their role in the wider world outside of the home.

> The exclusive responsibility of women for their children exacerbates conflicts about masculinity in men. As long as women mother, a stable sense of masculine self is always more problematic than a stable sense of feminine self. Yet cross culturally the more father absence (or absence of adult men) in the family, the most severe are the conflicts about masculinity and fear of women. (Chodorow 1978, p. 213)

This emphasis on the conflicts of masculinity occurs throughout these counselling sessions. However, what occurs is not a desire by these men for their fathers to stay at home but rather what will occur when they do return. I will contend their masculine identities form through having to make a choice between empathy for their mothers and their need for self-protection. It is this, I believe, which creates the latent emotional wounds which are then carried into these men's adult lives, hampering their ability to empathise and therefore to develop emotionally. The younger men's defining problem becomes not the fact that women mother, but that the father is unable to nurture his family.

In explaining how violence has shaped these masculinities, the conflict between love and violence engendered in these families connects to Laing's (1960, 1961) ideas on schizophrenia. Whereas in Laing's analysis schizophrenics retreated from reality, I began to see how these men had found another solution, described by Khantzian (1974,1995) as "self medication".

Pain, Violence and Dissociation

This aspect of Laing's work resonated for me with a later study undertaken by De Zulueta, "From Pain To Violence" (1993), illuminating the effect of trauma and dissociation.

> People who react to stress by carrying on as though nothing has happened dissociate themselves from the reality of their pain, terror or humiliation, but at a price: the self becomes divided and the process of dissociation becomes part of the patient's identity, to be brought back into action when faced with further stress or even situations that are only

reminiscent of the original stress. As a result of this repeated dissociative process, the victim becomes emotionally constricted and cannot experience the full range of feelings within the same state of consciousness. (De Zulueta 1993, p. 180)

This idea of the splitting allows unpleasant events to be 'masked'. I saw a connection between Winnicott (1965), Laing (1960, 1961) and Thewelait (1977, 1978), providing an insight into the conceptualising of 'self-medication' (Khantzian 1974, 1995) and its relationship to the concept of masculinities that I am exploring. Substance misuse within these sessions appears to reinforce this split, with 'dissociation' being used to cope with trauma. Tension arises when the drug is no longer available, memories and emotions surface, and the constructed masculine image 'fragments'. Masculine identity, based upon the gendered split Nancy Chodorow (1978) describes, resonates with the divergence between the masculine 'front' and what has been 'masked' – the emotional nurturing provided primarily by mothers. However, 'masculinities' is not an issue extensively explored in Laing (1960, 1961), Winnicott (1965) or Khantzian (1974,1995), and this research builds on Thewelait's (1977, 1978) research to concentrate on how these men use substances in order to cope with their feelings and emotions.

The Deptford masculinities I explore in this research are derived from these men's relationships with all aspects of their social, physical and emotional environment.

These masculinities are created through interactions with their peers, their mothers and fathers, and the institutions aiming to create 'docile bodies', a term drawn from Foucault's "Discipline and Punish" (1977). In reviewing the sessions, it is apparent the school, police, judiciary, probation authorities and all the other social agents who have acted upon these men, have not conceptualised these men's emotional worlds. This is analogous to the description Sereny (1998) provided concerning the institutional inability to investigate the background of Mary Bell, highlighting how this issue is not only specifically gendered (Sereny 1998), but class-based, and perhaps, from a psychological viewpoint, highlights an institutional 'resistance'. This institutional resistance and its relationship to a masculine 'resistance' is an issue I explore within this research in the chapter "Fathers and Coping Strategies".

'Dissociation', derived from De Zulueta (1993), becomes a key theme for understanding these men's words, as they all describe forms of isolation. In the past, social institutions have disciplined (Foucault 1977) the 'front' with minimal recognition of these men's emotional worlds, and they continue to do so.

As Rod and Billy described their school days, their stories resonated with ideas expressed in Foucault's "Discipline and Punish" (1977). Rod described how he switched off from school whilst Billy decided to pit himself against the system. Billy then described his own emotional battles against the police, prison, and other men as a fight for his self-esteem. Within this process of trying to understand how masculinity and men's emotional loves fitted within a sociological context, Vic Seidler's "Rediscovering Masculinity" (1989) allowed me to conceptualise these men's emotional lives within a sociological framework.

Counter Transference within Research

In thinking through how this relational methodology helped me to conceptualise my research experience, I began to understand some of the problems inherent in participant observation research through reading Connell's, "Masculinities" (1995). He studied a biker gang in Australia, drawing on the methodological pioneering work of Paul Willis (1978). Connell (1995) honestly describes how he found it difficult to empathise with his subjects, which reminded me of a chapter in Yalom's "Love's Executioner (1989) describing the process of 'counter transference':

> Sometimes counter transference is dramatic and makes deep therapy impossible: imagine a Jew treating a Nazi, or a woman who has once been sexually assaulted treating a rapist. But in milder form, counter transference insinuates itself into every course of psychotherapy. (Yalom 1989, p. 87)

I would contend that it is not entirely impossible, as Sereny highlights in "Albert Speer, His Battle with Truth" (1995). Speer did receive therapeutic support from Jewish writers and therapists, as well as other victims of the Nazi extermination, in coming to terms with his part in the Holocaust. Yalom (1989) also recognised his strong feelings towards his client, Betty, who was grossly overweight. These feelings stemmed not from seeing her as a human being, but from his own internalised feelings towards women, derived from his idealisation of the feminine.

> I have always been repelled by fat women. I find them disgusting; their absurd waddle, their absence of body

contour - breasts, laps, buttocks, shoulders, jawlines
cheekbones, *everything...* (Yalom 1989, p. 87-88)

Yalom (1989) realises he has reached the limit of his empathy when Betty asks him for help and he struggles to offer her 'unconditional regard'. However, through the process of working with her he begins to find out more about himself and, paradoxically, she begins to lose weight – one of the goals she set herself. At the end, he reveals to Betty that he has had problems in providing her with 'unconditional regard' and Betty replies that she knew, highlighting the multiplicity of dynamics taking place within relationships. These feelings of distaste emerge in Connell's (1995) description of a gang of bikers:

The outstanding feature of this group's experience of power relations is violence. To a sheltered academic observer, there seems a great deal of violence in these lives. The interviews mention bullying and outrageous canings at school, assaulting a teacher, fights with siblings and parents, brawls in playgrounds and at parties, assaults in reform school and gaol, bashings of women and gay men, individual fist fights and pulling a knife. (Connell 1995, p. 98-99)

Connell (1995) acknowledges his difficulty as a "sheltered academic observer" as he lists a series of violent early life experiences where "there is a lot of concern with face, a lot of work put into keeping up a front" (Connell 1995, p. 111). He has an implicit understanding of what he is describing, but then I feel his own counter transference issues arise as he judges them as having "apparently rigid personalit[ies] compliant to the demands of the milieu, behind which there is no organized character at all" (Connell 1995, p. 111).

This, I feel, marks a limit in this form of participant observation research, as issues of 'counter transference', although acknowledged, are not explored and overcome. It was also an issue I had to contend with in working with these men in Deptford who knew how to display their 'front', thereby deflecting inquiry into their emotional worlds. The bikers in Connell's "Masculinities" (1995) had seemingly spoken to the researcher about their past histories, which resonates with the stories of the men in this study as they describe their childhoods and adolescence. However, through the use of the therapeutic method I was able to become aware of some, though not all, of the 'counter transference' issues arising within this study. In reading Connell (1995), I felt that he tended to impose a pre-determined theoretical system upon his subjects instead of hearing the men's voices. They have provided him with the details of their early lives, shifting their 'fronts' to see if trust could be built; however, I believe Connell (1995) did not pick up on the signals. This is an issue I had to work with from the very beginning of this research as I aimed to move beyond the organised defences of clients to the emotional worlds beyond.

Connell (1995) highlights the need for political action as a way of changing the world, but I am unsure where this leaves the emotional worlds of the subjects. This marks a tension between Gidden's (1991) critique of therapy for the purpose of adjusting men and women to a flawed system and Connell's (1995) notion that the political world shapes the subject.

One of the challenges Connell (1995) inadvertently lays down in his exploration of this type of masculinity is:

"There seems to be no standard developmental path into it, apart from the level of tension created by poverty and an ambience of violence" (Connell 1995, p. 111). In response to this, the time and trust built over the years with the men in this study has allowed me to shift my initial conceptions, my own 'counter transference'. This allowed me to approach the research wanting to understand these men's lives, rather than condemning them to the academic margins.

III. FATHERS AND SONS

In this chapter, I will be drawing primarily on the five sessions taped with Billy, Gary, Simon, and John, all of whom were raised in Deptford. The dominant theme of this chapter is the violence these men suffered from their fathers and how this impacted on their developing masculinities.

The first section is an excerpt from Billy that relates his family dynamics, introducing the key themes of the chapter: his father's violence, the 'masking' of feelings, the use of violence and alcohol, and his fear of 'fragmentation'. I will then develop the conceptual tools I introduced in the "Theory and Methods" chapter to provide an insight into the emotional impact of Billy and Gary's 'fronts', 'masks' and 'fragmentation'.

In the second part of the chapter, I will introduce Gary and Simon, who describe their internal family dynamics, thereby providing an insight into their childhood pain, enveloped in silence until they spoke here. This allowed me to reflect on the links between their drug use, violence and their masculinity as a 'front'.

Gary talks of seeing his mother being beaten, his intervention, and his father directing violence onto him. In analysing this relationship, I draw on both Deleuze and Guattari's (1972) analysis of the 'Oedipus Complex' as well as Gary's own words to understand the after effects of this violence.

In attempting to understand the emotional resonances of suffering violence, I draw on Anthony Giddens's "Modernity and Self Identity" (1991) and Cannetti's

"Crowds and Power" (1960). Giddens describes the nurturing effect of the parental bond, which helps the child to feel valued, positing an ideal. Cannetti (1960) introduces the concept of the 'stings' of humiliation, leading to my understanding of how this bond is torn.

One after-effect I explore is the 'emotional tear' between empathy and anger. R.D. Laing's (1961) work on the 'double bind' illuminates how the constant stress of being forced to act upon the differing demands of parents affects children's self-esteem, as Gary and Simon describe how they constantly navigate themselves between empathy for and hatred toward their families. In developing their own strategies of coping within this 'double bind', Gary, Simon, John and Billy describe how they create masculine 'fronts' though 'masking' feelings of empathy and connection with drug use.

The latter part of the chapter combines these men's words with Khantzian's 'self-medication' (1995) hypothesis and Lockley's (1995) work in counselling drug users in Edinburgh. John, Simon and Gary describe the reasons why they use as "blocking things out", 'masking' memories of the pain induced by recollection. Within the context of this research, these masculine identities link directly to silence as an act of strength.

Billy's family life

Billy spoke fleetingly and disparagingly to me about his father. However, he provides links to the dynamics operating in Gary, Simon and John's families through having a strong, empathic bond with his mother and a violent, alcoholic father.

Billy: "… It wasn't my Mum's fault like, I was like, truanting, I mean ummm. I mean she had it hard mate, she had seven kids and my Dad used to drink a lot, and at that time he wasn't much help, that's why she had to go out and shoplift.

Dean: He was drinking all the money.

Billy: Yeah.

Dean: Was he working at the time?

Billy: Yeah, he was working. He used to give her some money, but you know what I mean? Not.

Dean: Not a lot?

Billy: Not a lot.

Dean: That's quite similar to a lot of people that come here isn't it?

Billy: Ehhh.

Dean: Was he disruptive around the house or just quietly pissed?

Billy: He used to have a shout but he never, he didn't ever used to hit us, you know what I mean? He used to hit my Mum, he hit my Mum a few times, yeah.

Dean: Did you see it?

Billy: Yeah, I see it a couple of times. Me and my brother jumped on him one time when he was hitting my Mum, you know what I mean?

In hearing Billy describe his family, I was struck by the contrasting relationship with his mother and father. He speaks of his mother's sacrifice, going to prison to feed her children. Through his words, she becomes pivotal in the provision of care and nurturing, whilst his father is *drinking all the money*. Billy's empathy emerges in the quote, *"she had it hard mate"*. He never spoke of his father tenderly, instead revealing how his father drank to solve his problems whilst his mother shoplifted to ensure the family had enough to eat. His mother's behaviour constituted an emotional sacrifice, which, up until this point, had been carefully hidden from outside view – *"that's why she had to go out and shoplift"*. She tries to resolve the fundamental economic question of having enough money to able to eat. Billy recognises this sacrifice through acknowledging his care for her; a two-way flow.

I began to see connections between his father's behaviour and Billy's emerging masculine identity in the form of his father's use of alcohol as a way of blocking out problems intertwined with his violence. Billy's father's alcoholism highlights a pattern reoccurring in these counselling sessions that resonates with Potter-Efron in "Anger, Alcoholism and Addiction", (1991) where the power an alcoholic holds in a family is described.

> The important point is that chronic anger/aggression alcoholism/addiction may add to an individual's power over and control of others. When both are present, the angry addict may gain an even greater advantage over his sober and less angry associates. (Potter-Effron 1991, p.12)

I began to see how alcohol use becomes a catalyst for the externalisation of frustration. Within this study, Billy tries to protect his father stating, *"my Dad used to drink a lot"*. At this point, he does not seem ready to connect the emotional effects of this activity upon him, just upon how it affected his mother. Billy says: *"He used to hit my Mum, he hit my Mum a few times, yeah"*. This violence stopped when he and his brother *"jumped on him"*. This highlights another major theme: the use of violence to combat violence; a strategy of revenge. As a child, Billy became caught up within competing demands: to be tough and bear the pain his father inflicted – whether physical, emotional or economic – in silence, but also to handle himself in the outside world. He takes his place in a social environment where men learn to sustain a silence around their own family dynamics for fear of outside intervention. This in itself becomes a currency of strength.

Billy's empathic bond with his mother makes him vulnerable to pain. The lesson his father provides is that power creates dominance, generating respect through fear. Billy learns the survival skills of manhood: the need to be tough through suppressing this emotional empathy. However, he does not want to eradicate this bond with his mother, even as an adult. His solution is to 'mask' this bond through forgetting and then display a 'front' of violence. This has links to the masculine power displayed by his father, except the drug of choice has changed and Billy's violence is directed outside his family, whilst his father's violence was primarily directed within.

Fronts

I will develop the concept of 'front' in this section in relation to Gary and Simon. I first came across the term 'front' when I asked Gary how he viewed the counselling and whether he talked to other men about his personal history. He replied: *"as soon as we leave here, we put our fronts on"*. What I had long suspected was confirmed: talking to me allowed him to connect with his feelings, but as soon as he left, he suppressed them. I began to see the counselling operating in a tension between what can be revealed in therapy and the pressures to conform to the wider world of peers.

Gary's remark drew me to Goffman's "The Presentation of the Self in Everyday Life" (1959). Thinking of these men's performances as an act constrained within the idea of a 'front' helps to explain the difference between their presentation of their masculine roles in everyday life and how they speak in these sessions. For Goffman (1959), a 'front' is

> ...that part of the individual's performance which regularly functions in a general and fixed fashion to define the situation for those who observe the performance. (Goffman 1959, p. 32)

A 'front' is a performance that is 'fixed' and played out for onlookers. I reflected on the performance and what lay underneath; the disparity between how these men acted and how they spoke with me. Through listening and observing, I saw it was a form of camouflage, diverting the gaze of the onlooker.

I also observed how they related to each other in the waiting room prior to individual counselling. They would talk about *"who was away"*, i.e. what prison they were in, what they were in for and for how long. The speech would be clipped and harsh. In the counselling room, once they had relaxed, a different type of speech emerged. I should point out that these men were under no pressure to talk and could leave at any time.

It was clear their behaviour 'on the street' was different than when they spoke to me. The difference becomes important for understanding the differing masculinities as 'fronts'. Through the counselling, I realised these acts were more than performances; they were charged with a certain type of energy, integral to sustaining self-esteem and identity. The 'front' is created for onlookers, to mark a distance between what lies in these men's bodies/minds and what the spectator perceives. This performance provides a reward, with status and power providing the rationale for sustaining the 'front'. I began to see why these men found counselling challenging, as it entails a shift, a dissolving of the image, and then reflecting on what has been 'masked', allowing emotions previously hidden to 'flow'.

A commonality appeared in all of the sessions – the development of a 'front' continuously upheld by masculine 'acts', providing little room for other forms of emotional display. I was conscious that Gary presented a 'front', and I was aware I needed to build trust with him in order to shift his 'mask'. I initially explored the relationship between his drug use and his emotional world, but I hit a wall where he told me there was no connection:

No, I don't think so. I'd been taking drugs since I was thirteen, fourteen. I think it was a natural progression sort of thing, rather than a major trauma sorta thing. I dunno what it was. I can't remember anything big happening to make me start taking drugs, nothing like that. I remember taking drugs anyway and people being round people who took drugs.

His answer stated his drug use was his choice, a 'stepping stone' approach, graduating from cannabis, to pills, to cocaine and finally, heroin. The other aspects of his life remained unconnected to his drug use. In his words, it was due to the people surrounding him – his peers who influenced him.

One of the underlying emotional foundations of the 'front' is silence, a masking of personal pain. With Goffman (1959), there is little notion of the 'front' being linked to an emotional state. It was through Thewelait (1977, 1978) and

Cannetti (1960) that I began to understand the relationship between the 'front' and the 'masking' of feelings.

Masks

Silence and the lack of emotional communication, other than anger and laughter, pervade these men's accounts. Underneath this 'front', I began to see another process: the relationship between what had been silenced by the 'mask' and the 'front' created by freezing and sublimating feelings – actively forgetting. All of these white men's masculine roles consciously depend on creating a performance based on the projection of violence in order to keep the spectator from seeing the emotional turmoil lying underneath. This quote from Cannetti (1960) explains the power of the 'mask' seen from the outside, by the spectator, whilst holding back the 'unknown':

> The mask is clear and certain but is loaded with the terror of uncertainty. Its power derives from the fact that it itself is known, while what it covers is never known. The mask is only known from the outside, or, as it were from **the front.**

> The real use of the mask is not in isolation but in ceremonies, and if it then behaves in a familiar and expected manner it can also have a reassuring effect. Here it stands behind the dangerous power, which is behind it and the spectator. If properly treated it can keep this power away from him. It can gather this danger into itself and contain it, only allowing to overflow in one manner - the manner corresponding to its own shape. Once the spectator has established

a relationship with the mask, he can behave in an appropriate way. Once these have been learnt, once one knows how much distance it demands, it acts as a protection against the dangerous power contained within itself. (Crowds and Power, Cannetti 1960, p. 436) (My emphasis in bold)

The 'mask' hides "the terror of uncertainty" – feelings kept hidden. When viewing the 'mask' from the 'front', this terror is never revealed. This provides the link between the 'front' and the 'mask', as the onlooker only sees the latter from the 'front', not knowing what is being 'masked', because the act played out to sustain it is taken to be the reality, held intact by the unleashing of emotions keeping the onlooker away. In sustaining this performance, only certain emotions are allowed to "overflow in one manner - the manner corresponding to its own shape". Within this research, this shape is controlled by the expectations of these men's perceptions of their masculine identities – what is deemed acceptable and what is not. I began to see the formations of masculine 'fronts' as straightjackets blocking emotional releases other than anger.

Anger and violence are allowed to 'overflow' through 'masking', implying a bodily control of the emotions through the tensing of the inner body described in this quote from Laura Dillon (1976). She draws upon a neo-Reichian concept concerning the body containing energy fields as a

human energy field…the biological, emotional and mental energetic activities of the organism. The energy field is known to pulsate, that is to contract and expand, to charge or take in energy, and to discharge energy. (Dillon, in Boadella (ed.) 1976, p. 251)

Within this paradigm, 'masking' also implies a contraction within the body, leading to the emotions becoming embodied in an act of 'shrinking' (Miller 1987).

> Fear is a contraction into the core of the body and a drawing into the self from the outside world. The body pulsation of the person blocking fear is "stuck" on the inward or contracted direction. As the fear is felt and expressed, the inward stroke is completed and the body is again free to pulsate fully. (Dillon, in Boadella (ed.) 1976, p. 258)

This quote embodies the concepts of 'masking' and 'flows' as they impact upon the body, employing the notions of contractions and pulsations. I prefer to use the former terms because they also imply a social embodiment of the concept, contained in the social interactions of male and female bodies interrelating – the end result of a group of individuals pulsating and contracting their emotions, creating a social dynamic, a nexus of 'flows'.

The sons learn to construct their own 'masks' from seeing and feeling the effects of their fathers' 'fronts'. These are the after-effects of the manifested physical and emotional power they have witnessed as they feel the fear and terror it creates. I see the 'mask' forming through these men contracting within, thereby impacting upon their ability to pulsate, stopping empathic emotions flowing.

The Mask as a Physical Act of Silence

Apart from anger – the explosion – the 'front' is also formed through 'masked' silence. Silence becomes a currency of strength, using energy for its repression. I see the residual masked emotion(s) 'overflow' into sustaining the 'front'. The role of silence is illustrated here when I asked Gary if he spoke with his family about his father.

No, we will talk about things. We laugh about most things, d'y know what I mean? We all sit there talking; me, me Mum, me sister and me Brother and that. We'll be sitting there one day and something will come up, and it'll lead onto that errm, and we'll just laugh, with tellys out through the window. I can remember the whole street going like it, like you can go in a house and it ain't happening. We've never sat down and seriously talked about it.

Gary describes how past events are laughed at, creating an emotional silence. I also asked Billy if he had seen similarities between his family and his friends, wanting to know if they had ever discussed it.

Dean: That's quite similar Dad to a lot of people that come here isn't it?
Billy: Ehhh?

The freezing of feelings continues within the family dynamic; pain is hidden in the present. I did not pursue this any further with Billy, as it was clear he did not want me to press any further, thereby distancing himself from this pain.

Fragmentation

The need to halt 'fragmentation' becomes key to understanding how violence sustains the 'front' in channelling emotions in "the manner corresponding to its own shape". It is a dialectical relationship, as 'masking' unleashes anger, keeping the 'front' intact – the reputation and fear engendered by a hard man.

Whilst violence sustains the 'front' from the outside, substance misuse keeps emotions 'masked' on the inside by dousing memories. When these strategies are not available, the 'mask' begins to 'fragment', and when it is no longer held together, the hidden emotions emerge. 'Fragmentation' is the psychological impact of withdrawal that accompanies the physical effect.

Gary's description of his father's withdrawal from alcohol arose after I asked him what happened when his father stopped drinking, which occurred for a brief period after his wife and children left him. This extract describes his father's turmoil in wanting to connect with his family but also wanting to 'mask' his emotions through the use of alcohol.

Dean: So your Dad was really torn then about his behaviour?
Gary: He knew, he knew that he couldn't control it in the slightest...

He *"couldn't control it"*, and I began to realise that he had invested so much of himself in sustaining his 'front'. When it 'fragments', he becomes torn between his feelings, wanting to connect emotionally and fearing rejection, but eventually returning to a strategy that he knows works – a reinstatement of the 'front' through 'masking' his feelings.

The term 'fragmentation', derived from Thewelait's "Male Fantasies" (1977,1978), involves the dissolving of the 'mask' and the unleashing of emotions. Gary spoke about a period when he stopped and *"Cried over the most stupid of things"*, a statement, which resonates with many other men I have worked with.

This also resonates with Thewelait (1977, 1978), drawing on Cannetti (1960), who described other forms of masculinity where German men fused their identities within the hierarchy of the German army. Here, en masse, they presented a 'front' – a mass phalanx of physical brutality, their individuality subsumed within the Freikorps – a presentation to the outside world. Thewelait (1977, 1978) describes this phalanx of masculinity as being based upon the suppression of empathy and memory, specifically the wounds contained within emotions. It is this split between power and force, and away from the emotional ties that mark other forms of 'masculinity'.

I will explore how the men in this research halt their 'fragmentation' through discharging anger and taking drugs. This quote from Thewelait (1977, 1978) marks another form of 'fragmentation' linking violence to hierarchy and being controlled by the 'disciplines' – the social institutions. The connections to Gary's account lie in the masking of emotions and the projection of a 'front'.

> His constant goal is to avoid the experience of fragmentation by fusing himself into a unity in which he remains on top. Only this can make him whole. He seems to love the whole greatly though his love is hardly selfless however much he may like to represent it as such. (Thewelait 1977, p. 98)

'Fronts' are sustained and bounded by institutions emerging in historical epochs that in turn create the epoch in a dialectical process. Thewelait (1977, 1978) describes how the soldier creates an identity through obeying an order, fusing with the crowd, the platoon. This masculine ideal moulds a mass of men into a gang or a troop, projecting violence, and bound within a hierarchy with minimal space for self-reflection. This marks the divorce between an inner emotional life and the need for men's masks to fit into a pre-determining hierarchical order and moulding into a unity. Emotional release is discharged through killing and promotion, passing on 'stings' to others (Cannetti 1960).

Thewelait (1977) portrays the struggle that takes place in sustaining this 'front' in order to keep the emotional world 'masked'. Gary's remarks reveal his father's lack of control when he stopped drinking. His strategy was to fuse with alcohol, halting his 'fragmentation'. In this respect, the fusing of a 'thing' shores up a man who does not want to think about the past, thereby providing a meaning for the present.

Violence, as Phil shows in "Mother and Son", stems the process of emotional 'fragmentation'. This relates directly to Thewelait's (1977, 1978) research on German masculinities, with violence becoming the discharge of frustration. However, the continued discharge of violence isolates the man from empathic connection. When Gary, Simon and Billy were talking, I visualised how lonely and cut off their fathers were from empathic emotional contact.

The Unspoken Fears of Gary and Simon

Within the session, Gary allowed a carefully camouflaged emotional life to flow as trust developed, allowing his recollections to emerge.

"There was no one else who had a better life, do you know what I mean, than anyone else? I remember four of us from four different families scared to go home, it was like a Friday night or something like that. Well, not scared to go, but we didn't want to go home, 'cos we knew what was going to be indoors. It was like a Friday about eight o' clock, had to be havin' a bath about eight or nine, or something like that. We were all sitting by the corner near the pub, we'd just finished football or something like that, it was getting dark and it was time to go in, we were being called and it was exactly the same thing that night, for every one of us. I remember tellys..., one night me Dad throwing the telly through the window and then in about four days all me mates had their windows gone through (Oghhh). Things had been smashed, it was the same for everyone, there was no difference. Didn't see happy families, do you know what I mean? Holding hands and going out together".

There is a difference in how Gary reflects on the past with me and how he does this with his family. When he sits with his family reflecting on the past, they shrug off the past events with laughter. When he talks to me, he reveals his terror in his narration of a series of traumatic events that dominated his early life. The emotional picture is one of desolation as the violence in his friends' families dominates their social environment. *"There was no one else who had a better life, do you know what I mean, than anyone else?"* He remembers his fear of returning home, finding it difficult to articulate, reflecting his inner turmoil: *"Well, not scared to go, but we didn't want to go home, 'cos we knew what was going to be indoors".* This hesitancy highlights the tension in his recall. However, in breaking the silence and allowing subsumed memories to surface, he alters the shape of his 'mask'. He shows an empathy with the other boys as he describes the televisions going through the windows, a 'collective hysteria', with fathers competing in their brutality, a 'ceremony' of violence: *"...in about four days, all me mates had their windows gone through"*. The imagery provides an insight into how violent displays are used for creating awe in the spectator and to keep them at a distance, as well as being a discharge of anger.

One of the effects of the violence was isolation. As violence and anger was so widespread in the locality, there was apparently no one to whom Gary could communicate his feelings. There was a fear of talking to outsiders, a sense of shame about what had happened, fear of what the authorities might do, and pride in keeping the silence. Simon, who lived on the same street, has similar memories.

"...I mean, I see what my Dad did to my Mum, and always it used to happen on Sundays, Fridays and Saturdays, say the two, three days near the weekend. Friday I was a bag of nerves, 'cos I used to have football the next day, and all the other boys, their Dad used to take them, but who used to take me? No one".

Years later, Simon relates being a *"bag of nerves"*, waiting for the violence to occur. In this extract, his feelings stem from his "terror of uncertainty"; he hopes it will not happen again, but he knows it will. These fathers appear as strong, violent men dominating through physical power, verbal aggression and alcohol. These children had unspoken fears about returning to their family homes, each being aware, yet unable to communicate this terror to each other.

In relating their fears, Gary and Simon illuminate their inner emotional worlds, showing that they exist even if they are 'masked'. This feeling of deficit of care became heightened when they played football away from the locality. Simon relates: *"cos I used to have football the next day, and all the other boys, their Dad used to take them, but who used to take me? No one"*. Gary similarly told me, *"It was embarrassing, Dean, we'd turn up in plimsolls and they would have shiny new boots with their Dads cheering 'em on"*. Football cemented these boys' initial relationship, with Simon and John having trials with Millwall. It was through their love of sport that they created a male comradeship lacking in their families, fracturing when their drug use escalated.

Gary and Simon spoke of their fears returning home and Gary revealed what had been 'masked'. Just before the following conversation took place, he had told me he had suffered no major traumas.

Dean: Was your Dad an alcoholic?
Gary: Yeah, and when it weren't pubs, it was parties indoors and it's end up with the house getting smashed up (Exhales loudly)…and me Mum getting hit and things like that. It just meant, when I was little, pubs are just…one thing about pubs, and parties and that, one thing I remember is me Mum getting hit and the house getting smashed up, do you know what I mean? Or there'd be shouting and things like that. At the weekend you weren't gonna get any sleep anyway or even in the week, in the end, really, sometimes.

The parties dominate his memories – the smashing of the house and the attacks on his mother, as the parties shifted from the weekend to the week, his family "adapting" to their father's social life.

Efron and Efron (1991) describe how aggression travels from the most powerful members of the family – in this context the fathers – to the weaker members of the family, the children and the mothers: " These relationships become normalised, so that families, organisations, and friendship groups begin to function as "alcoholic families" (Steinglas et al. 1987) or addictive organisations (Efron and Efron 1991, p. 27).

Gary and Simon's families adapted to their father's drinking, but they were still terrified inside the home, as well as having to cope with the shame of trying to keep the problem concealed from outsiders. The descriptions of their locality portray an area of ritualised violence, a ceremony of 'fronts'. Each man displays his 'front' through cowing his wife and his children in a collective pattern of violence.

Violence Enforcing Masculinity

When Gary and Simon related the witnessed violence, this created levels of high anxiety. As Gary began to recollect, he began to smoke, helping to erect a barrier against me in the present. Despite telling me earlier he could not recollect a major trauma, he went on to describe a life in which he had been constantly under emotional and physical stress. I went on to explore with him its lasting effects. The level and scale of aggression led me to consider how the interlocking dynamics of fathers and sons are sustained. Simon described a strategy of diverting his father away from beating his mother. Both Gary and Simon demonstrated their desire to support their mothers, showing a strong empathic bond between mother and son.

I began to think through how institutions defined behaviour and began to examine the latent effects of the application of the Oedipal Complex in understanding these men's development. This helped me to understand how the violence in Gary and Simon's families defined their ability to engage in emotional expression. In rereading the myth through the writings of Deleuze and Guattari (1972), I began to see how Gary's father's violence affected him. Deleuze and Guattari (1972) directly challenge Freud (1910), criticising his reading of the original myth.

> The complex which is formed is doomed to early repression; but it continues to exercise a great and lasting influence from the unconscious. It is to be suspected that, together with its extensions, it constitutes the *nuclear complex* of every neurosis, and we may expect to find it no less actively at work in other regions of mental life. The myth of King Oedipus, who killed his father and took his mother, reveals, with little modification, the infantile wish, which is later opposed and repudiated by *the barrier against incest*. (Freud, Two Short Accounts of Psychoanalysis, Penguin 1910, reprinted 1984, p. 77-78)

I will explore the basic outlines of the complex and then draw on Clare's "On Men, Masculinity in Crisis" (2000) for another possible explanation.

> Freud, in his creation of the so-called Oedipus Complex, claimed the myth revealed the unconscious desire of every son to kill his father and marry his mother. It has, however, been pointed out that the story of Oedipus is possibly darker than Freud's interpretation would have it. It is, after all a story of gross paternal aggression and abuse. The tragedy starts with a father, Laius, ordering his own son to be killed and tells of the intense, potentially destructive conflict between the generations - the young Oedipus and the old

Laius competing to cross the bridge. But the story of Laius himself is relevant. Like Hamlet, Laius was a son displaced by his uncle. Laius took refuge with the neighbouring King Pelops and ended up sexually abusing the King's young son. In turn, King Pelops cursed Laius predicting, correctly, that he would be killed by his own son. Subsequently, Laius became King of Thebes and conceived Oedipus unwillingly (his wife got him drunk and seduced him). He then commanded her to kill the child by exposure and she initially complied but later relented. Woven into this tragic myth are many of today's most elemental preoccupations and anxieties - child abuse, paternal violence, colluded with and participated in by mothers, jealousy and revenge within the family and the sexual humiliation of women by men. (Clare 2000, p. 168)

The struggle between father and son in the story lacks any intention, subconscious or conscious, of the desire Freud invests here: "it constitutes the *nuclear complex* of every neurosis". What does appear startling is how the above rereading provided me with the courage to believe Gary's account of what he revealed in his session.

Deleuze and Guattari's (1972) critique of the Oedipal complex describes how it has created a barrier to the understanding of family dynamics in psychoanalysis. For them, the discipline rests upon a fundamental error: the role of the son in relation to his father. The resonance of Freud's (1910) formulation has influenced institutional interventions upon these men, explored in the chapter on violence and the use of discipline.

> Oedipus itself would be nothing without the identifications of the parents with the children; and the fact cannot be hidden that everything begins in the mind of the father; isn't that what you want, to kill me, to sleep with your mother? It is first of all a father's idea; thus Laius. It is the father who raises hell, and who brandishes the law (the mother tends to be obliging, we mustn't make this into a scene, it's only a dream, a territoriality). (Deleuze and Guattari 1972, p. 273)

In looking again at the myth and its use by Freud (1910), they contend that "everything begins in the mind of the father", leading to the following analysis.

> The paranoiac father oedipalizes the son. Guilt is an idea projected by the father before it is an inner feeling experienced by the son. The first error of psychoanalysis is in acting as if things began with the child. This leads to the absurd fantasy, in terms of which the father, the mother and their real actions and passions must be understood as "fantasies" of the child (The Freudian abandonment of the theory of seduction). (Deleuze and Guattari 1972, p. 275)

Gary describes in the following session how his father became violent towards him, which has a resonance with the ideas of Deleuze and Guattari (1972). Up until this point, it seems that no one had asked Gary why he had been involved in drugs and crime, spending most of his adolescence and early adult life in institutions. It transpired that Gary had 'masked' his memories of the events of his childhood. He related to me how he wanted to protect his mother from the violence, how he felt as the eldest boy he had to intervene, feeling torn between his mother and his father, running a whole gamut of emotions he had never expressed before that he would describe in this session.

Dean: *How did your Mum put up with...*
Gary: *She hated it.*
Dean: *coping?*
Gary: *She hated it yer...at first she stuck it out as long as she could and then, we all left, a couple of times, but ermm, once she was going to divorce him, but she couldn't carry it through, she couldn't get on with it. But I wanted her to, I really wanted her, yer know to leave him, start somewhere else.*
Dean: *So at that point you didn't like your Dad?*
Gary: *I'd 'ad enough, I just blew up, I can't remember deciding, me body just went within. I was in bed and it was just going, and it'd been a really bad couple of days, dreading the doorbell going and things like that, or the car pulling up, or whatever, at the time. The dogs would go an' all. Before he walked through the door the dogs would cower. He never hit the dogs or nothing, but it was the shouting. I can remember sitting there on Sunday afternoons or Sunday evenings and that err... watching something, it was school the next day, and things like that. And I'd hear a car pull up, and I couldn't tell if it was a car or not, but the dogs would go. They'd run and things like that. The atmosphere would change. (Exhales deeply). LIKE THAT (Snaps fingers). And it was different, and everyone would sort of go quiet, and there was no joking then, you know what I mean?*
Some people would say: "I'm going to bed now".
But you didn't wanna. One person, whoever got up first was the luckiest, they'd get up, upstairs out the

way. But we couldn't run and leave me Mum and that.

One time I was in bed, I don't know if I'd gone into bed early or not, probably. Sam [his younger brother] was in the other bed. I could hear them shouting. The next thing I was down there, and he had a hammer in his hand, and he had me Mum on the settee, holding her like that, by the collar, and he wasn't hitting her, he was threatening to hit her with it. I run in there and he grabbed me by the throat:

"What do you want?"

Do you know what I mean?

I can remember that, and then after that I can't remember. I know I kept going downstairs though.

Dean: *How did you get out of the situation though?*

Gary: *I can't remember, I think me Mum probably grabbed him, something like that. But I remember thinking I'm not going to run, do you know what I mean? I'm just going to stand there, whatever. Me Mum stopped him and I don't know what happened after that, and then it was always (get) Dad off, well not always, sometimes I didn't go down. I think it was. I didn't sit there thinking I'll go down, it was just the anger, you know what I mean? The anger would be gone, I remember sitting there thinking: "Hope it stops in a minute".*

Then I'd be going downstairs, I couldn't stop meself. I went down there and ermmm...

Then after that when things got worse for me, the worst was when I woke up one night with his hands round my throat, do you know what I mean? One night. And then the first thing, he always thought I was going to hit him. He always expected me to hit him, because he had a fight with his Dad or something. He had this thing about me and him having a fight, or something like that. And then one night, another night, I woke up with him really hitting me. I couldn't breathe at all. That was the first time. I hit him as well, as a punch, more of a push. But I run and I didn't stand there, fuck I run. I was getting to the front door, I only had me boxer shorts on, getting to the front door, getting to the front door, shutting it, and this lump of wood coming through, square, like a lump of four be four, sort of thing, coming through the glass. Sticking like a knife it was, wired glass it smashed through. If it'd been a second earlier, it would've hit me, do you know what I mean? I didn't go home right then. I stayed over me sister's all night, and, I don't know, it just seemed to calm down after that.

Dean: *After you hit him back?*

Gary: *Yeah, I mean no, things used to happen after that, but ermmm...*

Dean: *Is it because you and your brother were getting more powerful?*

Gary: *I think so, I don't know. No, no he was, he knew he'd sort of let himself, let it bother him. It doesn't matter if there were eight of us, he wouldn't let it stop like that. But ermm... I don't know, maybe he was getting weaker. I don't know cos... just after that, just before that, we found out he got it after a second time, and they was trying to treat it with chemotherapy and all that again. That's what. I can remember that."*

The Double bind of empathy and fear

Gary began to recollect memories. He later told me this had been happening for five to sixteen years. I was also struck by another resonance in R.D. Laing's (1961) work on the 'double bind'. When Gary's dad returned home drunk, Gary became trapped between two competing demands: hiding from his father by going upstairs, or protecting his mother from being hurt – *"But we couldn't run and leave me Mum and that"*. He wrestled with this every time his father returned home intoxicated. This 'double bind' is explored in "Self and Others" (1961):

> One person conveys to the other that he should do something, and at the same time conveys on another level that he should not, or that he should do something else incompatible with it. The situation is sealed off for the 'victim' by a further injunction forbidding him or her to get out of the situation, or to dissolve it by commenting upon it. The 'victim' is thus in an 'untenable' position. He cannot make a move without catastrophe. (Laing 1961, p. 145-146)

This became the starting point for my understanding of Gary's conflict. He describes his entrapment, and wanting to help his mother, but also wanting to flee for his own safety.

Gary wants to help her by having an empathic connection with her pain, but is caught between his love/empathy and his personal safety; he is "thus in an untenable position". He cannot make a move "without catastrophe". He can either go upstairs, trying to pretend it is not happening, or incur his father's violence by staying.

Gary waits upstairs and listens, trying to judge how far the violence is going to spread before he confronts it. Once he has challenged his father, he feels compelled to think about doing it again: *"Then I'd be going downstairs, I couldn't stop meself."* I asked Gary why he stood up to his father. He replies that he:*" can't remember deciding, me body just went within"*. He describes how his mind was numbed, being led by his "body". The flow of emotions and the anger inside Gary became so intense that he was propelled downstairs. His first strategy was to stand there and act as a witness to his father's act, afraid to intervene directly.

The anger initially inflicted upon his mother is then directed onto him. Gary's intervention challenges his father's dominance, as Gary understands that his father bases his sense of his identity on his physical prowess. The answer to the question, "Which comes first, the Oedipalising son or the paranoiac father?" is described here: "... *I woke up one night with his hands round my throat, do you know what I mean?"*

This resonates with Deleuze and Guattari's (1972): "Guilt is an idea projected by the father before it is an inner feeling projected by the son". Like Laius, Gary's father perceives his son as a threat and wants to destroy him. He has developed his 'front' based upon the continuous need to uphold his authority within his family. Any perceived challenge becomes a threat leading to a 'fragmentation' of this 'front'. His father clings to it with desperation, willing to destroy everything around him to keep it intact.

The connection between Gary's predicament and the Oedipal myth is contained in these words: "... *he always thought I was going to hit him. He always expected me to hit him, because he had a fight with his Dad or something. He had this thing about me and him having a fight, or something like that"*. Gary's father has an expectation his son will attack him so he attacks first, showing him who is stronger. This resonates with Deleuze and Guattari (p. 274): *Oedipus is the first idea of an adult paranoiac, before it is the childhood feeling of a neurotic"* (Italics author's own).

His father is paranoid, believing his son wants to attack and hurt him. *"And then one night, another night, I woke up with him really hitting me. I couldn't breathe at all"*. At this point, Gary realised his father was trying to kill him. He stopped short, but these actions were repeated. His father is creating the conditions for his son to seek revenge against these attacks, culminating in: *" I hit him as well, as a punch, more of a push. But I run and I didn't stand there, fuck I run."*

What he had feared has become a reality: his son engaging him in violence. This resonates with the myth, as Oedipus responds to his father's violence at the crossroads. When he did fight back, Gary's father tried to seriously injury him by throwing a piece of wood that nearly speared him in the back. Seemingly, the projection of his son hitting him and his attempts to thwart this has led to what he feared most, even as he felt himself disintegrating from cancer.

The lessons Gary learns at this age resonate with Billy, where violence can only be combated by further violence – the immediate solution to the 'double bind'. However, this creates another 'double-bind' based upon an empathic connection and a growing hatred of his father. He also had confused feelings for his mother, whom he wanted to leave his father, which I was not able to explore.

Deflection of Violence and the Internalisation of Pain

Simon revealed how he deflected the violence aimed at his mother. Simon was not the eldest, but, similarly to Billy's case, there was a revenge attack undertaken by his older brother on their father, after the latter had once again attacked their mother. Here, he describes an incident that occurred when he was 9 years old.

Simon: I cut my wrists down to him, Dean, so he would stop fighting, so he would stop fighting and take me to the hospital, because at first he...(I'm not getting out of telling you about Sara [his ex-wife], *I'll tell you that.)... The blood came out slowly, it came out very slowly, AND ALL OF A SUDDEN, IT WAS LIKE A WATER PISTOL, it just went SHHHH. And I thought, nice one Simon, you've hit it, they've got to take me to the hospital now.*
Dean: Was that when your old man was beating up your Mum?
Simon: Yeah, the bastard, yeah. I had a very disturbed childhood, but my Mum made up for everything, she did, she's one in a million".

Simon's family was scarred by his father's alcoholic rages. He has a high regard for his mother –*"one in a million"* – and a distaste for his father – *"the bastard"*, coupled with empathy for his loneliness. Simon's solution to his 'double bind' was to self-mutilate, in an effort to prevent his mother from being beaten. He seemingly takes his mother's pain into his own body, providing for him an important lesson in self-sacrifice. He is diverting his father's attention, showing how the "paranoiac father" establishes the conditions for his son's pain. Simon's violence seemingly protects his emotional connection with his mother. However, these boys also have to learn to survive in the local environment, where their fathers display violence to ward off potential threats.

Stings

Simon and Gary created 'masks', thereby maintaining a silence concerning their family lives, subsequently becoming violent as adolescents, then carrying this into their adult lives. In trying to think through how their 'masks' were created, I will examine the resonances of these events.

> Linkage of chemical dependency, family violence and family disruption creates a situation of multiple stresses that increases the risk to children (Johnson and Montgomery 1990) and adults for continuing mental health problems. (Potter-Efron and Potter-Efron 1991, p. 27)

I have already shown how these men had to contend with 'double binds'. I see these acts as the "multiple stressors" impacting upon their mental health. I will explore how the anger impacts on the body and mind of these men, drawing on the work of Cannetti (1960) and Giddens (1991) on how these men create and sustain 'fronts'.

McIntyre, in "Feminism and Addiction" (1991), raises some important issues surrounding the effects of being raised in a chemically addicted family and how the humiliations become stored in the memory. This relates to Cannetti's (1960) concept of 'stings' and how they affect the psychology of men.

> Being a man usually means there is little space for anxiety, hesitation, fear, vulnerability, ambiguity or any (open-ended emotional process). The digression, deliberately set in parentheses, is important to the understanding of the psychology of men. Men are often filled with hundreds of parentheses of memories of not being good enough, memories of possible humiliations where they did not feel competent, in control. (McIntyre, Bepko (ed.), 1991, p. 215)

McIntyre (1991) shows the expectations of a 'front' and what lies beyond it. The recollections become polluted with scenarios of humiliation, heightened by the distance between the humiliated boy and the man of control. These memories of humiliation become more acute because of the premium placed on adult men to control, entailing a need to forget and also revenge past humiliations, which constitute invasions upon self-esteem. Drawing on Cannetti (1960) and his analysis of commands, I want to analyse these effects. Cannetti (1960), writing in the aftermath of the Second World War, and in particular the Holocaust, was concerned with understanding national psychologies.

He was also particularly concerned with the power of the command and the effect it had on a child. His pioneering work helped me to understand the role of Giddens' (1991) ideas concerning the 'protective cocoon'. I will examine how the 'arrows' and 'stings' of commands tear this apart. This will aid in exploring the emotional worlds of Simon and Gary. The following quotes are from "Crowds and Power" (Cannetti 1960):

> Every command consists of momentum and sting. The momentum forces the recipient to act, and to act in accordance with the content of the command; the stings remain behind in him...
> ...But the sting sinks deeper into the person who has carried out the command and remains in him unchanged...
> ...The fulfilment of a command is not the end; it remains stored up forever. Those most beset by commands are children. It is a miracle they ever survive the pressure and do not collapse under the burdens of

commands laid on them by their parents
and teachers (Cannetti 1960, p. 354)

I draw on Cannetti (1960) to understand how the command impacts upon the giver and the receiver, thus marking the physical and psychological impact upon both. The 'sting' lodges in the recipient, remaining within him "unchanged", a mark of the power of the giver. The 'sting' of the command impacts both physically and emotionally upon the recipient. The commands given to these men when they were children were emotionally charged with prospective violence, which was contained in their father's "momentum". The effects of these commands created an after-effect, a 'sting', as Gary and Simon felt the weight of this power. These resonate with the 'stings' of fright Simon and Gary describe, giving a sense of being emotionally hurt. The problem for them is that they are trapped in a 'double bind' where they cannot discharge the 'stings', which then pile up one on top of another as they endure the violence silently. The result is the formation of sites of pain where "No child, not even the most ordinary, forgets or forgives a single one of the commands inflicted on it" (Cannetti 1960, p. 355).

Gary's father created his 'front' and took firm control of the power flowing from it. He feared revenge from his son, and so exerted his power to contain this threat by attacking him. Cannetti (1960) points to why Gary's father continued to dominate his son, fearing that if he ceased to act then the revenge on him would be exacting. It explains the actions of the paranoiac who has no sense of emotional connection.

A command which threatens death and then does
not kill leaves the memory of threat. Some threats

miss their target, but others find it and it is these which are never forgotten; anyone who has fled from a threat, or given into it, will invariably revenge himself when the moment comes. The man who threatens is always conscious of this and will do everything he can to make such a reversal impossible. (Cannetti 1960, p. 358)

The "paranoiac father" locked into firing stings into his son feels he has to sustain this act because he has never forgotten the 'stings' fired into him by his father. He fears his son will seek retribution, continuing the cycle of revenge. There is a connection between the violence Gary's father suffered and the discharge of his 'stings' as humiliations onto his son. He has found a way to dislodge his own humiliation through re-creating similar conditions (Winnicott 1965), but they are not the same. However, the momentum of unleashing the sting creates a resonance in the protagonist: one of shame. These are the "flows of (dis)connection" operating in these father-son relationships.

In Gary's extract, he talks of bearing the brunt of these attacks, as his father seeks to "do everything he can to make such a reversal impossible", fearing his son may turn on him.

However, in locking himself into this 'front', like Laius, he is creating the conditions for revenge. This began with Gary going downstairs to help his mother, resulting in him punching his father.

Protective Cocoon

Trust in the existential anchorings of reality in an emotional, and to some degree in a cognitive sense rests on confidence in the reliability of persons, acquired in the early experiences of the infant. (Giddens 1991, p. 38)

I became interested in discovering where Gary and Simon's ability to reflect and empathise stemmed from, given the levels of violence both had experienced. One of the ideas I worked with, given their empathy with their mothers, resulted from an "existential anchoring", a sense of value ruptured by their father's violence. These men's ability to develop trust in these sessions led me to believe they had trusted at some point in their lives. As they described their infancy and adolescence, I found that this "trust" had existed within parameters. Their mothers provided nurturing between periods of recovery from violence, in contrast to their relationships with their fathers. The following incident shows how minimal the sense of connection is between Simon and his father:

"...Go on, go out, and whatever". He gave me a lemon and said: "Eat that boy, that will bring you vitamins". And like a silly fool I ate a lemon, a whole lemon. He was laughing 'cos he thought that was quite a big joke. I didn't know, Dean, I was taking it all into heart, the he's a bas...

This incident assumes great importance for Simon. He trusted his father, but was made into a fool. His father had commanded him to eat the lemon and Simon ate it because he felt it was an example of his father's care, but it turned into a joke, to see how gullible he was. His father had fired a 'sting' into him through a command, marking Simon's humiliation and powerlessness.

The previous extracts, when set against an ideal, show the deficit of care these boys experienced. Giddens (1991) posits how an ideal parent-child relationship would operate, where the care is an

> ...emotional inoculation against existential anxieties - a protection against future threats and dangers which allow the individual to sustain hope and courage in the face of whatever debilitating circumstances she or he might later confront. It is the main device in relation to risks and dangers in surrounding settings of action and interaction. It is the main emotional support of a defensive caprice or protective cocoon which all normal individuals carry around with them as means whereby they are able to get on with the affairs of day to day life. (Giddens 1991, p. 39-40)

The "protective cocoon" is something "which all normal individuals carry around with them"; a store of memories a person can retrieve from occasions where they felt valued. Through the years I worked with him. Simon could not recount any positive experiences with his father. The "lemon" incident was trivial compared with numerous other incidents Simon related. This shows how little emotional support flowed from his father, even though Simon was desperate for it.

Simon described another event that occurred after his father returned from the pub:

Simon: It's true once when I was a kid he picked me up, paralytic drunk, he was, when we used to live in Trafalgar St. in Deptford, before we moved to Jutland

St. He picked me up over the balcony [60 ft up], paralytic drunk. He never had hold of me like that (demonstrates by grabbing hold of his collar). He had me by the scruff. Now if that had've ripped, I would've been history, you know?

Simon's trust was already minimal because of the violence he had endured. He became animated as he described this event, terrified by the potential consequences. It marked another humiliation, as he was swung in the air in full view of the neighbours.

What emerges from these sessions is how the 'arrows' from Simon and Gary's fathers tore apart their 'protective cocoon', creating a state of continuous anxiety. There was a breach of trust between father and son. The anger of the fathers, fired as arrows, left 'stings', held as memories. The main target of their anger was the mother-son relationship, and, drawing on Giddens (1991) and Cannetti (1960), these arrows tore at their sons' protective cocoons, creating an enforced brutalisation. This engendered feelings of humiliation and shame, as described in these sessions. This provides a rationale for Gary and Simon's use of drugs as a means for creating their own 'protective cocoons'.

That sense of invulnerability which blocks off negative possibilities in favour of a generalised attitude of hope derives from basic trust. The protective cocoon is essentially a sense of unreality rather than a firm conviction of security; it is a bracketing, on the level of practice, of possible events which could threaten the bodily or psychological integrity of the agent. (Giddens 1991, p. 40)

This helps to explain the masking process created by drug and alcohol use, which blocks off negative possibilities, creating bliss and a solution to the 'double bind' (Laing 1960) through obliteration of memory, but also creating a constant psychological need to 'self-medicate'.

Stings in the Memory

Gary recollected a 'sting' fired into him when he tried to connect with his father in hospital. He talked of his distress at seeing his father lying before him, not feeling it as a moment of Oedipal triumph, but wanting to connect with his father, despite feeling hesitant.

Gary: It didn't really hit me until the operation, until he had to go in. They tried everything else, but it didn't work, like chemotherapy, radiotherapy and all that. That didn't work, so they had to attach himself to a voice box. And err, his thyroid gland, and all that. And err, he had to have it out, and left him with a hole in his throat to breathe through, so he couldn't talk. And the day after the operation, when we went to see him, I couldn't go up the hospital, just be on my own. I was sitting on me own with a... errr...He felt embarrassed, I think, which made me feel embarrassed, do you know what I mean?
I think he felt like a...It was a big operation he had, because they had to rebuild his neck, and they had to take a muscle out of his leg or something like that, and rebuild it. I think he felt that he had most of his self cut away, which made him feel...He always got certificates indoors for what weights he lifted and how he was a soldier and that, during the last year of the war, and I think it just cut more of him away, and just physically

took a lot out of him. I think he felt embarrassed about it. So did I. When I realised, I actually sat on the bed with him, there was blood dripping and I was trying to wipe it, and he was saying "Leave it alone". Do you know what I mean? And it really upset me. I went down and couldn't go back in. For about three weeks I couldn't go back to the hospital. And, err, after that I couldn't remember much about it.

Gary realised the emotional effect the operation had had upon his father. With his physical deterioration came a psychological one, the ebbing of his self-esteem, illuminated in these two quotes: *"I think he felt that he had most of his self cut away, which made him feel..."* and *"...I think it just cut more of him away, and just physically took a lot out of him".*

The physical cuts on his body created psychological cuts. Gary's father prided himself upon his physical power. Once this began to ebb, so did his self-identity as the powerful man, the boxer, the athlete – all these notions began to disintegrate along with his physical power. The operation was cutting him away, not saving him, and it was leaving less each time he went into hospital. This led to further 'fragmentation' of his identity, creating a deep unease. His son saw him stripped of his 'front', losing his physical power and needing help.

Gary relates his feelings of awkwardness as *"I think he felt embarrassed about it. So did I."* Gary describes his feelings of empathy and care, but his father felt helpless before his son. The dynamics in the relationship had altered, and what his father had always feared was transpiring before him: his disintegration, and his son appearing more powerful. Still wanting to hold on to his self-esteem, he denies his son any sense of connection, telling him to *"Leave it alone"* as Gary tries to help him. The 'sting' was instantaneous, as described here: *"And it really upset me. I went down and couldn't go back in"*. It was a humiliation, as he had tried to reach out to his father but had been rebuffed. He was to find his own solution to this pain through drug use – an obliteration of the world.

Self-medication and Masks

Cannetti (1960) describes the 'stings' as resonating within the present as well as being layered through memories in the past. Simon's brother John talks about how he is haunted by his childhood. At this time, John had moved out of his mother's home and was living in shared accommodation. However, he became scared one night and related these feelings to me.

I 'ad enough of this with my fucking Dad, coming back pissed, beating me Mum up, having to worry whether he's gonna start tonight, you know what I mean ? SLEEP LIGHT ! I'm a very light sleeper, as soon as I hear a noise, I'm up. Christ, is that man coming in? It brings it all back when my Dad used to beat my Mum up and everything.

Fifteen years later, John relives the violence of his family, obsessed by the experiences reoccurring in his dreams. This has led to sleeping problems, which also affect Simon. John had spoken previously about his family and the violence his father inflicted on his wife and sons. Similarly to Gary, he shows how he is constantly alert to the prospect of violence – a link back to his family life. The sleeping problems become a trigger for memories, which John has been trying to block out by taking large amounts of Temazepam. Even though he is on a large dose, bought illicitly, he does not sleep.

John's memories are triggered by an older man, drunkenness and the potential for violence. This shows how the past comes to impact upon the present. The recollection of memories of pain – the 'stings' of the past – creates anxiety now soothed through drug use. John's solution – using more drugs to try and block out memories – becomes key.

The journey to this point explains what lies beneath the presenting problem. Now I want to show the connection between these events and drug use. In looking at the role of drugs in these men's lives, I will draw on three excerpts from the sessions involving John, Simon and Gary to look at the link between the past and their present feelings of isolation.

One of the defining links of their experience of adolescence was being aware of their father's actions being a problem for the family. This link between a father's alcoholism and a son's drug use has been explained by Lockley (1995).

> Most common is heavy alcohol use by one or both parents, which occurs in a high percentage of the families containing chronic heroin users. Such alcohol use, seen from an early age, makes the children accustomed to seeing people under the influence. In time they come to accept such behaviour, or at least become hardened to it. Alcohol may produce a model of how to solve everyday problems... (Lockley 1995, p. 27)

Simon, Gary, Billy and John's fathers' alcoholism was more than just a way of solving problems; it was used to obliterate emotional pain. However, it failed to deal with the original causes, ensuring they remained emotionally isolated – the process of 'masking'. These fathers were unable to connect with their sons. Their alcoholism intertwined with all aspects of family life. It impacted economically through *"drinking all the money"* and it also operated on an emotional level. These men's fathers' were not just quietly inebriated, but full of rage, projecting a 'front' of fear to their children. This strategy had after-effects, in that the violence externalised upon Gary, Simon, Billy and John was never accepted as just. The families may have adjusted to cope with this dynamic, but they were torn between love and hate – a 'double bind' (Laing 1961). The sons developed their own coping strategies in dealing with the 'stings' of humiliation and pain they were enduring; they developed masking strategies and began to create 'fronts' of invulnerability.

Their drug use developed as a form of 'masking'. They also developed strategies for passing on the 'stings' of humiliation. All of these men were violent as adolescents, spending time in prison and detention centres for burglaries, shoplifting and car theft. They also fought other boys – Deptford had a considerable reputation across South East London for its gangs and their propensity for violence.

The links between drug use and violence is highlighted here. Whilst violence becomes an external act leading to an internal resolution, drug use is primarily an internal act having an external effect. The role of drug use and its link to the emotional state of the person is described by Lockley (1995):

> Opioids are the best drugs at defusing anxiety, at surmounting many of the difficulties that arise for young people, but depressants such as alcohol or benzodiazepines can also do the job.

However depressants, because of their lesser efficiency in anxiety suppression, have to be taken in larger amounts. (Lockley 1995, p. 44)

This resonates with the findings of Khantzian (1995), who described drug use as being a form of "self-medication".

... self-medication hypothesis holds that substance-dependent individuals are predisposed to use and to become dependent on substances primarily as a result of ego impairments and disturbances in their sense of self, involving difficulties with drive and affecting defense, self care, dependency and need satisfaction. (Murphy and Khantzian, Washton (ed.), 1995, p. 164)

Opiates defuse anxiety, linking drug use to the emotional life as a form of 'self-medication'. In this research, I have explored where this anxiety stems from looking at the relationship between fathers and sons. It is through masking their emotions thereby stopping the feelings surging forward they keep their 'fronts' intact.

John's Mask

John described why he used drugs, linking it to his fear of isolation. He is aware that his anger is ready to explode, highlighting the relationship between self-medication and anger.

Dean: Why are you taking them then?
John: I suppose to block things out.
Dean: Oh right... yes.

John: To block things out. As I said to you, Dean, I never 'ad
no one to talk, y'know what I mean? Counselling, about
anything for my childhood, know what I mean?
Dean: Yeah.
John: And upwards. I 'ad no one. I say I'd explode. It's like
a lemonade bottle, where you shake it and shake it.
It only takes so much and then it blows, don't it?
That's what frightens me, how much more can I take?
'fore I blow. I've been stabbed, is that pushing me? It
frightens me, it frightens me, to think what's gonna
'appen next. What's round the next fuckin' corner? It
does freak me out. I just don't see no light at the end
of the tunnel. I really don't. I don't want to end up in
prison, Dean. (coughs) I wanna move. I dunno, I can't
see nothing in my life.

John's sense of being emotionally anchored is fragile; never being able to verbalise his emotional pain, the past remains as a trauma, as a source of shame restricting him in the present. His strategy has been to keep it within.

He reflects on how he should have had counselling for what he had experienced as a child. This is a new concept for dealing with pain that John is verbalising. This shows his desire to connect with someone else about his experiences, someone he can talk to, so that he can validate his feelings and defuse his anger. He talks about never having anyone, of feeling a deep sense of isolation, and being trapped in his memories. This marked a major shift in John's attitude towards counselling, recognising that he has a deep-seated anger towards his assailant for nearly killing him. At this point, there was little I could offer him in the form of consolation, as his view of the future was bleak. The only strategy I had was to allow him to talk and to recognise the validity of his feelings, so that he had at least one person to talk to.

Simon's Mask

These extracts drawn from Simon's session show how he moved beyond his 'front'. I asked Simon if his childhood had contributed to where he was now.

Simon: What, the way that things've worked out, you mean ? Yeah, I think… people like thinking you should have an excuse for the way you are, but I ain't got an excuse, that's the saddest thing about it…I haven't got an excuse.

Simon presents me with another version of his 'front' – seeing his drug use as his way of taking control, since no one forced him to do it. This notion of control is another key theme, as he states he has *"no excuse"*. This resonates with Gary's initial statement about having no major traumas. I decided to press Simon by getting him to reflect upon why so many other members of his family were using.

Dean: How come nearly all your family is on drugs then?
Simon: Meaning John, Sue and Paul. Richard is the only one (who isn't). I dunno, them I don't…I'm not trying to cover them up or nothing but I don't know why they are on drugs.

Simon struggles between hating his father and empathising with him. Despite the violence he has endured, he attaches no blame to his father. The idea of being in control of your own addiction is important for

Simon's identity, and he refuses to make the connections between his predicament and that of other family members.

...I don't blame my old man, Dean, being an alcoholic, 'cos look at how many alcoholics there are, and they've got famous, and they got famous sons or whatever, haven't touched a drug. Well I don't know. I think they don't do drugs. They're just clever, aren't they?

Simon points out that just because his father drank does not mean he would follow suit. The notion of 'cleverness' and its opposite – 'thickness' – is a strongly held internalised belief relating to his lack of self-esteem. Simon has a strong notion he is thick, explaining his present predicament. He has read about famous people in the media and their struggles and feels his family cannot be the cause of his problems. This prompts questions about how celebrities' problems are reported in the media and the effect on people such as Simon, but this is beyond the scope of this research. However, in seeing so many men with drug problems narrating connected family histories, I asked him about his friend's families, trying to get him to make the connections.

Dean: What about Jutland St? How many people down there?
Simon: There was quite a lot of alcoholics down there
Dean: How many of those kids ended up on drugs?
Simon: Quite a lot
Dean: Is there any reason why the two are connected?
Simon: What, alcohol and drugs? errr, I don't know, I think alcohol is the same as methadone, Dean. It blocks out your worries, but your worries are still there in the next day. This is why they take it, they take drugs to block out whatever, but it's still going to be there at the end of the day. I took drugs more after she left me, just to

block it out my head. But then when I was 100 per cent normal, it was so clear to me, what was happening, it frightened me, it really did.

When I asked Simon about his friends, I received a different reply. Simon made the connection as he reflected on his childhood living in Jutland St: *"I think alcohol is the same as methadone, Dean. It blocks out your worries, but your worries are still there in the next day".* Simon makes the link between alcohol/methadone being used to *"block out worries"*, but the feelings remain; they are only masked by the substance use, not dissolved.

Simon's drug use initially stabilised when he married, began to rise again when his child was born, and spiralled out of control when his partner left him. He coped by taking substances to alleviate the emotional pain of isolation, another form of 'self-medication', analysed in greater depth in "Relationships". 'Self-medication' and the defusing of anxiety is explained in the following extract, as I pressed Simon on why his father drank.

Simon: He couldn't face up to reality, Dean. That's why I take it …I can't face up to reality.
Dean: What was so bad about his reality though?
Simon: I dunno Dean, I dunno. I really dunno. They was all bruisers, all of them. The one who won £150,000 on the Lottery, had two Mercs. He's a boozer, Larry is a boozer, Pat was a boozer but he's (dead), and me old man is definitely a boozer.

Money did not solve his uncle's emotional problems. When he had more money he drank more alcohol, highlighting a problem existing beyond poverty. Not being able to face up to *"reality"*, becomes the key to understanding these men's substance misuse. These extracts highlight how this reality corresponds to the emotional pain they hold inside.

I see the connection between his father's alcoholism and Simon's drug use – it is a strategy to stop thinking, to defuse anxiety – and needing constant administration to stop the flow of thoughts, stifling 'fragmentation'. I began to see how chronic drug use, in whatever form, becomes a method of fending off reality by creating a split. This split is engendered by the constant 'double binds', the connections and flows of love, and the need to hide this for fear of being humiliated. These men learned to create this split in their families, and their drug use can be seen as a continuation of this strategy.

Gary's Mask

Gary moved from experimentation with heroin to addiction whilst his father was dying. He began to use drugs heavily after being released from a Detention Centre following a 'sharp shock' of discipline. I explored with Gary how his drug use coincided with his father's illness. I begin to think his drug use was connected with his feelings that emerged during the illness and subsequent bereavement.

Dean: So you started taking it again after you came out of D.C.?
Gary: Yeah.
Dean: That's when your Dad was ill, wasn't he?
Gary: He was ill before that, he'd already had a, had his voice box taken out, the cancer taken out already.
Dean: How did that affect you then, his illness?
Gary: That was a shock. I dunno, it affected me Mum and all that and er, it gutted me. At first I went to ermm...

see him. I knew he had, I remember him, saying and all that he had it and the treatment he was having and all that. I can't remember back to be honest, I can remember just carrying on, just like how he was at the time, just carrying on like that.

Through his words, Gary shows his pain: *"er it gutted me"*. There was no one to communicate his pain to; he had tried to connect with his father, but failed. After this rejection, he internalised his feelings, following his father's example. He has little recollection of the situation, only a feeling of being numbed, finding it difficult to articulate: *"I can't remember back, to be honest"*. In the end, he describes it as *"just carrying on, just like how he was at the time, just carrying on like that"*. It is here the father-son strategies intersect through forms of coping: his father heavily sedated for physical and emotional pain, whilst his son increases his drug use, trying to forget. The 'masking' of emotion creates a silence between them, a silence held until Gary spoke about it here. After his father died, his drug use spiralled as Gary spent years in prison for crimes he committed to sustain his drug use.

In this chapter, I have illuminated the lack of emotional connection between fathers and sons emerging in these sessions. Nevertheless, these sons retain and hide the bonds they have with their mothers. These are hidden because they have been under attack from their father, forcing these men to define their masculinities in a tough working class environment where physical prowess and the ability to wield violence are prized. What has emerged is how this violence has helped to shape their adult lives and how they have used heroin as a coping strategy in order to cope with the 'double binds' they have endured.

What has been key in this process has been working with these men to develop empathic relationships so that they have felt secure enough to talk about themselves and their experiences, dissolving the 'front' they present to the outside world, which sustains their self-esteem. The memories of their fathers' actions have left emotional scars, which have been 'masked'. When trust is built in these sessions, it allows the memories to flow.

However, I am also left to address the problem of how their fathers developed such destructive behaviour and why they chose to inflict this violence on their families. Through the sessions with Pete and Gary in the following chapter, I will explore why their fathers drank so heavily. Why did they want to escape from reality?

IV. FATHERS AND STRATEGIES FOR COPING

I will draw upon two themes emerging in the previous chapter and explore these through the words of Gary and Peter. The first theme, derived from the concept of 'stings', is the anger directed from father to son, flowing from an inability to verbalise life events. Secondly, I want to link individual male silence to institutional silence surrounding a specific event: the Second World War, as both Gary and Pete's fathers served in the war. Thirdly, I will look at the role of alcohol – its relation to 'masking' and its connection to institutional silence.

In looking at how historical events have impacted upon and bounded Gary and Pete's fathers' emotional worlds, I will draw on Deleuze and Guattari (1972), shifting from a focus on family dynamics to recognising the wider social nexus and how this shaped them.

In the methodology chapter I analysed how soldiers returning from WW1 (Arthur 2002) found it almost impossible to relate their war experiences to non-combatants. I am interested to show in this chapter how this inability to communicate comes to be perceived as an act of strength. I also explore how institutional forces, through the micro actions of people, also uphold this notion. Drawing on the concepts of 'masks' and 'fronts', I will analyse how historical forces shaped these fathers' masculinities by sustaining silences, projected as male 'strength'. These issues emerged when I explored Pete and Gary's fathers' personal histories when I was working with Gary to gain an understanding of the underlying facets of Gary's father's anger, and with Pete to try and understand why his father drank himself to death. This chapter is primarily concerned with the views of two men who were heavily involved in the drug subculture reflecting on their fathers' emotional lives.

Previously I described the fathers' behaviour primarily from Gary, Simon, Billy and John's point of view, but here I want to draw on the empathy Peter and Gary felt for their fathers in trying to understand them. I want to show how their fathers also had emotional lives, shaped by the historical epoch they lived in as well as their family dynamics, moving away from demonising fathers to understanding them. This is vital for comprehending masculinity as a process flowing between generations of men as a strategy of coping.

Historical Forces

Deleuze and Guattari (1972) illuminate the impact of historical events upon individual men and women:

> The family does not engender its own ruptures. Families are filled with gaps and transected by breaks that are not familial: the Commune, the Dreyfus Affair, religion and atheism, the Spanish Civil War, the rise of Fascism, Stalinism, the Vietnam War, May 68 - all these things form complexes of the unconscious, more effective than everlasting Oedipus". (Deleuze and Guattari 1972, p. 97)

This marks a break with traditional psychotherapy, as both Rogers (1967) and Freud (1908) are largely silent about the impact of historical forces, in particular the Vietnam War, Korean War, Second World War and the First World

War on their clients and patients. Deleuze and Guattari (1972) challenge this silence, recognising that families are affected by historical events. I became interested as to why this silence has occurred. It has shaped psychology and what can be brought into therapeutic sessions, as analysed in De Zulueta's "From Pain to Violence" (1993) and Heinl's "Splintered Families"(2001). However, it is not only war that effects memory – I began to see how more mundane events, emerging in retrospect when new conditions have arisen, and against which the old can be judged in comparison, have also shaped emotional lives. One of these resonant forces was the grinding poverty of the interwar years, where families survived on meagre wages, with limited birth control, poor sanitation, disease and the ever-present threat of war. They also coped with the after effects of the First and Second World Wars. Also, there were patterns of migration, occurring all over the UK, as families fleeing poverty and persecution relocated to London from Ireland, the English countryside and from Europe, plus the evacuation of children to the countryside during the Second World War (Wicks 1988). Within the context of this research, I am aware the experiences of racism, for example the experiences of Irish migrants, are not raised in this chapter. This marks a limit of the research explored in later sessions.

Gary and Peter describe their fathers' emotional worlds as being shaped by their experiences and shrouded in a smouldering silence. I began to see how this silence operates on an individual and institutional level, which Siegfried Sassoon (1972), one of the first men to reflect upon the impact on the psyche of the First World War, described in his memoirs as men implicitly learning to self-censor their letters, thereby creating a silence and masking their experiences (also explored in Arthur 2002).

Sassoon (1972) describes how the letters of dead officers in WW1 were used to enhance patriotic feelings back home.

> I had often read those farewell letters from second lieutenants to their relatives which the newspapers were so fond of printing. "Never has life brought me such an abundance of feelings", and so on. I had always found it difficult to believe that these young men had really felt happy with death staring them in the face, and I resented any sentimentalising of infantry attacks. (Sassoon 1972, p. 420)

When Sassoon (1972) returned home, he could not relate his war experiences to non-combatants, keeping them to himself. He describes the 'mask': "But every one of us had something in his mind which he couldn't utter, even to his best friend" (Sassoon 1972, p. 423). He also describes his 'front' and shows the relationship between the 'front' and the 'mask' in this quote, showing how these concepts transcended class and culture, albeit taking different forms. This provides an English historical context for the silences I explore in this research. "I must play at being a hero in shining armour, as I'd done last year; if I didn't, I might crumple up altogether". (Sassoon 1972, p. 421)

Sassoon shows how masculine roles are part of a historical process, helping me to think through the English experiences of war, after having drawn heavily on the German experiences described in Miller (1987) and Thewelait (1996). Sassoon's masculinity, his 'front', marked by his social class, sexuality and culture, took on a different form to that of the men in this study. Sassoon highlights how 'fronts' have a wider social implication than that explored in the scope of this study, but his importance for me is in his recognition of how men are psychologically affected by war, helping me to conceptualise the experiences of Pete and Gary's fathers.

This helped me to understand the ideas Bettelheim was exploring in "The Informed Heart" (1960) and how this institutional silence constricted language and how debates were shaped, thereby stifling the ability to talk about the past. This relates to many different aspects of Pete and Gary's life, ranging from conditions at children's homes, working class poverty, and readjustment to civilian life after returning from war.

Return to Oedipus

In "Fathers and Sons", the Oedipus myth became central to understanding Gary's father. I want to explain how Deleuze and Guattari's (1972) analysis helped me understand the 'flows' of violence intersecting the fathers and sons in this study. In the previous chapter, Gary recalled his father's belief that someday they were going to have a fight. Gary related how his grandfather had uttered the same words to his son: a prophecy from the past, internalised as a fear – a 'sting' waiting to be unleashed. Gary's grandfather acts akin to Laius, sending his son, Gary's father, away to a 'Home'. Deleuze and Guattari (1972) asked what came first, the "paranoiac father" or the "Oedipalising son"? The message transmitted to Gary's father flowed from his father, highlighting how beliefs are passed down, contained in a 'flow' of 'stings'.

Freud's (1910) "Oedipus Complex" offers an analysis of father-son relationships, which, in "Inhibitions, Symptoms and Anxiety" (Freud 1926a, republished in 1993) seemingly sanctions discipline against sons. There are a number of assumptions here that impose a framework of meaning on the client.

> Let us imagine that he is a young servant who is in love with the mistress of the house and has received some tokens of her favour. He hates his master, who is more powerful than he is, and would like to have him out the way. It would then be eminently natural for him to dread his master's vengeance and to develop a fear of him - just as 'Little Hans', being in love with his mother, had shown fear of his father, we should say he had no right to have a neurosis or phobia. His emotional reaction would have been entirely comprehensible. What made it a neurosis was one thing alone: the replacement of his father by a horse. (Freud 1993, p. 256)

The voice of 'Little Hans' has become lost within Freud's analysis, as Freud's framework enforces a meaning that I will argue has led to the institutional silencing of the subject, since the analysis has drowned the subject. The link to this study is that the imposition of meaning has resulted in the subjects' experiences having become lost, as they do not have the language to challenge the meanings imposed upon them. This resonates with the lost voices of men such as Gary and Pete's fathers.

Gary described his father's family life, showing how his father's behaviour arose as a reaction to his public rejection, which he could not verbalise. I will analyse his 'flow' of anger, created by his holding of this humiliation and externalised as 'stings' into his family. Gary explored with me how his father's behaviour patterns were formed, describing how discipline was perceived within his family pre-Second World War.

Dean: *Do you have any knowledge why he'd behave like that?*
Gary: *Yeah, drinking.*
Dean: *Yeah, but...*
Gary: *Whisky.*
Dean: *Yeah, but were his family?*
Gary: *He weren't... I dunno, it weren't his family. His dad was really strict, I can remember him saying that to me. His dad beat him and, but in the end he got rid of him, because he was the middle child sort of thing. There were brothers older than him and sisters older than him, and both sisters and brothers younger than him. He was the middle one and they put him in Barnardo's, for no reas... I think he didn't get over that. He couldn't understand why he was dug out to go. If it'd been the older one, if it had been the eldest or the youngest, I think he would've accepted it more, but I think he was really ang...What pissed him off, they just got rid of him. He said that : "I wasn't any more trouble than any of the others". Yer know what I mean, the older ones were probably more trouble than anyone else? but ermmm...*

When I asked Gary why his father behaved violently, initially I hit a barrier. Gary stated, *"I dunno, it weren't his family. His Dad was really strict"*. Due to the relationship we had developed over the years, we were able to use a shared language of emotions. This allowed our conversation to shift.

Then Gary related a depressing story about his father's childhood. His grandfather chose Gary's father, the middle child, to go into a children's home in the late 1930s. Prior to being sent away, Gary speaks of his grandfather's reaction to his father: *"His dad beat him and, but in the end he got rid of him, because he was the middle child sort of thing"*. He describes this, not in a language of abuse, but as a form of discipline, a language of care and the enforcing of boundaries. His grandfather was very *"strict"* and in enforcing this strictness, he picked out his middle child to be sent away and receive care and discipline in a 'Children's Home'.

Initially I thought he was chosen because the family were in financial difficulties and they could not afford to feed their children. However, in retrospect, I see another dynamic. I reflected on Gary's words about his father's fear of him. This fear, drawing on the concept of 'stings', was possibly due to Gary's grandfather being scared of his son. This fear created a connection between the generations, as each created the conditions for their son's hatred, externalised in a flow of 'stings'.

The result was an initial feeling of bewilderment: *"I think he didn't get over that. He couldn't understand why he was dug out to go."* The way he was expelled from the family acted as an 'arrow', shattering his 'protective cocoon'; a 'sting' that became irreversible.

Rejection

Gary's father never developed 'self-esteem' or self-love because his family had never valued him (Bowlby 1973). I began to piece together what had occurred as Gary spoke of the beatings his father endured. In this period, many families used what is now considered, to have constituted excessive force in disciplining their children. However, what magnified his pain was being taken away, being forcibly rejected: ...*"but I think he was really ang...What pissed him off, they just got rid of him"*.

I wanted to think through the effect of this rejection on Gary's father's self-esteem.

> What has become increasingly apparent, is just how much individuals depend on the attachment relationships of their formative years to build up their self-esteem and their capacity to form satisfactory attunement relationships. These psychobiological developments are themselves rooted in the psychobiology of the attachment system. (De Zulueta 1993, p. 187)

De Zulueta (1993) provides an insight into the effects of rejection, since within the 'Home' there would have been many orphaned children – the result of poverty, war and disease. Many people were suffering from trauma due to the loss of their parents after WW1. However, drawing on Bowlby (1973), I believe the experience of being rejected by parents who are still alive – the severing of attachment with the full knowledge you are not wanted – is potentially even more disastrous. It is this act, which decimated Gary's father's 'protective cocoon', and severed his 'basic trust'. This would begin to explain his internal rage, where "violence can be seen as the manifestation of attachment gone wrong" (De Zulueta 1993, p. 188).

The Resonance of Rejection - the Reversal of Stings

England was recovering from a major loss of life after the war, and many families existed in conditions of absolute poverty. Drawing on De Zulueta (1993), I would contend that 'masking' arises from conditions of poverty due to the high mortality rate of infants, death of women in childbirth and men in war. Working class people, afflicted by a series of bereavements, coped by 'just getting on with it'– a grim stoicism where pain was masked to cope with the present. However, as Heinl (2001) shows in "Splintered Families", just because the problem is ignored does not mean that there are no after-effects.

> The shock-waves of a devastating and widespread 'wipeout of fathers' in one generation would be felt in the next generation. The trauma of losses is not limited to one generation but 'spills over' into the next one, displaying a transgenerational effect. The fatherless children will eventually grow into adults, yet deep in their hearts they may have remained children who continue to yearn for the father model for their own children; they search for being fathered themselves. (Peter Heinl 2001, p. 75)

Heinl' s (2001) description of the transgenerational effect of loss provides a further insight into how historical events, noted by Deleuze and Guattari (1972), shape emotional lives. The strategies young people develop to cope with family loss are only currently being recognised (Heinl 2001). When Gary's father was placed in a 'Home', the full impact of his circumstances would have been catastrophic, striking at the core of his self-identity. Gary does not say a court placed him there, and seemingly there was no sense of legitimacy: *"If it'd been the older one, if it had been the eldest or the youngest, I think he would've accepted it more, but I think he was really ang..."* His own family sent him away, with no one to advocate on his behalf. I perceived his feelings, forming as wounds, were held in silence, as he had no avenues of escape or even a conceptual language to verbalise his pain. This illuminates the role of the institutional concept of silence and its impact in 'masking emotions'. De Zulueta (1993) reveals the effect of this rejection:

> Attempts are now being made to understand how children can and do suffer from post traumatic stress disorder. What has become clear is that children react to psychological trauma much as adults do. (De Zulueta 1993, p. 188)

The notion that children have emotions and react to stressful conditions draws on the work of Burlingham and Freud (1944), and is currently being further researched, rendering the notion of "post traumatic stress disorder" (De Zulueta 1993) more fully understood.

The resonances of rejection are also explored in Alice Miller's "For Your Own Good" (1987). This helped me to understand the emotional impact on Gary's father of being sent to a 'Home'.

> The greatest cruelty that can be inflicted on children is to refuse to let them express their anger and suffering except at the risk of losing their parents' love and affection. The anger stemming from early childhood is stored up in the unconscious, and since it basically represents a healthy, vital source of energy, an equal amount of energy must be expended in order to repress it. (Miller 1987, p. 10)

This process describes how the 'stings' of anger become stored in the individual and are then bounded by institutional silences. Within this context, the 'masking' of emotions takes place, because there are no avenues to express them so they are held internally. 'Masking' develops from being 'stung' and then not being able to discharge the 'sting', creating anger that cannot be discharged. A 'front' of violence can then ward off further 'hurts' through retaliating first or through a recreation of the same dynamics, except this time the man who was the victim of childhood violence is now in control, the discharger of 'stings'. This, I feel, begins to explain Gary's father's 'front' of violence.

The 'mask', in this context, forms when the 'protective cocoon', the condition of 'basic trust', is severed. What emerges is Gary's father's need to defend against any perceived attack. Alice Miller (1987) shows the internal processes of an individual building a dam against his memories of humiliation. Employing this concept, I can understand how Gary's father created his own 'protective cocoon'. This creates a rationale for his 'self-medication', his use of alcohol as a form of 'masking' and his violence in sustaining a masculine 'front'.

Gary's father's alcohol use helped to 'mask' the original trauma, but not without leaving a resonance – the use of 'vital' energy to repress his pain.

> Forgetting one's experiences. It is easy for a man who thinks a lot - and objectively - to forget his own experiences, but not the thoughts evoked by them". (Nietzsche, reprinted 1984, p. 239)

The original memory may be lost as a result of self-willing or inebriation, but the resonance of the wound still creates his need to keep continually dousing it. The original trauma may be forgotten. As these sessions show, many forgotten childhood memories are repressed, in particular those that contain pain. The act of forgetting needs energy in order to seal off the past. The passage of time allows memories to become over-layered with other events, but the resonance remains behind in the form of thoughts. These are doused with substances, alleviating the anxiety generated by these thoughts. The act of forgetting becomes an endless Russian doll, as layer builds upon layer, highlighting Gary's father's use of alcohol as 'self-medication' (Murphy and Khantzian 1995).

An aunt and uncle began to provide support, but as soon as Gary's father was able to join the Army, he left South East London to fight in the War, an after-effect of his family rejection.

Dean: He felt rejected.

Gary: Yeah, there was Barnardo's, sort of brought up by his cousins, a load of us live in Sydenham, and errr, he went into the Army when he was sixteen, made out he was eighteen. And that was it. After that, he got into a lot of trouble, just after that. He got nicked and went into Barnardo's a few times. After he went into the Army, he was in and out of Nick all the time, but errmm… I think that really pissed him off, that err, even now he don't get on with, even now before he dies and everything, he didn't get on with his brothers, like the others got on, do you know? They really got on, he was sort of always, I dunno, boys had things to say about him. They'd talk when he went up there and things like that, his younger brother's house, and, but most of them are dead by now, by that time. One left I think, and there were two sisters left at the time, but they're all dead now. But it pissed him off about that.

Gary's has an intuitive understanding both of his father's coping strategies and his anger.

Gary is silent about his father's war experiences, but depicts his father's life being bounded by institutions, leaving one to join another: the 'Home', the Army, and then prison; a 'cocoon' bounded by the command of powerful others (Cannetti 1960). This 'discipline', far from correcting him, did little to halt his flow of anger. Whilst the institutions contained him, his anger seemingly became 'masked' through routine and discipline (Cannetti 1960; Thewelait 1977, 1978).

As well as being rejected by his parents, his brothers and sisters also continued to rebuff him after he left the 'Home': *"boys had things to say about him. They'd talk when he went up there and things like that, his younger brother's house"*. The imposed silence ruptured his bond. Miller (1987) wrote of the energy needed to repress the 'flows' of anger with the use of 'healthy energy'. I see a parallel in Gary's father's relationship with his son as he severs the father-son bond when they are both in the hospital. This illustrates how patterns become stored, re-emerging in different contexts: the denial of connection and the sustaining of silence to stop the 'front' from 'fragmenting'.

Gary describes the link, highlighted in the quotes from De Zulueta (1993), between his father's anger and his rejection by his family. Through learning to sustain a silence, reinforced by his family, Gary's father's emotions emerge as anger. Anger in this context becomes a strategy for sustaining a 'front', a result of the stresses brought about by the thoughts created by the act of forgetting, creating emotional distance, upholding self-esteem and warding off other potential threats of humiliation.

This psychological issue comes to the fore as he develops his body as a force for warding off potential attackers. Gary's father idealizes his body, winning medals for boxing. He asserted his esteem through his muscle power and the ability to inflict violence. Gary's description of his father contains a number of connected themes: rejection, pain, anger, bodybuilding and violence. What lies underneath this embodied 'front' of violence are 'masked' emotions and being *"pissed off"*.

Silence and Wounds

Gary's father's anger shifted from being directed at people outside the family to becoming a force wielded within the family. His anger and violence, directed at other men in pubs and on the street, helped him to sustain his self-esteem as a giver of 'stings', as opposed to being a victim in childhood.

However, Gary is haunted by the question, *"I don't know why he took it out on me Mum?"* Gary understood that despite what had happened, his father had choices – he could have used his experience to ensure there was no reoccurrence of violence in his own family. However, he chose to re-enact the violence.

Dean: So there was a huge sense of anger and rejection inside him then?

Gary: Yeah, yeah, he talked about...ermm, about leaving Barnardo's and how strict they was there, do you know what I mean? It's nothing like it is now, it was just a Boy's Home, simple as that, he was stuck in, and that was that. And err, he never said how he felt about it,

*or nothing like that, he just got on with it, do you know
what I mean?*

*Dean: It sounds as though he bottled it all up and it came out
through his drinking*

*Gary: Mmmm, I don't know why he took it on me Mum,
there was other people to take it out on for, take it out
on people.*

Gary has an intuitive understanding concerning his
father's experiences and I will explore this connection
between his early childhood trauma and his adult
violence, drawing on Alice Miller (1987). She explores
how 'silence' and the inability to respond to an attack
affects mental health, which connects to Gary and
Simon's experiences of feeling the 'stings' of their father's
anger, caught within a constant 'double bind', where
they learn to forget their pain but not the thoughts
evoked by the forgetting. This, as Laing (1960, 1961)
highlights, would have had a significant impact upon the
recipients' mental health, described here by Miller (1987):

Those who were permitted to react appropriately
throughout their childhood – i.e. with anger -
to pain, wrongs and denial inflicted upon them
either consciously or unconsciously will retain
this ability to react appropriately in later life too.
When someone wounds them as adults, they will
be able to recognise and express this verbally. But
they will not feel the need to lash out in response.
This need arises only for people who must always
be on their guard to keep the dam that restrains
their feelings from breaking. For if this dam
breaks, everything becomes unpredictable. Thus,
it is understandable that some of these people,

fearing unpredictable consequences, will shrink from any spontaneous reaction; the others will experience occasional outbursts of inexplicable rage directed against substitute objects or will resort repeatedly to violent behaviour such as murder or acts of terrorism. (Miller 1987, p. 64)

Miller (1987) describes the wounds created in both the protagonist and the recipient through experiencing anger leading to a physical reaction. This forms a wound in the memory, the arrows of the command entailing pain (Cannetti 1960). This pain may be healed if it is deflected by the recipient pointing out to the protagonist they are being wounded. However, Gary's grandfather ostracised any potential threat to his power, ensuring his victory over his son was complete by banishing him.

Alice Miller (1987) portrays how these wounds layer themselves, as 'stings', one on top of the other, where they cannot be deflected and the 'arrows' cannot be removed, thereby becoming sealed in silence. Gary's father received many 'stings': the beatings from his father, the rejection, possible beatings in the 'Home', the drill of the army and the prison regime. Drawing on Thewelait (1996), I would see his father's identity as being sustained through receiving commands, and I feel he may have begun to experience himself only through the words of powerful others after his familial rejection. This process would have led him to denigrate his own feelings as he received commands, fusing himself with the regime. The regimes of power, operating hierarchically, would therefore reinforce his emotional silence.

When the commands were no longer forthcoming after he left the army, he would have been in the position of a tightly bound man, suddenly released. The only world he would have known up to that point was that of discipline and command (Cannetti 1960).

"Emotional Arrows"

For Gary's father to assert his masculinity as a form of self-esteem and to avenge his pain, he would have needed to rid himself of his 'stings'. This provides a possible explanation for why he chose to fire them into the people closest to him. Miller (1987) writes of two strategies flowing from humiliation: 'shrinking' and 'exploding'. The former becomes analogous to Gary's father's alcohol use, sublimating his pain through 'masking'. Through violence, he is able to project his pain externally onto others, making the explosion – a firing of 'arrows' – a form of revenge. This allows him to externalise his anger and sustain a masculine 'front', whereby instant retaliation wards off other threats. Gary's father uses both strategies: sustaining his silence, and holding back his childhood memories where he was constantly hurt. He then discharges his anger.

I began to think about the role of the family in Gary's father's life, especially when children are born: the sense of loss and envy, his wife's attention being torn away from him; he is now competing for her love in emotional silence. Gary's father chose to terrorise his family, his inexplicable rages coming to be directed onto 'substitute objects' in a form of re-enactment. This can be seen in the way he visualises his son as an antagonist, just as his father had perceived him. It also reinstated the conditions of the past, a dynamic of pain by which he had been bounded, except now he was the aggressor instead of the victim, and he was firing his arrows into weaker bodies.

The flows of anger – the arrows – are contained in the vibration of sounds and the releasing of body chemicals (Boyesen 1976). Coupled with the flow of anger is the physical connection with bodies: the infliction of physical pain reinforces the psychological pain in the expression of power and command. The receiving body reacts to the physical pain in the form of messages being sent across the skin and through the nervous system. The memory holds the wound. The body becomes formed through the physical blows and the retention of this psychological grief. Gary's father's rage can be explained through the use of such concepts, as he wounds through the memory of his humiliation.

Although he had a fight with him, Gary's father was unable to fully reverse the 'stings' from his own father, so he displaced these onto his own family. He sees his son's growing power as a direct threat, and his empathic emotions create a dichotomy for him, since his own family had continuously isolated him. Consequently, he is not used to intimate communication. I see his inability to express his empathic emotions as a fear of being rejected once again. Not feeling 'good enough', he aims to establish the conditions he knows through constant testing of his wife's care by pushing it to the limits with his abuse, revenging his childhood humiliation. In becoming the aggressor instead of the victim, he gains control in the family, and it ensures he receives the attention he craves. I began to see how he might have been jealous of the mother-child bond – something denied to him – gauging his presence through the damage he inflicts. The whole process points to him using his wife and children as objects of his jealousy, in an act of psychic revenge.

Transecting Historical Events - Death Camp

Deleuze and Guattari (1972) comment on how the family grouping is where historical actions ripple over the participants as their micro actions flow through friendship, work and kin networks, connecting to other people. The historical silence operating on family dynamics has been explored by Heinl (2001) and, drawing on Peter's session, I began to understand how a significant event could have a continuing resonance through his family dynamics, shaping his notion of 'strength'.

I explore how the after-effects of this historical event shaped Pete's Dad and Pete's perception of him. The connection between these events and the family is analysed, drawing on the concept of 'flows'. This allowed me to see the silence of the past re-emerging in behavioural forms, linking to Nietzsche (1984). Active forgetting requires 'vital energy' in the form of going to the pub, buying alcohol and using this to forget. Pete provides an intuitive understanding of his father's strategy and is full of admiration for his strength. This form of masculinity becomes related to 'masking' events and holding memories at bay.

Peter's account of his father, based on an extreme event, is one account I have taped. Other non-taped sessions ranged across numerous war experiences. Bri spoke of his mother's experiences of near-death. Ross spoke about his father fighting the 'dirty war' in Burma and then having to resettle back into civilian life. Vietnamese men have spoken directly about their experience of the American War. Therefore, this account is part of a whole narrative of differing life experiences, which become related in the counselling sessions.

I explored Peter's feelings for his father after previously looking at his family background. He had spoken about his family and his adolescence, but we had never really looked at his childhood, although I knew some snippets of his family history. In this session, we explored this topic further, discussing how his father coped with his emotions after his release from Auschwitz.

Dean: Your Dad must've had a lot of coping to do, getting his mind round coming back from Germany to...

Peter: Poland.

Dean: Poland, to settling down here.

Peter: Yeah, because as soon as he got released from prison, after being in a War Camp all those years, the first thing you'd do is have a Light Ale isn't it? Bam, bam, in a couple of years he went from eight stone to fourteen stone and he never missed work till the day he died.

Dean: He didn't have a very good war did he?

Peter: He won, but cor, did he, did he really? I mean what did he get out of it? Not even a thank you really.

Dean: Was he quite bitter about his war experience?

Peter: He wouldn't talk about it. To me Mum he did, but he wouldn't talk about it. I'd tap him, tap him, tap him, and then he'd tell me things. Oh yeah, very bitter, yeah.

Peter's Dad returned to England after being incarcerated in a concentration camp. We did not explore how he arrived there. When Pete first told me, I was disbelieving. A British P.O.W. at Auschwitz? Why had no one had mentioned this before? It had not arisen in any of the historical documents I had read, so I was puzzled. However, Peter was adamant he was there and this raised issues for me about historical silences. I do know his family did not

145

belong to one of the deliberately targeted groups such as the Gypsies, Slavs, Gays, Communists or Jewish people. He was a British P.O.W., captured just prior to Dunkirk.

In exploring this with Peter, I had an underlying sense he was very uneasy talking about himself, just as his father had been. My strategy was to speak with understatement. For example, I mentioned to him that his father did not have a 'good war', knowing he had been in Auschwitz. It took me some time to adjust to what he was saying and we both communicated in this manner as Pete replied about his Dad having a "Light Ale" when released. We moved away from this shared meaning, an understanding of codes, to explore some of the deeper emotional issues.

I know from personal experience with family friends that war memories are extremely painful. This section will show one aspect of this pain, drawing on a concept introduced at the beginning of the chapter: having the conceptual tools to narrate past events.

When wars finish, men such as Pete and Gary's fathers have to readjust to civilian life. An unspoken expectation of a soldier is that they resume just as they had left it. In the twentieth century, however, the concept of war changed. Industrialisation brought the mass targeting of civilians, genocidal conflicts and national terror. This created psychological problems as well as requiring economic adjustment for whole populations after both the First and Second World Wars.

Even today, despite all that has been learnt about battle related traumatic stress disorders, British soldiers who fought in the Falklands War,

Northern Ireland and the Gulf War are not being given proper health care and self help facilities by the Ministry of Defence. A voluntary Crisis Line, set up for these men and their families in the UK provides evidence that there is a large and invisible population of these war trauma sufferers who present with unusual and sometimes violent behaviour when they return home. (De Zulueta 1993, p. 168)

It is clear the conditions of war produce psychological stresses held in the memory.

Men were caught up in the euphoria, and many like Pete's father volunteered to fight for their country, inspired by patriotism; or, in Gary's' father's case, a desire to leave his 'Home'. When the war ended, they had to return to a changed country, and this experience of adjustment was problematic. During wartime, killing is legitimated – the antithesis the situation in peacetime. In recognising this adjustment problem, the MoD has diagnosed post traumatic stress disorder (PTSD), a significant change from previous epochs, but this is still increasingly perceived as a medical condition rather than a psychological state.

Pete talks of his father's sacrifice, not being acknowledged by a *"thank you"*, which left him *"very bitter"*, breeding feelings of resentment. Both Gary's father and Pete's father had to make their own readjustments through "drinking to forget", but not forgetting the thoughts evoked by them. This establishes a relationship between the 'masking' and the performed 'front'. It is this process of rehabilitation to civilian life that Peter relates below:

Dean: How did you learn that he was in Poland then?

Peter: Me... I've always known, me Mum told me he was in Auschwitz or Belsen for about two months and then to Auschwitz. He was in Auschwitz until they freed 'em all at the end of it. If I was a sixteenth strong as my Dad, I'd be some man, you know in that way?

Dean: How did he rehabilitate himself then?

Peter: (Exhales deeply)...just got on with life, I suppose, just accepted it, just a case of having to, isn't it. It's happening, so what can you do?

Dean: Must give you a totally different outlook on life?

Peter: Oh yeah it's got to ermm...

Dean: And then going back to the same place where you were brought up. How did he end up there?

Peter: I don't know really, Dean. I know the war had been going on four days, it had been kicking off four days and bang he was captured, he was held somewhere in Northern France for a little while, and then he was took to Poland, and then he went to Belsen, then some other place and then to Auschwitz for three and a half years. Cos we're going to the pictures for relaxation on Friday, and they asked us what film we want to see. Well I suggested that Schindler's List. I've never seen it but I'd like to. It's all about that isn't it?

I never did get Peter to explain how his father's different outlook on life affected him. He has a clear regard for his father and the latter's ability to cope and survive. In explaining how that behaviour translated itself in adjustment to civilian life, Peter trails off. We did, however, explore his father's alcoholism, which emerged as his coping strategy.

There is a connection between Pete and his father, but he does not directly emulate his father's drinking, as he is a chronic 'speed' user, and, as with most chronic amphetamine users, now derives little effect from the drug. Initially, it provided him with a euphoric self-confidence, which is now merely part of his routine. I explored with Pete why he does not drink.

Peter: *Reason why I don't, maybe yeah, maybe ehmmmm, and me Dad 'cos of his liver. That's part of the reason he died.*

Dean: *Was it cirrhosis?*

Peter: *It rotted or something.*

Dean: *Yeah, cirrhosis.*

Peter: *Yehmmm, that's another reason.*

Dean: *He didn't drink bad though did he?*

Peter: *No, but it was hard for a man sixty-eight years old who'd been drinking since he got released from the war, perhaps he was drinking before then yeah. Yeah, but like, to stop if you know what I'm saying,' cos it's been so long, and it's not illegal is it you know? If you're an alcoholic, it must be terrible, Dean, you know? Drugs and things you've got to look for, but beer you can get anywhere, can't you? Anywhere you can get it from, can't you?*

Dean: *How much was he drinking then?*

Peter: *He used to be the life and soul of the party, that was his buzz.*

Dean: *Right.*

Peter: *Yeah, when he was like in his prime... four, maybe five nights a week, he and me Mum would go out who knows, fifty pints whatever, throughout that space. I don't really know, then when he started getting problems with his health, he was like drinking, four or five bottles of Pils a week. Dinnertime go up the pub have his bottle of Pils and then come back home, you know?*

Dean: *That's maybe how he overcame his trauma then?*

Peter: *YEAH, mmm, mmm, probably yeah.*

Dean: By drinking it off.

Peter: Which, really, there's nothing wrong with that is there? If it can help him with that, you know what I mean? Yeah it must've been horrific, the things that were going through his mind.

Dean: Yeah, and then he was having to keep a lid on it because he didn't want to tell, tell you or your...

Peter: Mum yeah.

Dean: He told your Mum things?

Peter: He told me Mum, but like she still had to tap him, and but like they was married, but like I really used to press him to, come on what about this, and then he'd tell me a few things. He'd never come out and start the conversation, never, you know?

Dean: So you'd always have to keep digging at him.

Peter: I imagine there was some right bad things that happened, that he never told anybody about. I must imagine yeah?

Dean: Oh yeah, I would've thought so.

Peter: Like when he told me one of his jobs was chucking his dead mates onto the back of a lorry, yeah. You could see his eyes just fill with tears, as he was saying it. I just thought stop Dad, you know, 'cos my mind just went whummmp, fuckin' hell, you know?

This shows how drinking to forget painful memories, sustains a 'front' and physically masks pain, thereby eradicating memories. Peter reveals how his father coped underneath his 'front' of stoicism, portraying a father who contained his memories through drinking. What is apparent is that everyone seemingly knew why he was drinking. *"Yeah it must've been horrific, the things that were going through his mind"*.

One of the problems Peter's father faced was to find a vocabulary to express his memories. It would have been completely beyond most people's life experiences. (Sassoon 1972; Arthur 2002) There were no trauma groups for survivors, despite the fact that now there is "evidence that there is a large and invisible population of these war trauma sufferers" (De Zulueta 1993). Pete describes his father's coping mechanisms: *"just got on with life, I suppose, just accepted it, just a case of having to, isn't it* Whilst Pete's father may have carried on, the effects were ever present. Heinl (2001) describes the latent effects of war.

> The staggering loss of millions of fathers during the Second World War produced many orphans. Yet there is another disturbing war-related issue which is underrated, although it appears to me of great significance. This is the issue which I define as 'emotional fatherlessness'. What I am referring to are fathers who survived but were badly damaged psychologically by the experience of war and the prisoner of war years so that they were rendered unable to fulfil a father's role in a way which would have been beneficial for their children. (Heinl 2001, p. 75)

Peter's father's experiences were ones of extreme suffering in the camps, and he coped the best he could when he returned home by using alcohol.

Recoil from Pain

The concept of emotions being contained within memory – as being part of it – are portrayed in Pete's comment about the horrors in his father's mind. There is the moving account of his father's eyes watering at the recollection of his memories. *"You could see his eyes just fill with tears, as he was saying it"*. The flood of emotions begins to fragment the 'front', but Pete feels his own 'mask' also shift. *"I just thought, stop Dad, you know, 'cos my mind just went whummmp, fuckin' hell, you know?"* Pete wants his Dad to stop because he experiences his father's pain, which throws Pete into turmoil, watching his father's 'fragmentation' as masked emotions begin to emerge. This fractures Pete's view of his father as a bearer of pain, a man of strength.

Pete's father 'masks' his tears before they break into a flow, by exerting energy in trying to forget; this is maintained by his alcohol use, as crying is not seen as part of an appropriate male response. One of the lessons Peter's father provides is how he copes with overwhelming emotional situations through silence. His father's use of alcohol provides a solution to coping with psychic pain.

This is a pattern that Gary's father drew upon in coping with his emotional strains. However, there is a link, as Deleuze and Guattari (1972) reveal, with the strategies employed by institutions, which uphold strategies of emotional coping by relying on the need to maintain a 'silence'.

Institutional Silence

Despite having concentrated on individual accounts, I am also aware of institutional responses to trauma. Personal silence is bounded by institutionalised silence. If there had been an open discussion of the after-effects of war, especially the emotional cost, then this may have had some impact upon Gary and Pete's fathers' ability to verbalise their experiences. In trying to understand why this had not occurred, I was struck by Bettelheim's (1960) "Informed Heart", which describes his experiences in the death camps.

Sassoon (1972) highlights the emotional silence created during and after WW1. Bettelheim (1960) explores how this silence was sustained after WW2. I began to understand the link between this lack of acknowledgement of traumatic memories and the use of alcohol by these older men. Coupled with their war memories were the humiliations of abject poverty, the feelings of loss of home and people, as well as feelings of terror (Heinl 2001).

Drawing on Deleuze and Guattari (1972) and Bettelheim (1960), I began to reflect on why historical resonances were largely ignored in psychotherapy and how institutions denied horror. This helped me to understand the role of Pete's Dad's use of alcohol as a way of coping. Bettelheim (1960) described the formation of a silence after WW2 after the discovery of the camps across Europe after 1945:

> "Three different psychological mechanisms were most frequently used for dealing with the phenomenon of the concentration camp:
>
> a) its applicability to man in general was denied by asserting (contrary to available evidence) that acts of torture were committed by a small group of insane or perverted persons, b) the truth of the reports were denied by ascribing them to deliberate propaganda. This method was favoured by the German government which called all reports on terror in the camps, horror propaganda (Greuelpropaganda), c) the reports were believed, but the knowledge of the terror was repressed as soon as possible.

All three mechanisms could be seen at work after the liberation. At first, after the discovery of the camps, a wave of extreme outrage swept the allied nations. It was soon followed by a general repression of the discovery. (Bettelheim 1960, p. 252)

This repression of horror has been consistently employed by social agencies and can be traced back to the First World War (Sassoon 1972), where deliberate attempts were made to control reports about war conditions.

The space to talk about and explore personal feelings becomes constrained as the prevailing media have already colonised perception. Sassoon (1972) wrote in anger as he challenged the media on how they reported the conditions in the trenches to the people back home. This provides a resonance with Bettelheim's (1960) observations on how the horrors of the death camps were reported.

What was this camouflage war which was manufactured by the press to aid the imaginations of the people who had never seen the real thing? Many of them probably said the papers gave them a sane and vigorous view of the overwhelming tragedy. "Naturally", they would remark, "the lads from the front are inclined to be a little morbid about it; one expects that, after all they've been through. Their close contact with the War has diminished their realization of its spiritual aspects". (Sassoon 1972, p. 464)

The quote from Bettelheim, "a wave of extreme outrage swept the allied nations. It was soon followed by a general repression of the discovery" (Bettelheim 1960), relates to Pete's father's inability to express himself. This left Pete's father isolated, trapped within his memories, as no one wanted to talk about what had occurred. The newspapers had already colonised the imagination, and Sassoon (1972) sees an attempt to describe his view of the conditions silenced, with him eventually being placed in a 'hospital' to aid his psychological recovery.

Within this context, I was able to understand Peter's father 'masking' his past. The Bettelheim (1960) quote shows the quandaries thrown up for the survivors. For Peter's father to find a language to express himself would have been difficult enough if his problems could have been discussed openly; but as his masculine identity, as Pete describes, is based on strength, this discussion would have diminished his ability to receive pain and not break down. In the culture he grew up in, possibly knowing of other men's fathers who fought in the First World War, returning soldiers re-entered family life to 'get on with it', their traumatic stories resurfacing years later (Heinl 2001; Arnold 2001).

The relationship between Pete and his father differs from that between Gary and his Dad. Pete's relationship is one of idolisation. He speaks of his father's strength. He carries his remembrance of his father's death in the form of a tattoo marking the event. However, Peter never felt comfortable exploring this dynamic between father and son. In the sessions, he would sweat profusely and become agitated and the conversation would turn away whenever we came close to looking at this relationship. I had an intuition that there was a pain he could not face, which would need a great deal of nurturing for him to explore. This was only an intuitive feeling on my part, and not something that I could get Peter to explore, marking the limits of our relationship.

His father is perceived as a powerful man, surviving one of the most horrific cauldrons of brutality: *"If I was a sixteenth strong as my Dad, I'd be some man, you know in that way?"* Pete identities with his father's ability to survive and then control his emotions, although he knows it is sustained by alcohol use, *"which, really, there's nothing wrong with that is there? If it can help him with that, you know what I mean?"* Masculinity in this context becomes directly related to the ability to isolate oneself and hold memories within, helped by substance use.

In this chapter, the aims were to look at men's emotional pain and see how they coped. Although the experiences of the men's fathers were different, they both used alcohol to cope in dealing with emotional and physical violence. Peter never revealed how his father acted towards him when he was drunk apart from being the *"life and soul of the party",* and that alcohol was his *"buzz"*. Gary's account in the previous chapter is graphic.

The two accounts show how the fathers developed strategies for coping. Gary's father, rejected at a young age by his family, had little emotional support around him. He became bounded by institutional forces; but when released, he began to come into conflict with them. The anger at having been rejected that he held inside became directed at the people closest to him as he came to fear the emotional connections he had created. He felt they would turn on him, but his actions only ensured that his fears would become a reality. He was in a position where he could exercise those 'stings' lodged within and enact a form of revenge in which he would be the protagonist and not the victim, thereby avenging his own humiliation.

Peter's father internalised his anger, but a bitterness remained in his feeling that his country had forgotten him. He was also consumed with the memories of what he had witnessed. His solution, drawing on Pete's description, was to eradicate his bitterness and memories through using alcohol. This shows the role of the pub in this generation of men's lives; Pete's dad was perceived as a 'social drinker', but the cumulative effect of his drinking and the holding in of his emotions severely weakened his system until it killed him.

V. MOTHER AND SON

This chapter focuses primarily on Phil's difficulties in relating his empathic feelings to his mother. Phil allows only those emotions to flow outwardly that reinforce his self-image, as he directs his anger to create a 'front' he hides behind. This highlights the tension between his 'front' and what has been 'masked' within an intimate relationship, with Phil describing his coping strategies.

This chapter is therefore split into two parts. The first introduces the theoretical concepts I employ in analysing Phil's relationship. This is his 'mask' (Cannetti 1960), here viewed from the inside, with Phil describing the links between his verbal and physical violence and his inner torment. This marks a shift from the previous chapters where I looked at the violence being inflicted upon these men.

Trapped within his 'mask', Phil relates his feelings concerning his *"blocked emotions"* and his stifled ability to communicate with his mother. I see these as masked 'flows' of emotions. Here, I will develop the points raised in the chapter on "Fathers and Sons" to look at the 'flows' and 'breaks' between a mother and her son.

Then I will look at how Phil, instead of being a recipient of 'stings', becomes a protagonist, a marked shift from his status in the "Fathers and Sons" chapter. Phil describes the abuse of his mother, revealing the functions of his 'mask' and relating to me his inability to communicate and his frustration. He talks of his overwhelming feelings, wanting to cry, then 'masking' his 'flow' of tears, reinstating his 'front', transmuting these feelings into anger, verbally wounding his mother, then witnessing the effect and feeling his 'recoil' – his remorse after seeing her hurt. He then attempts to reinstate control by using anger and violence as an explosion of 'stings' onto others. His other strategy is to use drugs, thereby becoming pacified by heroin, again and 'masking' his feelings, 'shrinking' away from contact (Miller 1987). He is engaging in a 'self-medication' (Khantzian 1995).

Latterly, Phil describes another strategy he utilises in dissolving the 'sting' (Cannetti 1960), showing how violence and drug use can be overcome.

It's Hard to Say I Love You

This first section looks at the defining issue of this chapter, Phil's inability to communicate emotions. This session began with initial small talk, but as we proceeded I was caught by surprise as Phil began to talk about his relationship with his mother.

Phil: Well I don't know but, see, I'm a funny person you know.
Dean: 'Cos you've spoken before about how you were unable to show your emotions at all.
Phil: Yeah, yeah, I find that hard, to do that. Specially to me Mum - people like that. It's funny, it's hard to say, "I love you". Things like that.

Phil relates it being 'hard' to communicate with his mother. We went on to examine some of the underlying issues and I drew upon my knowledge of Phil's involvement in gang violence to explore his anger.

Dean: You're able to show some emotions aren't you, like anger?

Phil: Yeah, but they're wrong emotions.

Dean: So you can't say the nice emotions.

Phil Yeah the nice emotions, like.

Dean: Why do you think that is?

Phil: I dunno, like when we argue, say me and my sister argue, or after, I say sorry I didn't mean that, which maybe instead of saying I..., it's there telling me too, I can't.

Two major themes arise from this extract, the first revealed here: *"it's there telling me too, I can't"*, illuminating his inner turmoil, the power of his 'mask' and the deep-rooted nature of his 'front'. He wants to change and communicate his feelings, but his need to sustain his self-image stops him.

The second theme, connected to this, is his moral framework. He describes his anger as one of the *"wrong emotions"*, and his inability to communicate *"nice emotions"*. This relates to his self-perception of being a *"funny person"*. Phil has reflected upon himself and his behaviour, seeing himself as odd; therefore, the 'front' Phil portrays to his mother and other members of his 'family' is not really how he perceives himself. He feels alienated from this presentation.

Wearing a Mask

What lies underneath Phil's 'front' is something intangible, inhibiting his connection to his mother, as he is trapped in an image. In viewing Phil's behaviour as a 'front', I will analyse his performance (Goffman 1959) in order to examine what is 'masked' as Phil unravels the layers. Again, drawing on Cannetti (1960), he describes the 'mask' from the inside, rather than viewing it externally.

> The wearer knows perfectly well who he really is; but his task is to *act* the mask. While doing so he must remain within certain limits, corresponding to the mask that he wears. The mask is something put on, something external. As a physical object it remains quite distinct from the man who wears it. He feels it on him as something foreign, something that never wholly becomes part of himself; it hinders and constricts him. As long as he wears it he is two things, himself and the mask. The more he has worn it and the better he knows it, the more of himself will flow into the figure it represents. But there is always one part of him that necessarily remains separate from it: the part that fears discovery, the part which knows that the terror he spreads is not due. The secret he represents to those who see the mask from the outside must also have an effect on himself inside it, but it is clearly not the same effect. *They* are afraid of the unknown, *he* is afraid of being unmasked. (Cannetti 1960, p. 436)

Phil has not eradicated his empathic feelings; they still exist, carefully camouflaged – a 'mask', as "his task is to *act* the mask", becoming engaged in behavioural forms "foreign" to him. The mask "hinders and constricts him", stopping him from communicating with his mother and his sister, thereby becoming "two things": the Phil who projects a 'front' of violence and another Phil who wants to connect, but feels shy and embarrassed. He feels a certain safety in his 'mask' and sustains it by spreading terror.

The split occurs when he feels the 'recoil' of shame after his actions. His 'mask' gives him power, but at a cost. He must constantly keep it intact, using vital energy in the creation of fear and distance to repress the consequences of his actions (Miller 1987). This becomes the link between what is perceived from the 'front' and the 'mask' itself. I began to see how he 'masks' himself, because he is afraid the people around him will see his underlying emotional turmoil: being shy, wanting to cry, feeling gutted and keeping control through inflicting violence and taking heroin. Ultimately, "*he* is afraid of being unmasked".

Flows

In reflecting on Phil's ability to empathise, I will explain the concept of 'flows', derived from Deleuze and Guattari's "Anti-Oedipus" (1972):

> It is the desiring production of the unconscious whose streams pour out over the "body without organs" (matter that has not yet been socialised, "nature") in order to produce, populate and change that body in accordance with the flow of desires. Desire splits off and joins; streams of desire join up with other streams, then separates from them again. The unconscious is a flow and a desiring-machine, the human being a system of couplings, with which he/she can couple onto, and uncouple from, continuing processes: "Now what?" - those are the questions and streams of desire. Through the streams of connection with objects, institutions, continents, and other bodies, new desiring machines arise and begin to function, opening up territories, crossing

borders, then breaking up again or destroying themselves. (Thewelait 1977, p. 255-256)

Deleuze and Guattari (1972) posit that humans have unlimited potential to connect with the outside world, that these flows are the 'streams of desire' where "The unconscious is a flow and a desiring-machine". This links to the themes already discussed, such as Dillon's (1978) ideas on contraction and pulsation, Boyesen's (1978) 'streamings' and Miller's (1987) notion of 'vital energy'. I see all three connecting to the emotional power that surges through the body, contained in its chemical biology.

Phil blocks his unlimited potential to connect, afraid to show his emotions because he feels embarrassed and lacks confidence in his self-expression. There is a tension between his desire to act how he believes a man should behave and his own personal desires. This is seemingly blocked by outside forces such as the expectations of his family, peer pressure and social institutions as well as from within. I see this as the connection to his masculine presentation.

The block can be seen when Phil states, "*it's telling me to*" *and* "*I can't*"; the split is between his internal desire to communicate and his self-imposed censure. I feel this connects to his need to forget the past, but he cannot forget the thoughts evoked by this forgetting. His 'mask' inhibits his self-transformation by containing and redirecting these desires. Phil then becomes frustrated with himself, redirecting his shame into anger and stifling the flow of empathic connection.

Phil's 'mask' is embodied in his act of using his facial muscles to stop himself crying. Anger then becomes a surrogate release of this tension, an 'explosion' (Miller 1987; Thewelait 1977).

Phil loves his mother, but he is scared to show it. He dares not say the word, highlighting his fear of 'fragmentation' and of the transformation that would ensue concerning how he would be perceived. However, in talking to me, Phil draws on an inner emotional language, not expressed outwardly to his mother, showing he has the ability to be self-reflexive and empathic and highlighting how he is camouflaging himself, paradoxically enough through talking about his inability to express himself: *"It's funny, it's hard to say, "I love you. Things like that"*. His emotional language languishes as a prisoner in his self-made dungeon. Language has the potential to communicate the flows of his care, but Phil instead relates his inability to express himself and he wrestles with the consequent personal cost to him.

Emotional Language

In "Fathers and Sons", anger emerged as a dominant force in family life, creating fear through its rupturing of the 'flows' of care and empathy. The sons are the recipients who erect their own defences around emotional expression, using violence to halt violence, and severing emotional ties. This session explored Phil's emotional life, shifting his layers of defence to show what was hidden. My aim was to work with him to alleviate his need for violence and drug use. Having learned the value of communication myself, I felt it would flow when conditions of trust had been created. Paradoxically, this can only be created through communication. The process entails small steps in building up trust until Phil feels safe enough to communicate in emotional language.

Emotional language is visceral and this creates a conundrum for research evidence, as it is felt rather than being measured. In these extracts Phil does not tell me he is feeling emotional. It emerges as a shared meaning, the product of the trust established between us. When he talks he reveals his empathy for his mother and this highlights his internal moral framework as he knows he is hurting her and this creates a repercussion.

In reflecting on how emotions are engendered and where his empathy flows from, I see Phil's mother's support as providing a crucial role. As with most of the other men in this study, Phil opted out of school in early adolescence and so cannot remember a favourite teacher who may have provided care. The main person who sustained his emotional language of connection was his mother.

In the "Methodology" chapter, I discussed the insights Nancy Chodorow (1978) and Carol Gilligan (1989) provided, and the 'protective cocoon' (Giddens 1995) formed though the Mother/Son relationship that enables conditions of empathy to 'flow'. I began to see how emotions developed through 'flows' of care. Emotional Language and the flows that sustain these bonds are concepts crucial to understanding the role of violence and drug use in Phil's life.

This first extract from Nancy Chodorow's "Reproduction of Mothering" (1978) explains how the 'double bind' (Laing 1961) creates problems for Phil's ability to express himself. Nancy Chodorow (1978) illustrates how the development of masculine values evolves as a reaction to the feminine world of initial care. The masculine/feminine split explains how the 'mask' becomes 'foreign to the wearer' as an 'act'. Phil's 'mask' becomes constructed, in a shift away from his connection with his mother. In Phil's case, this has entailed the need to project a clear identity, increasingly based upon his use of power and force rather than the initial emotional world that sustained him (Chodorow 1978). This is not to say his relationship with his mother was not without problems prior to this attack. Phil related later how his mother had to cope with her own issues, leading Phil to relate to me how he was determined he was going to act differently as a parent to his own children.

> A boy's identification processes are not likely to be so embedded in or mediated by a real affective relationship to his father. At the same time, he tends to deny identification with and relationship to his mother and rejects what he takes to be the feminine world; masculinity is defined as much negatively as positively. Masculine identification processes stress differentiation from others, the denial of affective relation and categorical universalistic components of the masculine role. Feminine identification processes are relational, whereas masculine processes tend to deny relationship. (Chodorow 1978, p. 176)

The above extract begins to explain how Phil creates his emotional world as an antithesis to the initial care provided by his mother. As Chodorow (1978) states, "Feminine identification processes are relational, whereas masculine processes tend to deny relationship". Chodorow (1978) contends that a boy's identification is with a distant father; but, drawing on the sessions, this does not clarify these personal histories. For example, in the chapter "Fathers

167

and Sons", the fathers are described as exerting power and control through violence fuelled by alcohol, severing empathic ties. In the chapter "Relationships", I look at why this occurs. There is an imposed rupture in the 'flow' of empathy resulting from the actions of the fathers.

When growing up in Deptford, the reflections of 'hard men' are mirrored all around Phil, as his friends and their families reflect their 'fronts' as part of a cultural pattern. Silence concerning the internal dynamics of family life helps to camouflage emotional pain, leading to the 'front' defining 'strength' rather than being perceived as a reaction to pain, since the onlooker sees only the 'front' (Cannetti 1960). From working with Phil, I began to see his masculine development being subject to four particular forces. He witnesses the power of his father, seeing his mother's lack of power in comparison, which shows how masculine power triumphs over emotional connection. Secondly, the physical force Phil and the boys endure as part of a toughening up process from their fathers and other members of their family (brothers and sisters as well as uncles, aunties and mothers) causes them to hide their emotions. Linked to the above are the expectations of his mother after the period of his infancy, when her son is faced with the need to conform to the outside world to prevent being hurt. The third, linked to this, is the peer pressure, which bounds emotional expression through taunts and force such as the fear of being called 'queer' by other boys and girls, or the idea of being different resulting in further humiliation. Number three and four are themes that emerge in the chapter on "Violence". The fourth represents the expectations of the institutions, who devalue the emotional world, resulting in further physical and verbal humiliations. These become bounded by silence in the need to maintain codes of honour.

Carol Gilligan (1988) develops Deleuze and Guattari's (1972) ideas concerning 'flows', providing an insight into how Phil's emotional life may have been nurtured. She highlights how empathy forms through 'flows'.

> The role of feelings in knowledge and attachment and detachment raises the question of how knowledge of feelings is gained and expanded. The infant, responding empathically to the feelings of others, demonstrates co-feeling in its most inchoate form. As the child develops, different experiences of human connection—with parents, siblings, friends, teachers, etc.—may deepen and widen the experience of feelings and increase his or her interest in knowing how people feel. (Gilligan 1988, p124)

Carol Gilligan (1988) continues to explain about the role of the parents within this process.

> For example, it is the child's and parent's responsiveness to each other that gives life to the relationship between them, imbuing it with the pleasure that comes from responsive engagement and creating an interplay of feelings that leads the child to wonder at the adult and the adult to delight in the child. Through the attachment or the connection they create between them, child and parent come to know one another's feelings and in this way discover how to comfort as well as how to hurt one another. When the responsiveness between parent and child decreases and their inequality comes to the fore, the child may feel ashamed or guilty in the eyes of the parent, and the parent, at best, looks on the

child with sympathy and feels compassion for his or her distress. (Carol Gilligan 1988, p. 124)

This extract shows how loving parent(s), through empathic responsiveness can create ideal conditions for nurturing a child. Being loved and valued as an infant encourages the growth of this dialectical bond. Emotional language is encapsulated as an initial flow from the parent to the child, reciprocated through this bond. Emotions are nurtured through trust, explaining why this initial care becomes so vital for the development of emotional empathy and the ability to form later attachments (Bowlby 1973). For all of the men, apart from Bri and Damien, it is their mothers who sustain this emotional attachment, since they traditionally stayed at home to provide care for their children.

One of the key themes in these excerpts is Phil's emotional empathy, developed through the mother-son attachment. As these extracts show, whilst he was hurting his mother, he also felt her pain.

Camouflaging Shyness

Phil's dissolving 'front' allows us to embark upon a journey through the 'masked' layers of his defences. Phil discloses that he verbally attacks his mother, but he is unsure why. I asked him why he did not apologise, to dissolve the 'sting'.

In re-reading the transcript I am aware I use a form of understatement in order not to make a judgement. From previous experiences, I know that if I make judgements, the trust will shatter. For me, the process is important, because Phil has begun to change according to his own wishes. I began by asking him why he never said sorry for his anger outbursts.

Dean: Is it because it would mean, you see yourself as surrendering?

Phil: No, it could be shyness, you know.

Dean: Do you think it's something a man doesn't do?

Phil: No, because it is, isn't it? Everyone must have some, some you know respect, I dunno. I just find it shy, I dunno. It's very funny, even to say sorry Mum, I love you.

Dean: Even when you call her cunts and fucks and things?

Phil: Yeah.

Dean: Did you apologise last time when you called her a cunt?

Phil: Yeah ermm, no I said, "Fuck off, you cunt". And it's a bad word, they just come out.

Dean: But did you apologise afterwards?

Phil: Ermm, did I? No, but she knows I do. She knows I don't... mean... because, it really does, no, that's why I don't want to do it more.

Dean: It's a bit disrespectful, isn't it?

Phil: Yeah, but I can't help it, Dean. I don't mean it, it just comes out. If I wasn't saying it to me Mum, I'd be saying it to….It weren't me Mum, yeah, or me aunts, it'd be the same thing that would come out: "Fuck off, you cunt".

Phil describes how his verbal abuse erupts: *"it just comes out"*. He believes his mother knows he *"doesn't really mean it"*, highlighting his faith in her, that she can see beyond it. I feel this assumption rests on an unspoken bond – the 'protective cocoon' where she grew him in her womb and then reared him. Despite the abuse, the bonds of empathy are strong between them. Through the intertwining of their personal histories, this metaphysical dynamic exists underneath his violence, but his words are still hurting her.

171

I initially misjudged his readiness to explore his relationship with his mother, viewing it as his stubborness to capitulate to his remorse, but Phil raises another emotion, seemingly at odds with the abuse he is heaping on his mother. He raises it tentatively to see how I would respond. Once he feels I am not going to mock him, even though I do not fully grasp the implications of what he is saying, he feels confident enough to proceed. He feels *"too shy"* to apologise for his attacks; the words become stuck within him.

This concept of shyness Phil uses, as I know from working with him, is another form of understatement. I see it as being linked to his feelings of 'lack', principally a lack of confidence, and a feeling of deep embarrassment or of seeming foolish or effeminate in wanting to display 'masked' emotions. He cannot speak to his family regarding this lack of confidence because he has built his 'front'. They too have created their own 'fronts', having also grown up in Deptford. He has invested so much of himself in sustaining this 'front' that he has become trapped in this shyness. While he can reveal this to me, he feels afraid to make a shift within his family, fearing the transformation and how he would ultimately appear, leading to an emotional paralysis.

The relationship of anger and violence to 'masking' appears in the above quote from Cannetti (1960). Phil becomes trapped, afraid he will be unmasked:. "the part which knows that the terror he spreads is not due". This explains the split in his behaviour between inflicting verbal violence and feeling the dread of his actions, being unable to shift from his 'double bind'. Phil fears discovery and maintains his 'mask' at all costs.

This shyness creates a sense of confusion for Phil. Within his culture, there is an underlying feeling that this form of vulnerability is to be mocked. Phil has been part of a gang, spent time in prison, and has been heavily involved in the criminal subculture, in addition to his chronic heroin use. He wants to try to overcome his deficit, not through the development of strategies to prevail over it, but to try and hide it.

The Mask of Shame

In feeling alone with his shyness, I see another dynamic emerging: a sense of shame. Around him are presentations of hard men – especially his older brothers – who appear not to suffer from the same self doubts: *"they just get on with it"*. Shyness becomes concealed; there are no spaces to talk about it. It cannot be spoken about with friends, who also conceal it. Exposure would create a crack in the presented façade, with the prospect of having to endure further feelings of shame. The fact that the other men in this study have created 'fronts' points to the phenomenon being a local cultural issue rather than an individual one. This also links to the wider issues of institutional silences I explored in the chapter on "Fathers and their Coping Strategies".

As the emotional world becomes sealed, shame appears to fill the vacuum. Shame takes many forms, but it primarily springs from feelings of personal inadequacy linked to having little self worth and a sense of the self being under threat. In reading James Gilligan's "Violence" (2000) I began to understand how shame creates another dialectical dynamic, compounded by a lack of communication of feelings and a subsequent sense of unease. For Gilligan (2000), shame fuels further feelings of shame, leading to increasing isolation and a complete lack of connection. This resonates with the split in male and female worlds Nancy Chodorow (1978) describes, where men learn to develop their masculinity in response to the feminine world they are born into. However, the dynamic engendering this split that I found from working with so many men over the years is built upon suffering violence and the humiliation of being an object, creating self-shame and a feeling of worthlessness.

Phil's verbal attacks push his mother away, but under this façade he still needs his bond with her. This becomes a way of understanding Phil's verbal abuse and the split within him. This process also helps to explain the dynamic in Chodorow's (1978) separation of male and female spheres, highlighted by Gilligan (2000):

> ...many men are so deeply ashamed of their wishes to be loved and taken care of, which they equate with being infantile, passive and dependent (as though there is anyone, no matter how mature, who does not need to be loved and taken care of), that their feelings of shame motivate them to ward off and repress these feelings by going to the opposite extreme. (Gilligan 2000, p. 131)

I see a connection between shame and how it affects Phil, because of his reliance on his mother. Whilst wanting her care, he also tries to "ward off and repress" these feelings, marking this distance through his wounding and denigrating of her, because he feels ashamed of his need. He is still living with her, feeling he is the man (man = power) in the house. However, his mother cleans, cooks and washes for him, still taking the role of infant carer. He wants to reciprocate, but does not know how to relay this to her, so he creates a distance between them. His identity can then be sustained through detachment. Shyness in this context can be seen as the result of having emotions, but not having the confidence to express them. He is held back by fear of misinterpretation and ridicule, the fear of being seen as effeminate. It is also an encumbrance to the maintenance of his 'front'.

In the next extract, this becomes the defining problem. Phil has to contend with his desire to cry, but does not want to show this to his mother, another part of the 'double bind', demonstrating the tension between empathy and detachment.

Crying

Phil describes the 'recoil' (Cannetti 1960) of his abuse producing his need to cry, but keeping his feelings of empathy held in check. I draw on the concepts of 'flows', encoded literally in his flow of tears, created by the emotions of sadness and sorrow produced by his actions. He discloses his ability to 'mask' this and turn his sorrow into anger, thereby re-instating his 'mask', by literally holding back the tears with his facial muscles, resonating with Pete's father. He needs to 'mask' his feelings to keep the 'front' intact, for fear of the shame at being perceived as weak. This fear of crying in front of others again bounds the masculine world, opposing the feminine. I asked him how other members of his family would react if he insulted them, wanting to know why he behaved like this toward his mother.

Phil: Well, it depends what ones. Some will take it bad, or some take no notice, but erm, I dunno I just, and when I say it, mean, cos that's why I try not to argue with

*my Mum. I walk out, I'm really angry, that's why I
bash doors and things.*

Dean: What, when you've been arguing with your Mum?

*Phil: Yeah and things like that. Instead of taking it out on the
telly or something, I would punch the door.*

*Dean: Cor, you must get yourself really wound up then to do
like that.*

Phil: No, I get wound up because of what I've said.

Dean: Oh, what you've said.

*Phil: I feel sorry after, I feel like crying, when I go up to my
upstairs I feel like crying.*

Dean: Why don't you buy her a card or something?

*Phil: I feel like crying and then when I walk out on the street,
I'm fucking boiling.*

Dean: Over what you've said?

*Phil: Yeah, and it takes any stranger to say anything to me
and I do something stupid. Get meself arrested, you
know what I mean? That's why I try a more seeing,
dangers of it an' all. I get myself in trouble doing it,
plus I shouldn't do it, number one, plus I find it hard
to say ermm sorry ,blah, blah and erm, it just rips me
up inside when I say it to her. I think, you cunt, what
are you saying that for? And I feel like that I want to
cry. I can't, but inside it's just like, like a block.*

I began to understand the alchemy of sadness turning
into violence (Seidler 1999). In stemming his crying, Phil
freezes his feelings, but they still remain. He provides a
display, converting sadness into anger and potential physical
violence as a form of discharge. Phil allows his feelings
to emerge in one particular manner, but "foreign to the
wearer" (Cannetti 1960). He does not want them to come
out this way; "*it just rips me up inside when I say it to her*".

Phil speaks of his *"block"*, where his body takes on a response his mind is trying to overcome, where crying – a display of sadness and a mark of helplessness – becomes a reminder of infancy. Crying involves a 'fragmentation' of the 'front', revealing hurt and sadness, – the opposite of the masculine qualities of toughness and exertion of power.

It is also interesting to see how it rests upon a polarity of anger, moving swiftly from one emotion to another in his attempt to try and stem the flow. This passage from Vic Seidler's "Working with Men for Change" (1999) encapsulates the process:

> This allows first boys and then men to feel that if their sadness, fear or vulnerability is not named, then it "does not exist". Often men learn to automatically transmute emerging feelings of sadness into anger or rage, before the incipient emotions are even acknowledged. The anger is "acceptable" because it affirms, rather than threatens, heterosexual male identities. (Seidler 1999. p. 189)

I see Phil's masculine identity as having been forged in an environment where there was little room for other forms of emotional expression. He constantly has to sustain his 'front' with displays of anger, resulting in his desire to discharge this anger onto a passing (male) stranger. Seidler (1999) illuminates the quandary Phil experiences: "Often men learn to automatically transmute emerging feelings of sadness into anger or rage". This displacement of feeling becomes a substitute for the original predicament. The culture of violence in which Phil has grown up becomes legitimated, directed onto the street, onto another man who looks at him, offering a challenge, "because it affirms, rather than threatens, heterosexual male identities". The dynamics operating in the family ripple and enmesh within a wider culture of violence, where anger and violence become sanctified, reasserting heterosexual masculine values of power and domination and creating respect and awe in the spectator. However, it is only a temporary release for him. The original problem is unresolved, as he still wants to talk to his mother. These are the 'strategies of revenge' that occur consistently in these sessions, where 'stings' are passed on rather than dissolved.

Gutted/Shame

Phil illuminates the stresses of non-communication and the bodily effect of the 'recoil' – the flows of adrenaline released by his anger. I see this as connecting back to Gerda Boyesen's (1976) observations on 'streamings', where emotions are trapped inside the body, leaving him "feeling ripped apart" by his actions. This shows the importance of the body in dealing with the aftermath of the emotional release. I explored with him how he coped with this impact, the 'recoil'.

Dean: *What happens, do you get a churning in your stomach?*
Phil: *Yeah.*
Dean: *Does it hurt?*
Phil: *Naa, I just feel gutted, you know, like gutted, ashamed.*
Dean: *Yeah and it affects your body.*
Phil: *Yeah, I feel ashamed of what I've said, I shouldn't have said that, ashamed.*
Dean: *You get angry with yourself?*
Phil: *I should have cunt, me tongue chopped out. My Mum does so much for me, and this and that, and I spin*

round and say: "Fuck you, cunt ", or whatever. I don't mean it, it ain't there to out, it just comes out, it's like there's no picture there. I wanna say: "fuck off, you cunt". It just comes out, and it comes out to the wrong people. Well, it shouldn't come out. I mean, I shouldn't be swearing, but it's the wrong people and plus it's mum blah blah. But erm, I don't know.

Phil connects his shame to *"being gutted"*, as though he holds his emotions in his stomach. The feeling of *"being gutted"* relates to being *"ripped apart"* – having the insides of his body removed. I noted how he controlled his facial muscles to stop himself from crying; here, he relates how his emotions affect his internal organs – the churning in his stomach created by his emotional turmoil and the image of wanting to chop off his tongue to control himself. He describes how he is making himself ill in an internal battle, demonstrating the deep split inside, as he is torn between his need to talk and his desire to inflict emotional damage.

Phil has never engaged in explicit self-harm such as cutting. He has put his life in danger by his violence and drug use, through gang fights and overdosing on heroin. However, his body becomes a vehicle for discharging his shame, expelling his anger through punching doors, almost certainly hurting himself in the process.

This embodiment of shame helps to contextualise his drug use, which soothes his body by obliterating his internal pain. Heroin alters his body chemistry, affecting the major organs, as well as releasing endorphins that soothe his mind. It literally becomes embodied in his relationship with his mother.

Wounded Mother

I asked Phil where this behaviour stemmed from. I nearly received an answer but felt we were at the edge of an emotional precipice and needed to draw back. What became clear was that Phil was the only family member who verbally abused his mother. He says he is a *"spoilt brat"*. It was left at that. I see Phil's verbal attacks as paradoxically trying to claim his mother's attention, thereby reinstating a form of connection, whilst maintaining distance; a half-way strategy. This highlights how his 'mask' creates codes almost impossible for anyone else to decipher, refracted through the prism of Phil's internal shame.

Dean: Where do you get that sort of language from?
Phil: It hurts her sometimes, that's what hurts me more. Sometimes I think, ermm, when we've argued, I think well, suppose she erm, suppose she passed away the next day. I think to meself: "fuckin hell that really, really would hurt me", you know? Knowing I could've said sorry or whatever.
Dean: You never say sorry though.
Phil: Yeah I know, but I can't, it'd be too late anyway, do you know? But, ermm, that's what I'd be doing, wishing that I'd've said it. I'll make meself ill or whatever, so I just try not to do that.
Dean: Where do you get that sort of language from though, the way you speak to your mum?
Phil: I dunno, maybe, I dunno.
Dean: Does anyone else speak to her like that?
Phil: No, no one, none of the other kids ever done it. No, Sammy, none of them. Joan, Jill none of them ever did it. I don't know where it comes from. Maybe because I was a spoiled brat or, whatever, I don't know, er,

no, the others were never like that, no. Sometimes I say some stupid things like, cunt and things like that. They're horrible words, but erm it just comes out. It ain't as if I see it, and say oh no, don't do that. Where I could fight it off or whatever. It just, it comes out and after I feel bad for what I've said.

Dean: So it's almost like a lack of control.

Phil: Yeah, but it plops and after I feel so bad for what I've ...

Dean: How does your Mum take it when you use those words?

Phil: Yeah bad, I see it in her face, you know.

Dean: So it wounds her then?

Phil: Like she's there thinking, I dunno, she's must be feeling: "How can you say that?" you know, "the things I do for you". And she goes, "I'm better off not here".

Phil's anger physically wounds his mother, as he sees it *"on her face"*. He wrestles with himself, trying to *"fight it off"*, to stop hurting her, describing his internal struggle. His mother feels denigrated by his words, telling him she does not want to live if he continues, an emotional revenge for the grief he is causing her, knowing it will wound him. This, however, does not stop him. He calls his mother a "cunt", a word of hate, a vilification of her sex to humiliate her, another form of revenge.

I will look at two methods Phil uses that become linked to the observations of Alice Miller (1987). Phil's outbursts of anger and the subsequent 'recoil' causes him to assert control through *"punching doors"*, the 'explosion' that brings about a release of adrenaline. His other strategy is obliteration through taking heroin, which has the effect of *"mellowing"* him out.

Anger

Anger is the easiest emotion for Phil to express. He has punched the door so many times his mother asked him to take it off.

Phil: Naa, I wanna door. The only reason why I ain't gotta door is it's been smashed.
Dean: And you smashed it.
Phil: Yeah, I smashed it, it's got holes in it. You can't have holes, big holes in it, so me mum said: "Take it off ", because there's people coming round, and they stay and use the toilet or the phone. It don't look nice, does it, big holes in the door. It looks like you've been having fucking mental nights fighting one another or whatever. But ermm...it's laziness, that's all it is. It really is, laziness. I don't know why I don't go and sort one out. I dunno. Ermm just for that bit of quietness, peaceness. When the door's closed I'm shut off. So what's going on out there it don't concern me.

He recognises that when he unleashes his anger on domestic objects it marks his mental state: *"It looks like you've been having fucking mental nights fighting one another or whatever."* Phil's exertion of control through violence is temporarily expedient: not wanting to replace the door because he knows he will smash it again. However, he acknowledges that when the door is shut, *"what's going on out there, it don't concern me"*. The paradoxical nature of isolation and connection appears again. His violence creates distance, whilst the physical aftermath reduces his privacy. Phil's need to be isolated is balanced by another, the need to know what is happening within the house; or, alternatively, he wants other people to see him.

Heroin

The other crucial strategy Phil uses is to 'mask' his feelings by going out after each argument and soothing himself by taking heroin. This is something his sister notices and ridicules. Drugs help him to suppress the feelings he holds inside. Here he mentions his need for isolation, part of his ongoing depression.

Phil: Ermm...I can get snappy, you know, I just wanna be left alone. I'd rather be in me room or anywhere, on me own, not see no one and not really talk to no one for a couple of days. Because, it ain't though I won't talk to anyone, 'cos I don't. If I did, it's obvious...if I don't want to talk for weeks on end, it ain't a good thing, and it ain't like.. . I ain't saying I don't want to talk to people, what it is, sometimes I just have to cut off for a little while, so I can 'ave my own thing, otherwise I get too snappy, ermm. Silly things, I got flu or something like that, you know er...Stupidness, lazy things, err...

Dean: So all these things affect you then, does it, giving you stress and that?

Phil: Mmm, not all, some of the things.

Dean: Where you errr, less stressed, when you were on drugs then?

Phil: Err...It's a funny thing, I'll 'ave a argument, with me sister, though not lately, but before now and then, and she'll say: "Ahhh, he's got his pills and his drugs down him, he'll be alright in a minute". But the funny thing is, I AM. (smiles)

Dean: You are?

Phil: Yeah, you know ermm, half-hour, I'm mellowed out.

Phil utilizes heroin and Valium to 'self-medicate' (Khantzian 1974, 1995; Lockley 1995) his emotions to cope with the present as well as the past, sustaining a 'protective cocoon' to insulate against anxiety. This is the transmutation of sorrow into addiction, healed through the soothing effect of opiates and tranquillisers that defuse anxiety. However, his drug addiction also engenders feelings of self-shame. He perceives his drug use as a weakness, the reason why he came for help, although not, interestingly, a form of weakness linked to effeminacy.

Although the use of the drug is heavily sanctioned in the local culture, it is a different form of sanction, one which does not rely upon violence but distance, ostracism and non-communication by other community members.

However, substance use offers only a temporary relief. The drug lasts for a limited period and then the dread of his actions grips him. The same problems occur when he uses violence. His solution has been to use more drugs to 'mask' these feelings. Heroin allows him to feel good for the time it interacts with his body. His drug use becomes embedded in his relationships, allowing him to interact from an emotional distance, eradicating his desire for violence.

Expressions of violence

Although Phil is engaged in limited problem-solving strategies, he is also reflective and knows that what he is doing is destructive to everyone around him, including himself. I worked with him to see if he could reinstate the connection.

Phil: And that really does make me go worser then. In me insides, sort of. It makes me feel: "Oh cunt, Phil," you know? rrm maybe because I go out and punch doors or whatever, I dunno, but ermm, I try to control myself, I take my anger out on that.

Dean: Wouldn't it be easier to say sorry then?

Phil: Yeah, but, I'm gonna try.

Dean: Can you say it?

Phil: If I ain't argued.

Dean: Can you actually say those words then?

Phil: Well, it's funny, right.

Dean: Go on then, have a go now.

Phil was unable to say sorry – the block was too great. I was asking him to drop his 'front' completely. At this point Phil shifted the conversation.

Dissolving Stings

Phil describes how he resolved an argument with his friend. The manner in which he spoke showed a huge shift had occurred in his self-perception. I would like to think it was because of the effect of the counselling, but what is clear is that whatever was happening, Phil was shifting his self-image.

Phil: Me and my mate had an argument the other day, at the Hall. It was so stupid how we come to clash, nearly fighting over stupidness, over money. But he said something, I took something the wrong way, and he's like, not fighting but like, ermm....we had an argument with each other. I'm there, just standing there, and he's standing there and there's all these people there who's seen it and that, blah blah. And I know I'm in the wrong. I know I was in the wrong...before he walks off

I was saying to myself, "I've got to stop him and shake hands and say sorry". Like I say… but I've got to do that before he walks, otherwise I might not do it after, or… (mumbles).

I would do it after. See, that's when I could do it, after. I (would) say: "sorry it's out of order". But at that time, when I'm boiling and got the hump or whatever… ermm…But it's me, I'm the one out of order, I've walked up to him and shook his hand and said: "Sorry, I was out of order". But I find it so hard.

Dean: *How did he take it?*

Phil: *Not hard, but easier than talking to me Mum, and saying sorry to me Mum, you know? See I'll tell you 'n all, how it is, I don't, because there is an embarrassment… a bit. Because when I'm saying it to him I feel shy, sort of, not shy, but embarrassed you know?*

Dean: *Why is that then?*

Phil: *It's like kids stuff innit? We shouldn't be arguing in the first place.*

Dean: *Right, but then to say sorry is harder.*

Phil: *See, I'm only just starting to realise, I realised it there, it come straight into me head, there and then instead of later: "You're out of order Phil, apologise". Do you know what I mean? I didn't usually get those things in me head until later on. But it's come in my head: "You're out of order, apologise before he walks away". 'Cos maybe I wasn't saying it, do you know what I mean? So I said…*

Dean: *Did you feel better after you apologised?*

Phil: *Yeahh, much better, 'cos I would've been standing there for the next hour or the next thingy, with that still on me mind, this argument. And people see us arguing you know, this… it'd be going on.*

Dean: *So you were able to clear it.*

Phil: *Yeah it made me feel good.*

Dean: And your mate accepted it.

Phil: Yeah, yeah that's what he wanted. Well, he never wanted that but he didn't want us to erm, fight and clash in the first place. But it made him feel better, and it made me feel better. It did make me feel good because I would have still carried that on my mind afterwards, do you know what I mean? Not that I'm saying that it would actually do me in, but I'm wondering if it will still be on my mind, do you know? I know I was out of order and I shouldn't have said that. I should be man enough to apologise to him in front of people who was there when we had the argument. So instead of calling him over, or seeing him later. That's what I would have done, seen him later, and he would've gone "oh sorry" and I would've gone "sorry we shouldn't have been arguing like that", me and him face to face, there was other people there.

Dean: So you backed down in front of everybody?

Phil: Yes, I done it. I said (to myself), "you've got to apologise now". So I went and shook his hand, and me other mate said, "That's what I like to see, that's what you should be doing instead of arguing with one another", but ermm…I shook his hand and I said "We shouldn't be doing this", blah blah, poxy this, but erm, he said "Yeah, that's fine". It made me feel good after. Like I got rid of it, instead of carrying it. I sorted out a problem out and got rid of it of instead of carrying it along.

Dean: Can't you do that with your Mum then next time?

Phil: Yeah I'm going to try, because how can I say? I'll go home, I will sit in the chair and say, "Oh fuck I shouldn't have said that to him, you know what I mean?" But I did not go home and do that because I dealt with it there and then and cut it off, not brought it home with me. There ain't nothing, nothing playing

*on me mind, that I've brought home with me, you
know, when I've gone in I'm sort of fresh, not fresh but
there's no "Ah fuckin' I shouldn't have said that to him
or no or, whatever".*

Dean: *So you're taking more responsibility for your own
actions?*

Phil: *Yeah and erm...er...but it ain't that when you erm...,
you got be grown up enough, to er... in front of people,
shake their hand and say " look, I was out of order,"
blah blah. See, I could not do that in front of other
people or whatever before, but er...I done it anyway.
I found it was better. Someone said: "Yer, that's what
I like to see, shake hands and make up". That's what
made me feel a bit better an' all.*

In fact, hearing this story made me feel better as well,
as all the work we had undertaken around his violence was
beginning to be integrated into his actions in his social
life. Previously Phil would have fought, no matter the
consequences, but here he narrates in a staccato, nervous
fashion how he was able to show his emotions in front of a
crowd of other men. What occurred then marked a startling
shift: he was applauded for his behaviour instead of being
mocked, creating a new dynamic within the snooker hall.
This allowed him to feel better, marking a shift away from his
previous strategies of taking heroin or inflicting violence.

Phil relates how he connected empathically with his
friend, whom he had hurt. He had to make a decision whether
he was going to keep his 'front' intact or lose his friendship.
Phil decided to listen to himself and take a chance on saying
sorry. He talks about what happened to him: *"It made me feel
good after. Like I got rid of it, instead of carrying it. I sorted out
a problem out and got rid of it of instead of carrying it along".*

The 'recoil' of anger dissolved through instating a connection. This marked a new strategy in dealing with conflict, illuminating how Phil had developed the confidence to show his emotions in front of his friends.

This chapter portrays the internal battle Phil undergoes as a result of not being able to communicate empathic emotions and how this becomes translated into anger and violence. It shows how the severance of connection and the creation of strategies of isolation sustain Phil's conception of his masculinity, now based upon his ability to discharge anger and take heroin. This discharge is based upon the suppression of flows of empathy, which Phil feels may be ridiculed if he ever shows them to his family.

Phil's relationship with his mother rests upon an unspoken bond: *"she knows I don't mean it"*. However, the effects of his wounding have a physical effect upon her. His strategies are to explode *"you cunt"*, and to shrink back to *"mellow out"*. However, there is a 'recoil' from each strategy - a sense of shame, which feeds into a further need to discharge his emotions through further acts of drug-taking and violence. This continuous 'double bind' entraps him.

He describes his inner turmoil as he wrestles with his emotions throughout the session. He finds his own resolution when I push him to demonstrate some emotion. He shifts the conversation to describe how he dissolved a 'sting' through creating a connection.

In the next chapter I will look at these men's relationships with their partners as they describe their 'masking processes' and how they too find it difficult to communicate feelings of tenderness.

VI. RELATIONSHIPS

In this chapter I will look at the issues arising from these men's heterosexual relationships. The analysis is based on the concepts weaving through this thesis: 'fronts' and 'masking' emotions. I will explore how these men's relationships developed and, in all cases, sadly disintegrated. In this exploration, the concept of 'fronts' becomes crucial in understanding how Wayne, Simon, Alex, Alan and Damien are caught in a 'double bind' of wanting to connect while retaining their 'fronts'.

This 'double bind' in particular highlights the dichotomy in their relationships with women. When they first meet their partners, they make an effort to create an emotional connection, a shift in the 'front' producing a flow of emotion (Jefferson 1994). This shift appears not to be sustainable, a quandary highlighted in Vic Seidler's "Rediscovering Masculinity" (1991).

> Possibly we sense that more contact with our emotional selves might threaten our sense of masculine identity, since it will show us as more vulnerable and more needy than we present ourselves to be. As men we are brought up to be independent and self-sufficient. (Seidler 1991, p. 50)

These men need to present the 'front' because they feel it is what the women in their lives want, a man who is "independent and self-sufficient", who can project strength. This is a problem Damien struggles with, as described in the second part of this chapter. This tension between masculine identity, presented as the 'front', being independent, and the desire to communicate tender emotions becomes a key component in understanding what has caused these relationships to collapse.

Initially, I will draw extensively on Wayne's reflections on his relationship. A number of themes arose here that are explored further in the discussions with Simon, Alex and Alan. Wayne described the pressures he felt related to his expectations of his partner, and the social pressures that "transect" (Deleuze and Guattari 1972) young families living in a consumer economy in the 1990s. This influenced their relationship, making him vulnerable to images of consumption and the consequent feeling of low-esteem. Wayne reveals the pressure of trying to hold onto his job so he can pay off these items. In turn, he demands a reciprocation of support from his partner. However, she does not fulfil this role and this leads to tension, as he feels let down.

Wayne described the pressure of raising children, which also emerged when I spoke to Alex and, to an extent, with Simon. Alex in particular explored this pressure when he revealed his jealousy when his son was born. In trying to think through the implications of this, I felt a resonance with Pasolini's "Oedipus Rex", filmed in 1967.

> We see two loving parents but also the birth of jealousy of the father, an army officer, stares into the baby's pram and realises that the baby is a rival for the mother's love. (Geoffrey Nowell-Smith, "Oedipus Rex" sleeve notes, 1999)

This version of the myth resonates with the theme that emerged in the chapter on "Fathers and

Sons", highlighting the problems fathers encounter in creating relationships within their own families.

Wayne's session highlighted the tensions that arose from arguing and how this tension connected to the reversal of 'stings', the strategies of revenge. What occurs is a 'tit for tat' desire for revenge from both partners, commencing a descent into a spiral of mistrust. The result is the collapse of the relationship. Drug misuse becomes his form of 'self-medication', an emotional insurance policy to block out his pain at the loss of his relationship through 'masking' feelings and reinstating the 'front'. A lack of care and a disconnection from emotional pain are apparent, which both Simon and Alan also reveal.

I then analyse another dynamic, the loss of a relationship and Damien's struggle as he tries to shift his addiction by exerting 'strength'. This highlights the tension and 'fragmentation' of identity that surfaces during withdrawal , as he tries to shift from drug user to father, trying to emotionally connect with his partner and his children.

Great Expectations

Wayne reflected on his relationship for the first time two years after it ended. Implicit within his description is that the basis of his relationship was in a traditional notion of breadwinner and housewife (Meth and Pasick 1990).

Dean: So there was a lot of pressure on two young people then?
Wayne: Well yeah, yeah there was but, erm...it didn't make no difference, in the sense...mm... maybe the pressure didn't help much. Could be, the pressure might not

have helped much. I don't really think two people living together anyway..., real pressure helps them. More pressure and more pressures, I don't know, I can't say I think that helped us at all. I say, we was young and erm, I mean, once we were living together and we had a kid and that, it was like, that was my whole life mapped out for me, so I suppose it was pressure. I can't say that, like, every minute of my waking life I was overjoyed thinking that this was my entire life in front of me. At the same time I never thought though: "Oh we can't stay together". I loved her, but I suppose, like, towards the end we was starting to like, row a lot, and it's no good rowing when you've got a kid anyway. I can't agree with all these people who say stay together for the kid, 'cos if the two of you aren't getting on, in a bad atmosphere, that's no good for the kid.

Wayne "loves" his partner, but this love is not enough to keep the relationship intact. He talks of feeling trapped: *"it was like, that was my whole life mapped out for me".* He cannot visualise that his life will ever change. He feels he is being worn down, caught in a treadmill under the pressure of having to support his family.

There were also other forms of 'pressure': *"More pressure and more pressures, I don't know, I can't say I think that helped us at all".* The baby was very ill, and Wayne had to go out to work, so his partner then felt trapped by her role as the carer. As Wayne told me later, he suspected that she was depressed.

In my own reflection on Wayne's description, I am drawn back to the earlier quote from Deleuze and Guattari's "Anti Oedipus" (1972), where they refer to the "historical forces" dissecting family life. These were also creating new pressures, which I will explore.

Changing roles

One of the major upheavals occurring in the late eighties/early nineties was the renegotiation of gender roles in working class communities. The changes were engendered by the advent of mass unemployment and the labour struggles across the UK involving the miners, print unions and the dockers. The effect of unemployment hit the wards of Deptford, Marlowe, Grinling Gibbons and Evelyn particularly hard. Nearby, there was a financial sector boom, which led to an influx of money into Bermondsey and Rotherhithe, particularly associated with building work and the relocation of the news industry. Although the building sector boomed, local unemployment remained high.

Another major impact came about as a result of an anomaly in the Social Security system. For many low-income families on state benefits, it actually became financially prudent not to marry or share the same address. Father and mother received more money as single people claiming separately. This also led to family breakdown, as the man had to act furtively, particularly so younger men, as his known presence led to a reduction in the family income. This became intrinsic to all of the relationships described in this chapter.

When Wayne was working, he was always under threat of losing his job. This would impact significantly on his lifestyle, as most of his possessions were on hire-purchase. When he was thrown out of work, he lost all of the things he had worked for, and with these possessions also went his status. It seemed he was working for nothing. This was one of the underlying reasons Wayne felt pressured trying to sustain his role. Employment was one of the few ways he could assert some form of control in his life and also express his care for his family.

> It is easier for a man to believe his own hard labour allows him to sit back and take it easy than to openly ask to be taken care of. Such a request would reveal the underlying vulnerability and fear of not being able to do it all, something men view as an important measure of masculinity. (Meth and Pasick 1990, p. 65)

Wayne's relationship with his partner rests upon an unspoken division, a pattern derived from his own family experience, but where the social conditions had changed. He discloses it here, but it took a great deal of patient work for him to begin to flow, as he still felt wounded. There was a limit to what he would reveal, as he had tried to forget the emotional pain he had endured and I was asking him to remember it so he could move on.

Dean: What were you rowing about, money?
Wayne: Ermm...
Dean: Did you want to go out and things like that?
Wayne: What was we rowing about? We could be rowing about, anything, you name it absolutely anything. Like rows.
Dean: Who watches TV?
Wayne: Yeah, it could be anything, one little thing can start and then everything that has been building up.
Dean: What were they really about, say if...what were they really about?
Wayne: We rowed about money. I was, all the time I was with her I worked, just over half the time I was with her I was working, and say about for over a year I wasn't

working, not even a year straight, four months here, four months there, so yeah, sometimes it was money. Not all the time it was money, sometimes I would be working and I'd come home from work and I'm tired and then she hasn't tidied up and I'd moan at her for not tidying up. I've got to say this, I was in the right and she was in the wrong there. Overall, I might be more in the wrong than her, towards the entire relationship breaking down. But in some ways, she never bothered tidying up, and I used to cop the hump when I came home from work. When I was working there was reasons to row, like I come home and she hasn't done nothing, and she use to cook me dinners most of the time. I remember one time I come home and she didn't cook no dinner, I just asked her, she had a go at me for asking her and that caused a big row. That's one example like, 'cos she didn't cook me no dinner. Not that I started a row off, 'cos she didn't cook it, but when I asked her, she had the hump like and said, "I ain't got to cook you dinner". Start a row over anything, but ermm, just like what me Dad says, at the end of the day, I think it's true: "You can't say you can live with someone for six months or a year and you're gonna be with them for the rest of your life". From being with someone like that and then being together with a kid at that age, like, you just break up. You don't like, you might love each other to start with, but you don't love each other enough to be two people that live together for the rest of your life. All the pressure and that, you just don't like it no more and things just aren't right and you end up rowing and whatever. Ermm... like I say, I know that at the end of the day, I will never get back with her. I couldn't live with her. I don't think she could live with me. I know myself I couldn't live with her. I'm not thinking like, I wanna get back with her or anything like that at all. And I'm seeing my son now, so in that respect I mean, at the end of the day, er, I, that's all in the past, it's all forgotten about. I mean, I don't, and even when I see her, I don't talk about anything. I might mention one or two things but that's more like looking back and laughing at it, like we were both like that, but we both know that we can't get back together. It would be like that again, but because we aren't back together we can look back on it and say: "Weren't we stupid the way we carried on?" but we both know that if we got back together, within six months we would both be like that again. So we both know we would never get back together and because of that, it's a bit easier. Cos there's no thinkin' I wanna get back with her, you know what I mean?

Pressure - the Desire for Money

Wayne expected his partner to look after their child and attend to the housework. Returning home and seeing this was not done, he felt let down and told her so. Having a job gave Wayne some power over his partner: *"When I was working there was reasons to row, like I come home and she hasn't done nothing"*. He did not ask her why she was not able to support him; instead, he felt justified in discharging his anger onto her, firing arrows and creating 'stings' in his partner. The pressures he was under to sustain his family were immense, as there were few anchor points or enough periods of relaxation and contentment for him to gain a sense of satisfaction. He felt he was striving for nothing, as everything was falling apart.

Simon also described his inability to provide money as placing a strain on his relationship from the beginning: *"I thought to be with Sally you needed to have a couple of thousand pounds in your pocket"*. Simon's lack of self-esteem derives from feeling he is not good enough, that she can only ever love him because of his earning potential. The pressure Simon is under also becomes linked to his ability to provide money and consumer goods for his partner, and he knows he will struggle to do this, inside of the law, because he does not have any vocational skills, leading him to the conclusion *"I don't think (know) what I had to offer her"*. It was not just the money, as he relates: *"she just used me to have my baby and go"*. The problem for Simon is his feelings of worthlessness, of not having what it takes. I can only speculate on the connection between his childhood and the feelings he talks about here. Simon has a sense of 'lack' that he has carried into his adult life; his emotional life seemingly only having been validated by his mother. His current use of drugs helps him to present a 'front', a disregard for emotional connection that is belied by the intense feelings he relates to me.

Wayne expresses ambivalence about his relationship, feeling he has settled down too young. His father tells him this and Wayne has internalised the message; the relationship is doomed anyway: *"You can't say you can live with someone for six months or a year and you're gonna be with them for the rest of your life"*. In retrospect, Wayne explored his devastation after the relationship had finished and began to use heroin to cope with the emotional after-effects. His sense of loss he carried in silence.

Wayne narrates a series of incidents, although he is initially hesitant about looking too deeply into his loss: *"that's all in the past, it's all forgotten about. I mean, I*

don't, and even when I see her I don't talk about anything".
Now he speaks of having a dialogue with his partner
and having a *"laugh"* about the past, *"I might mention
one or two things, but that's more like looking back and
laughing at it."* Wayne projected a 'front' of nonchalance
– the break-up of the relationship had not affected him, a
reinstatement of the 'front', with the past being 'masked'.
I am reminded of Gary's family's laughter when they
reflect, hiding the sadness contained in their memories.

This disavowal of the pain is encapsulated in this
quote from Vic Seidler (1991) in "Achilles Heel". It
illustrates how Wayne's strategy links to other forms
of masculinities and the desire to forget and move on:

> Within a relationship it can mean not dwelling
> on things when they are going badly. We
> learn to "turn over a new leaf" or "leave the
> past behind", for "there is no point in crying
> over spilt milk". We learn to look forward and
> disconnect from our experiences that have
> been painful or unhappy. (Seidler 1991, p. 6)

Wayne has not just forgotten about the past, he has
increased his drug use to obliterate his memories. As I worked
with him, he revealed his pain. It may have been easy for
me to accept Wayne's conclusion that his loss meant little
to him, but I was worried about his deteriorating mental
health. He had few friends and was living with no electricity
or gas. It appeared that apart from attending Orexis, he had
little outside social contact. He spoke of seeing his son, but
this was something we had worked upon together because he
seemed so bereft of support. He had effectively walled himself
off from the outside world, physically and emotionally.

A tension existed between his presentation, which I perceived as a 'front', and his concealed emotions, which I saw as being 'masked'. I began to see connections between the pressures Wayne described and the issues that arose in the sessions with the other men I worked with.

The Pressure of Fatherhood

Wayne highlighted the pressure of fatherhood, the expectation of acting as a parent. Traditionally, men have gone out to work to bring money home to sustain the family and women have stayed at home to look after the children. I would contend there has also been another subtle change – the end of the hedonism that defined teenage life, marked by the responsibilities of looking after a child.

Wayne and his partner were just out of their teenage years when their son was born, and Wayne felt he had few parenting skills to offer. He was young, without a steady income and had a prison record, which he felt ashamed of. The birth of his child produced a change in his relationship with his partner. Wayne's arguments escalated after their child was born, a dynamic that affected both Alex and Simon.

Wayne feels deskilled as a parent, so he leaves the responsibility to his partner. This boils over into frustration, further fuelling the rows, which intensify, and he has to make a choice between staying with his partner or separating. His choice is to separate, rationalised as *"a bad atmosphere, that's no good for the kid"*. He related the break-up to me as being in the best interests of the child, not as being good for Wayne himself. He left his son with his mother because he felt she could offer him the emotional support he was unable to give.

Alex and Simon also had a crisis when their children were born. This crisis was played out in silence and anger, masking of emotions and the firing of 'stings'. These stemmed from the desire to connect with their families but not knowing how to express this. A lack of confidence became shaped into anger. Implicit in these extracts are the effects of the arrival of a baby changing the dynamics, when suddenly the attention given by the woman to the man is now directed onto a new arrival. Wayne did not speak explicitly about this, only about his shock at the change.

Alex spoke explicitly of this transformation in his relationship. I felt in working with him that there was a distance between him and his son, typified by his references to the *"kid"*. This is the same term Wayne used in describing his son, highlighting for me the emotional distance established through the use of language. The birth is described as *"we had a kid"*. He does not use his son's name, nor does he show any sense of connection; it is as though he is referring to an object. At the same time, he spoke of his feelings of deep loss and subsequent joy in re-establishing contact, but he still felt he had nothing to give. We became stuck at this point, as I was unsure how to proceed.

Alex: Even before we had the kid we were close, before we were separated. We would fall out and she would want me back straightaway…but after the kid it was OK at first. She had postnatal depression, which I did not understand. I was trying my hardest, staying up all night with the kid, the kid's teething, then going to work, coming back in and doing the housework and everything, giving her money, you know "here's some money go and get yourself a pair of jeans or a jacket or something.

202

*That will cheer you up. But no. I was still, I wasn't anything
at all, not in her eyes. Getting under feet is what it seemed like.*

Alex describes his closeness with his partner before
the arrival of his son. After a row they would always
come back together, as their relationship rested upon an
emotional and sexual connection. When his son appeared
there was a shift in this dynamic where, *"it was OK at
first"*; then, as he explains, his partner began to experience
"Post-natal depression, which I did not understand". Alex
speaks openly about his feelings of loss – his partner
was no longer the same person as before. Alex tries to
cope by attempting to make the relationship work by
undertaking some of the roles normally associated with
women – after returning from work, he looks after the
"kid" and does the housework. This shows a different type
of intervention to Wayne's, who had defined ideas about
gender roles and spoke very little about trying to make his
relationship work. Alex, who is a little older than Wayne,
tries to alleviate the physical pressure on his partner.

What becomes held in silence is the disruption to his
sex life, the adjustment to sleepless nights, with the woman
recovering from the effects of childbirth both physically and
emotionally. Although I did not ask Alex, I would surmise
she was not as interested in him sexually as she was prior
to the birth of their son, especially since he stated that she
had post-natal depression. I began to see the difficulties
these men faced in adjusting to a new type of relationship,
one with minimal outside support, where the man is on
the outside of the mother-baby bond. His role is seemingly
reduced to working to provide money, and there is the need
to divert more of his income to feeding and clothing the
baby, who has taken away his wife's attention. Another
issue, highlighted by Winnicott (1957) in "The Child,

The Family and the Outside World", is the jealous feelings mothers have regarding the father-child relationship.

> It is well known that there is sometimes a vital bond between a father and his daughter. As a matter of fact, every little girl has it in her dream of being in mother's place, or at any rate to dream romantically. Mothers have to be very understanding when this sort of feeling is going on. Some mothers find it much easier to stand the friendship between father and son than between father and daughter. Yet it is a great pity if the close bond between father and daughter is interfered with by feelings of jealousy and rivalry instead of being allowed to develop naturally. (Winnicott 1957, p. 117)

Although Winnicott (1957) describes the problem of jealousy in terms of gender, the dynamics of the arrival of a newborn child may have the potential to create a complex counter-reaction, particularly if the mother and father have unresolved issues from their own childhoods that they then project onto the baby. Both partners may hold these feelings of jealousy in silence, leading to the child occupying the middle ground in a silent struggle. This creates long-term consequences for family stability, and requires further research.

Money as a "Flow of Care"

Alex spoke of the difficult childhood his partner had experienced and recognized the birth of the baby was creating problems for her that he was not able to understand. His second strategy was to try to please her by giving her money, a similar strategy to Wayne's. In this context, money becomes a substitute for emotional connection, touch and speech. The giving of money is seen as a form of care in itself: *"here's some money, go and get yourself a pair of jeans or a jacket or something. That will cheer you up."* When this failed, he felt deflated, thinking he had nothing to offer. As he explains, he did not understand the emotional after-effects of giving birth, the depression his partner went into and her feelings towards the baby and him. He thought he could buy her out of it.

Alex: I gave her everything I had, you know what I mean? I
    used to give her loads.
Dean: What, in terms of money?
Alex: (nods)
Dean: What about in terms of emotion?
Alex: She got that as well, she knew how much I cared for
    her.

I explored with Alex how he knew she cared for him and the answer became teleological: because he gave her money and she just did. Like Wayne, Alex also felt he could rely on the initial courtship memories to sustain their bond. As he explained how he provided emotion, he began to trail off. There is a similarity to Wayne's predicament, with rows becoming centred on money. Wayne's partner felt that he was not sharing his money. At this point, Wayne was not using drugs, but spending money on himself, on music and clothes. He was continuing the lifestyle of a single man.

Money plays a major role because the giving of money becomes a code for affection and emotional provision. I asked Wayne if he ever expressed his emotions to his partner. He told me, *"she knew I loved her"*. He felt it unnecessary to irrigate his relationship with expressions of emotion, instead relying on the initial bond and his memories of courtship. However, as I pointed out to him, the dynamics had changed.

Children and Jealousy

Ultimately, Alex's strategies failed and he felt useless and redundant, *"getting under her feet"*, getting in the way of the mother-son relationship. There was also another dimension to this – his feelings towards the birth of his son and the impact it had on his relationship. His strategy was to return to the lifestyle he had developed as a single man, except he was carrying the stress of not being good enough to provide for his family.

Alex: 'cos I used to get quite jealous, you know, at first, when the kid was born.
Dean: Did you?
Alex: The kid was getting the attention. Not jealous, jealous, but yeah, a bit left out. I had to accept it; I realized that. It took me a bit of time, but I had to realize it. It's a kid, so the kid gets the attention. I gave the kid a lot of attention as well. I gave the kid as much attention as her mother. I used to take the kid out all of the time…and the kid loves it at her Gran's".

Alex expresses his feelings of jealousy stemming from his growing sense of isolation from the mother and son relationship. This bond has been developed through the child growing in her womb and his reliance upon her for sustenance. Alex feels he is losing his partner to his son. He can retrieve the memories of when they both went out together, but the dynamics have now changed with the arrival of his baby. The attention he formerly received has diminished, and this is exacerbated by her depression.

Alex speaks of a developing rift. In feeling isolated, he wants to go out with his friends, which causes more problems, because she feels he is not supporting her. The lack of communication of emotions leads to a widening gulf between them, fuelling more conflict. A spiral of decline develops as the lack of communication causes each partner to engage in a strategy of revenge culminating in relationship breakdown.

I also want to look at the after-effects of this breakdown through the words of Simon. Alex's feelings of upheaval at the birth of his son are not unique to him. This sense of isolation is a common occurrence among men from differing social strata.

> With the birth of a new child, men often feel silently aggressive for having been displaced from their position within the relationship. Often people are unprepared for the new situation and the lack of freedom that a baby brings. Men unknowingly can seek revenge through a sullen withdrawal or sometimes through seeking a new relationship. With the birth of a new child women often want more emotional support from men, and men can find it difficult to provide it. It can be easy for men to feel that things should be the same as they were before, and so not to appreciate how radically changed the situation can be. It becomes important to negotiate emotional needs but if there is little experience of this, problems are created within the relationship which might only surface years later. (Seidler 1991, p. 10-11)

This feeling of being left out seemingly affects many fathers when their children are born, as the focus shifts from them to their sons and daughters. The men in this study have few coping skills and minimal parenting supports. I began to see this as creating a silent need in them to be at the centre of their partner's attention, because once they have found love, they find it extremely difficult to cope with the loss of attention without a total collapse of self-esteem, which begins to explain for me how the *"paranoiac father"* develops (Deleuze and Guattari 1972).

Within Seidler's extract, the man seeks his revenge outside of the family unit, feeling something has been denied to him in the current relationship. The dynamics may also be further complicated, drawing from Winnicott (1957), in that the mother also feels jealous of the father's role, thereby creating an actual or unwitting barrier to his involvement with his child.

The Pressures Released through Revenge

Simon also spoke of his feelings of being left out when his child was born. Seidler (1991) writes, "Men unknowingly can seek revenge" when their relationship is transformed. Simon's remedy was more drastic than Alex's. Here, he describes a polarity of emotions, ranging from his exultation when he was married to a desire to block something out.

Simon: ...My wedding day: it was ace, I was over the moon. I had the girl of my dreams and she was pregnant with my baby and I really thought I could work things out and all of a sudden (claps hands)...I got to see Dr. White one day and tell him like I'm cold and like I'm taking codeine linctus and he writ me out me first Methadone script. And but I'm not knocking him. I could've said no, but I took it, got immune to it,

*enjoyed it, and this is it, and now I've been on it now
or what...errr...it's gotta be about thirty coming up.*

Simon has spoken to me about how he failed to cope when his son was born. Feeling isolated, he went to see a doctor to put him back onto medication. He stopped using heroin when he was first married, but the strain of acting as a father was too much for him. This led to the decline of his relationship, which he speaks of in detail, noting the difference between his wedding day, which was "ace", and what happened afterwards: *"and I really thought I could work things out and all of a sudden (claps hands)"*.

I will explore Simon's reaction to the birth of his child as I trace the strategies of revenge that flow through relationships, leading to their collapse. These strategies emerge in the way relationships spiral into arguments as both sides try to assert control and revenge the 'stings' they are receiving.

Wayne recounted how he had arguments with his partner and how they escalated, often centred on money. Arguing, a discharge of anger, constantly arose when these men explored their relationships, as they were unable to communicate their sense of isolation and lack to their partners. Instead, verbal violence emerges as a means of establishing connection.

Alex's arguments did not resolve his fundamental problem; they only served to heighten the tension at home. At this point, I was asking Alex how he balanced his decision to leave his partner against his subsequent drug use, knowing he cared deeply for her.

Dean: So you'd rather have heroin than a girlfriend then?
*Alex: Naaa, I dunno, that depends what the girl is like. If
    it was like the one before and we're back to the good*

times, you know what I mean? 'Cos when I was with her things were good, know what I mean? And she ain't into things like dangerous drugs...And that was a good life with that woman for a number of years. Then that stopped and I started hanging around with my friends again who were junkies and it was just a matter of time and I was back on it again.

Dean: That relationship ended because you started arguing?

Alex: Yeah, petty arguments and that. I was paranoid basically, and she thought I was possessive, but I didn't think I was possessive. She was telling me lies, so I was watching her that bit. She never messed about behind my back, you know what I mean? 'Cos she did care a lot about me, you know. It was just I was getting too paranoid and I was accusing her of things and I was picking fights, you know what I mean? And that was annoying for both of us...

Alex's relationship spiralled out of control as he realised he had become possessive, leading to his own isolation as his partner's attention became directed onto their son. He felt she must have been up to something, because their dynamic had changed. Alex found it difficult to adjust, feeling *"that things should be the same as they were before"*. His "paranoia" emerged, exacerbating the conflict. He began to pick fights, aiming 'stings' at his partner, wounding her for attention. However, this was creating a 'recoil' in him. In his effort to control his disintegrating world, he began to use heroin to cope with the engulfing emotions of his 'double bind'. It was his strategy to punish his partner and himself, thereby emotionally escaping from the relationship decline. His drug use was also adding to this spiralling descent, as the need to escape now became the focus of his life.

Many of the themes I have explored in these extracts also surfaced in this session with Simon. This extract describes how he externalized his 'stings' through arguing in public. The counter attack from his wife was her pretending she had another man. His retort was to tell her he didn't care; her reply was to spit at him. Simon's triumphant "victory" was pawning his wedding ring to buy heroin. The 'strategies of revenge' flow backwards and forwards as 'stings' designed to wound one another emotionally. However, Simon reveals underneath this violence that he is crying, belying the 'front' he is presenting. His next strategy – the same as Alex's – is to increase his drug use in order to cope. Here he describes the final break-up of his marriage:

Dean: How did you fall out with Sally then? Did you get more and more out of control?

Simon: I was getting more and more out of control, err, things like I wasn', I used to work now and then totting with me brother. We bought a van, and...

Dean: Who was that, Paul?

Simon: No, Liam, the oldest one. We bought a van and we was earning good money. We was bootselling it, you know, a bootsale, and we was earning a bucket... And all of a sudden she told me she didn't love me no more, and I said OK. She spat in my face. And I went: "I'm going back to work". She went: "Well I don 't think I'll be back here when you come back". So anyway I, as I got back, as I'm working, I was working in Deptford. I was just knocking down this wall, you know the Dayfold Centre, just round the back there, so she knew where I was. She was f'ing and blinding at me, yeah. And when I said: "Well you didn't want to stay with me, you've met someone over the Docks, who's meant to have whatever". So I says: "see you later". That was lies 'cos she kept on saying: "I wanna make up". She was beating me and I wasn't going to hit her and she spat at whatever and me... It made me cry to be honest, and whatever. And she found it in her heart, that she was trying to make me jealous. But I did the baddest thing, didn't I? 'Cos I thought it was over, what did I go and do? Pawn me ring, the wedding ring, 'cos I thought it was all over.

Dean: *You didn't make much of an attempt to save it?*

Simon: *What, the marriage? Not really, 'cos I don't think what I had (was good enough) to offer her.*

Dean: *You didn't think you were good enough?*

Simon: *No I didn't. I thought it was though... ((looking at the table) me cups moving up and) ... I thought to be with Sally you needed to have a couple of thousand pounds in your pocket. But now she's, and then sometimes I think she just used me to have my baby and go. I've had a lot of things, Dean. You are the first one I've ever opened up to...You know, I've had a lot of things on my mind. I'm not mad. Like I say my prayers every night and things like that, but nothing seems to go right for me, Dean.*

Sally confronts Simon, wanting a demonstration of his emotions, *" cos she kept on saying: I wanna make up"*. Unbeknown to her, Simon was already on a script, from soon after the baby was born, as he could not cope with the loss of her care. Simon could not transform himself within a public space and reach out to his partner in front of his older brother. He had internalised the fact that she did not love him anymore, because he felt he had little to offer: this was an easy escape route out of the marriage.

Simon describes how Sally used emotional revenge: *"she was trying to make me jealous"*. He carried on working, presenting a 'front', even though he was torn inside by what was happening: *"It made me cry to be honest, and whatever"*. However, he did not show this to Sally, for fear of being seen as weak. After she left he began to cry. Simon then undertook his own form of revenge: *"But I did the baddest thing, didn't I? 'Cos I thought it was over, what did I go and do? Pawn me ring, the wedding ring, 'cos I thought it was all over"*. After he bought his heroin, he began to seal himself off from the emotional after-effects of his relationship.

Self-medication as an Emotional Insurance Policy

Within this context, Simon's response to his emotional crisis was to use drugs as his 'emotional insurance policy'. Once he felt events slipping away, he sought solace in active forgetting, 'masking' his feelings and taking control, leaving his partner feeling isolated, and then simply increasing his heroin use to shut her out. This created an emotional rift, which through the 'tit for tat' revenge cycle became a chasm of non-understanding, a break in the flow of love.

In the chapter on "Fathers and Sons" I explored the connection between emotional turmoil and drug use, drawing on the connection between Simon's father's use of alcohol and Simon's use of drugs. *"I took drugs more after she left me just to block it out me head"*. This also resonates with Alan's devastation, caught in a striking image from his session, after he split up with his partner. I asked him directly, years after the break-up, and after he had had time to reflect upon its effect. His reply was succinct.

Dean: Did the break up of that relationship affect you?
Alan: Ahh yeah fucking right. It took me a long, long time to get over it, you know?
Dean: Did your drug use escalate after that break-up?

213

*Alan: Well, when I was with her, I wasn't really using drugs.
I was more into motorbikes; that was the only sort of
errr.... My life revolved around motorbikes, you know.
After she left, the motorbike never moved, it just sat
there, you know.*

Alan's life ground to a halt and he went into a
depression. In order to compensate, he underwent a change
of direction, going to the pub to 'mask' his feelings by
getting drunk. There he met some other men who were
involved in the shipment of drugs, and from this crucial
juncture, his drug habit and involvement in the drugs
industry intensified. What becomes apparent in the two
accounts is how the 'recoil' of the break-up of Simon, Alex
and Alan's relationships became 'masked' by drug use. The
memory of the relationship is not eradicated completely,
so they have to keep up the habit so as not to remember.

The problem compounded, with Alex, Alan and Simon
relating how they had suffered various forms of emotional
neglect and abuse within their families. They have strong
needs, held silently because they fear being hurt and
perceived as weak. When they eventually make a bond, they
are caught within a dilemma: the terror of being unmasked,
and the feeling they are not good enough. A 'front' of
cool indifference camouflages this fear. When they form
relationships, this necessarily entails a transformation from
their previous male forms of behaviour; this implies the
establishment of an emotional connection, which becomes a
challenge to their self-perception. How can they remain hard
and cool on the outside and yet express love and tenderness
to a woman? They fear dropping the 'front' because it entails
a move into connection, and possibly becoming hurt in the
process. It also risks being perceived as effeminate as a

result of expressing love and concern. There is also another issue: the fear of whether the woman really loves them when they do not love themselves, having experienced little self-affirmation as children or as adolescents. These fears become secrets shrouded in silence, masked and subsumed into actions that uphold the 'front'. The situation becomes exacerbated, exemplified by Alex and Simon's descriptions of the difficult childhoods of their partners, which highlights the relationship complexities Winnicott (1957) explored. The lack of support in negotiating relationship difficulties is implicit in the following quote from Simon.

Dean: You know, if you'd had a stable upbringing though, that would have helped you to overcome the break-up of your relationship, if you could have talked to your Mum and Dad about it?
Simon: Yeah, but...
Dean: Being as you couldn't...
Simon: You hit it right on the head. I couldn't. I couldn't talk to them. When we was splitting up, 'cos my Mum and Dad are divorced, and it was sort of like you say: "You made your bed, you lie in it". And that's how it's been for the last four years.
Dean: So there's no one to give you support.
Simon: No I never had it.

The result is that Simon has to negotiate his emotional upheavals by himself, so he resorts to a strategy he has seen his father draw upon: the use of substances to 'self-medicate' (Khantzian 1995).

The Aftermath, Faith Destroyed

I explored with Simon and Alex how they were feeling now, and whether they felt strong enough to develop another relationship. The answer was invariably no. They did not feel good enough, their self-esteem was low and they were scared of being 'hurt' again.

Dean: How come it destroyed your faith in them?
Simon: I'm frightened to get hurt again Dean. I don't want to get hurt again.
Dean: How were you hurt by them?
Simon: Well, I'll always remember the day she come and she packed her gear and took the baby away from me. That was the last I see of her. That was why Micky was OK because we could talk about our missies. But I would go back out with her, but I would have to take it very gently. That is if she would take me obviously. But women are OK, but I'm frightened of them, very frightened. I'm frightened of getting hurt again.

Alex's lack of self-esteem is encapsulated in this quote:

Alex: No decent girls is gonna go for someone like me you know. Especially if they know I'm on drugs as well. That's it. I would maybe get away with it if I wasn't on drugs but when they found out you're a junkie, most girls won't touch you. Unless they're on the gear themselves. My ex-girlfriend, once she knew I was back into junk, that was it. She took me up the road and took me back, I think, to give me a chance to get back off it, but it didn't work out. She actually caught me doing it, that was it....

Alex has a strongly held idealization of decent girls who do not take drugs and a consequently negative view of "junkie girls", where the relationship becomes centred on drug use rather than emotional connection. The drug use helped to create a sense of isolation, of being walled off from emotion. In trying to shift from the drug subculture, Alex recognizes the difficulties. He has few opportunities to break out of his self-imposed world. Another difficulty in forming relationships emerges for Simon:

Dean: Would you rather be with a woman though, than take drugs?

Simon: Yeah, yeah, but I'd like her to understand me. Mean, I don't expect her to, don't expect her to, cos it ain't fair, drummin' drugs into girls that don't take it. It's like them drummin' things into me like: "Oh I done knitting today". And I'd go, I wouldn't listen to that, you know, knitting but. I can't talk to them about drugs cos I don't think it's putting it on 'em like. I don't think it's fair, you know? I would love to go with a girl when I'm off drugs but I don't think I've got it".

Simon wants a woman to understand him, but he does not want a drug user. He is caught within two competing demands, but I think what he really wants is for a woman to rescue him from himself. At the same time, he has no self-esteem: *"I would love to go with a girl when I'm off drugs, but I don't think I've got it"*. Simon does not believe he has anything to offer a prospective girlfriend; to some extent, in his present position and because of his sense of hopelessness, this is difficult to counter.

He has let everything in his life slide; hanging on to his flat has been the one positive aspect of his drug existence. He has never made contact with his ex-partner or his child, feeling too ashamed to talk to her. Instead, he has steadily increased his drug use in order to block everything out.

Strength

In exploring relationships, I will explore another dynamic, the concept of 'strength': its relationship to withdrawal and 'fragmentation' of an identity. Damien's session illuminates the general difficulties in ceasing drug use and the huge difficulties he faces in rebuilding his life.

Damien wants desperately to stop using drugs so he can rejoin his family. Similarly to Alex, Simon, Alan and Wayne, Damien's drug use escalated after his break-up, but now he wants to restore contact with his partner and he is caught in a 'double bind'. The following extract traces his internal struggle and the difficulties this throws up for him.

Ceasing drug use in order to rejoin a family is often stated as an aim in the sessions. However, for most of them this remains a fantasy, as their partners have had enough and have moved on to create other relationships. Damien proved to be the exception, as his partner genuinely wanted him to be with her if he could cease his drug use.

My objective in working with him was to allow him to gain more confidence to express emotions other than anger. He had earlier spoken about his abusive relationship with his mother, which we did not explore on the tape. By this time I had sustained a relationship with Damien for two years and after a considerable amount of trepidation on his part, being unconvinced that counselling could be effective. As his 'front' began to dissolve, Damien began to relate his feelings.

Dean: What happened, have you been in Halston?

Damien: Well, I've been in Halston all this time. I've been coming off, I've been back on it, coming off, getting back on it. All the time I've been staying with her, although like I've had my own place, round the corner... it just got too much in the end, you know what I mean? One minute I'm alright and the kids are playing with me, the next minute they can't come near me, up in the air and really, I'm just not strong enough. When I went down there I went through two weeks of fucking agony, coming off that Methadone and afterwards I just couldn't hack it no more, you know, so I went out and bought some heroin.

Dean: Did your partner know?

Damien: Yeah, yeah, I almost finished with her now. I was there, um, last week, it's been happening so many times that I've been telling her I'm coming off. I've been withdrawing for so long. I've been going out every night getting a bit of gear, handling it for a couple of days, coming back trying to get off of it, can't handle it, going out and getting more gear. It's been disrupting everything, she's been cunting me off, she's been horrific, she's felt like using herself.

Dean: What's so hard about coming off apart from the pain?

Damien: Well that's what it (laughs) I dunno. It seems to me that's doing me in.

Dean: So it's the pain of withdrawal. What kind of pain is it? Is it body pain or is it...

Damien: It's body pain. When I'm withdrawing, especially if I've got no money, I'm sitting there and my brain's going fucking mental, thinking how can I get some money, straighten myself out. I can't stop it from ticking over. When it's ticking like that it's like I haven't got to say anything, but it's like everything I'm feeling is all

219

*coming out of me, bouncing round the fucking house.
It's been like a fucking black cloud over my head, every
time I'm withdrawing, and it's just been fucking too
much, too much for me in the way I'm fucking there,
and I realise how much grief I'm causing, you know?*

Dean: *Mmm.*

Damien: *I can't go back to my place. I've got a shitty bedsit
down there. There's no way I can sit in there and come
off. I dunno. It's just I'm not strong enough, simple as
that: I thought I was strong enough. I'm not as strong
as what I thought I was.*

Dean: *Has it surprised you then?*

Damien: *Yeah I thought fucking, I could go through with it.
I thought if I want this relationship so much, I want
to be clean so much, that I could straighten myself up,
and be able to do it, but I just haven't been able to. The
breaking point comes, like I say, about a week a go. I
was round there and I'd been there for about two days,
when...I ain't gotta say anything, she knows I'm sitting
there, anxious and getting fucked up, you know? She
said: "If you leave this time". She said like, she said:
"If you go out the house, and score, I don't want to see
you again until you're clean".
You know, and er, well, I fucked up didn't I? I fucked
up.... I couldn't cope, the withdrawals. Just as much
as I love her and the kids, just as much a cunt I feel,
you know? I walked out and she's fucking bawling
her eyeballs out....(Pause) So I've got a mixture of a
gear and Methadone habit at the moment, that I'm
getting off the street, down in Hastings, er last time I
was up here I went to see Dr. X... and when was it?
Not the last time, the other week, I did a flying visit.
I would say nearly two month ago, Dr X was all funny
with me, you know, and he wanted. He just wouldn't
entertain me anymore, I dunno why. I don't think I*

did anything to upset him, but erm, but at the end of half an hour of arguing, he gave me a three-week prescription, and on yer way you know. He gave me a three-week prescription, well, I said, give me a three week prescription, like you've got to give me at least three weeks to er, sort out another doctor, so he gave me a three week prescription, you know? You see he's funny sometimes. Anyway, I went back there this morning, and the receptionist said:
"Oh you're off the books. He won't see you anymore". I really don't know what I've done to upset him. I don't know what to do, (Mumbles) I'm just not strong enough.

Dean: *So it's got a bigger power over you, the addiction then?*

Damien: *Yeah, I always knew that it had a strong physical hold over me. You know, the time I'm withdrawing, I'm bumping around just thinking, money, drugs, get on the street.*

Dean: *What about psychologically?*

Damien: *That's what I mean, that's what I mean, yeah it's got a fucking strong psychological hold over me. I'm just not strong enough. I thought I could come off, Dean, you know. When I come up here and you gave me that three-week prescription I had no intentions of going down there to find another doctor, because I thought I could use this lot to come off. I had that little lot which was over a thousand mls of Methadone, Valium. And I was intending to not use so much Valium and Temazepam. So at the end of it, a friend of mine gave me a bottle of a hundred mls, and two hundred DF118's. I thought I'd use them after the Methadone, the DF118's. I done all that, but I didn't, I mean, fucking, I suppose they lasted me about a month, a month, five weeks or something. Then, at the end of it, I was just fucking high and dry again. I thought at least because I'd broken the other Methadone habit, I broke it, even though I was still using, but it wasn't the Methadone, it was much deeper than that, mostly gear. I thought I was suffering, why it was so bad, because I'd never had withdrawals like it, like never come off Methadone before, only come off gear when I had to, ermm, and I thought it would be easier this time, because I was with her. But it was just the same. And as Joan said, the more you prolong it, the harder it gets. After that two weeks I didn't have none for two weeks, I felt really ill. At the end of the two weeks I could hardly fucking, I'm still a right mess now. Still haven't eaten properly, could hardly walk. If I was driving, I had no fucking. It was like I was an incoherent driver, driving across the fucking lanes. I didn't know whether I was coming or going. Early on, I was just thinking, just hang on and then I could get strong again. That is what I was thinking. After the two weeks, I went out and used, and felt better and er, instead of going for it again like I intended to, when I was free I was thinking, fuck going back to that again, you know? I should have left it alone then. Like now I'm using and trying to come off, going up and down trying to come off, and it's been like that since I've been down there, so I've split up with her for the time being.*

Dean: *So you kind of see yourself as not as strong as what you think then?*

Damien: *Not where the withdrawals are concerned, no. When I come out of er, the DDU that time, I think I could've done it. I think I could've done it. Especially if I'd've stayed in there, 'cos I came out, I went down there and I didn't have anything for four days and I felt rough, well, I felt like, I was capable, you know? I felt it would be like, but it was not, it was just too much and when I tried to cut myself down I obviously done it wrong. I was using, instead of waiting until I felt really on top mentally. I was waiting until I felt a little bit rough, and then taking enough to make me feel properly better, instead of just taking enough to, I dunno. I'm a greedy bollocks as well, that don't help, 'cos if I feel better I like to feel better, not fuckin' half better. (laughs)*

Dean: *Why do you think you're so weak then? 'Cos that can boost your habit up. You've been like that ever since you started using.*

Damien: *I think it's because I've always had, fucking quite a lot of money.*

Damien wants desperately to stop using, and he exerts his willpower to this end. We had worked on a plan for him to stop, and I was trying to give him responsibility for his detox. He said he could come off at his own pace, if only he were given a chance, as the relationship meant so much to him. I was caught between wanting to believe him but at the same time feeling the addiction had other layers to it. The discussion above showed me the importance of setting and negotiating realistic boundaries, as I reflected on the emotional pressures Damien described in his withdrawal.

One of these layers revolved around how he shifted his self-image. He shows a lot of trepidation at the prospect of shedding one identity and moving into another. He tries to detox as an act of strength. Damien had determination, but this was not enough: *"I'm just not strong enough"*. His masculinity becomes the battleground where he exerts his will, his strength. I felt he should perhaps have allowed his 'front' to dissolve, so he could become more emotionally expressive, but instead he wanted to overcome his addiction through will power.

Damien perceives his addiction as a kind of test, a trial which he was losing. He has a strong desire to cease his drug use and to re-connect with his family. This causes him further pain: *"Just as much as I love her and the kids, just as much a cunt I feel, you know?"* Trying to come off and failing merely heightens his feelings of weakness and downward spiralling self-esteem. I wanted to look at why Damien was forced back into using. In the above extract, there are two intertwining layers that emerge: body pains and emotional pains.

Damien states that the reason he cannot come off is that *"It's body pain"*. However, Damien also talks about where, *"I'm sitting there and my brain's going fucking mental, thinking how can I get some money, straighten myself out"*. His "brain" is telling him to go and get some money.

'Fragmentation' of one identity, that of the drug user, necessarily involves the creation of another, but this session highlights what occurs when the drug is no longer present. Damien's physical pain takes on a particular form where his emotions become externalized: *" but it's like everything I'm feeling is all coming out of me, bouncing round the fucking house"*. Many men I have worked with have described themselves as being *"in bits"*. This highlights another aspect of the process of 'fragmentation'. This following extract from Damien provides a physical description of the process by which his feelings become external realities. *"It's been like a fucking black cloud over my head, every time I'm withdrawing, and it's just been fucking too much, too much for me in the way"*. I began to see the process of withdrawal as much more than a physical process of endorphins leaving the body, but also a psychological disintegration, leading to the strong desire to re-create the 'mask' and sustain the 'front', thereby easing the physical discomfort. Damien becomes obsessed about the need to restore himself: *"I'm withdrawing, I'm bumping around just thinking, money, drugs, get on the street"*, which will take away the physical and the emotional pain that he is feeling.

However, Damien does not buy just enough to stop the pain; his drug use escalates: *"I'm a greedy bollocks as well, that don't help, 'cos if I feel better I like to feel better, not fuckin' half better" (laughs)*. This cyclic process of defeat caused his self-esteem to spiral downward as he fought to try and beat the habit. He seemingly restored his sense of masculine prowess by taking a large amount of heroin. However, what Damien found truly difficult was to articulate his feelings to his partner. He was trying to come off by himself. Although the reason for his detox was to be with her, he was not able to communicate what he was feeling whilst he was 'fragmenting'.

Making his Bed

Damien, unlike Wayne, tries to accommodate his partner, seeing his role as a 'house husband'. His partner has moved away from their former life and has rebuilt her world, but Damien has found he needs to catch up with her. This is a pressure he currently faces, the feeling of being left behind and not being able to transform himself. In this extract, he outlines a vision of himself and how he wants to adapt. He is torn between his need to 'mask' his emotions and allowing them to 'flow'. However, he is fearful of the consequences of this adaptation and draws back into the world he knows.

Damien: But I'd like to be doing something where we're sort of rotating, 'cos obviously she's not gonna be working, if she's counselling, it's not gonna be a nine to five. I'd like to be something along that sort of line. Ultimately have the kids, do you know what I mean? Right, look after the home. I wouldn't mind being a working house husband, for, you know what I mean, changing nappies. Not that I'd like doing that but it has to be done. That's what I'd like to be fucking, but I've fucked myself up, I've fucked everything up. It seems like I've no other choice; you've made your bed, now go and lie on it. I mean, what fucking idiot trades in a family for a bit of gear? That's exactly what I've done.

Damien reveals how he sees himself, providing a stark picture of the choices he has made that have led to his declining self-esteem as he tries to connect emotionally, but then feels he is not good enough. He feels shame about his shame, thereby compounding his self-esteem problems.

Ultimately, his attempt at connection ended when his heroin use escalated out of control. He was left with the consequences of not being able to connect with his family, having used heroin as a form of emotional insurance policy: *"what fucking idiot trades in a family for a bit of gear? That's exactly what I've done"*. He blocked out these feelings of loss, eventually dropping out of treatment as he plummeted into depression. I felt helpless watching him sink, knowing that he wanted to give up the drugs and establish a family life, but at the same time knowing his lack of self-esteem was wrecking his attempts. He wanted his partner to care for him as she did the children, but she wanted someone who could help her look after the family, not compete for her affections.

The power of the drug met his need to block out the past, which he had revealed to me in previous sessions. He had made some significant shifts during treatment, recognizing his anger and his violence, but at the same time he wanted to hang onto the status this conferred upon him. This was also part of the dynamic that made his vision of himself as the "house husband" so remarkable.

All of the above attempts at sustaining relationships ended in failure. After a brief period, Wayne again lost contact with his wife and son. However, he was able to build a relationship with another woman he met who was not involved in drug use. Simon never saw his son again. Alex lost contact with his partner and became increasingly isolated. Alan, mourning the loss of his relationship, never saw his partner again. Damien tried and failed to reconnect with his partner. Of the other men who had relationships, Bri tried to reconnect with his partner, but she made it clear she wanted nothing to do with him. Ross spoke of wanting to see his children again after they went into care and tried to make amends but found it was too late: *"they were like strangers"*. Billy did not have a partner long enough to sustain a relationship. Rod, to be discussed later, has never formed a relationship with a woman because he felt he had nothing to offer. Rob held down a relationship, but this became increasingly centred on heroin and crack use. John also tried and failed to sustain a relationship, vowing never to be hurt again after it had finished.

Two of the men who did undergo a shift and managed to hold down relationships were Phil and Gary, who, interestingly, were able to dissolve their anger and build up empathic relationships with women, moving away from 'willing' a relationship to work to engaging emotionally with their partners and talking to them about their problems. This, I feel, allowed them to enter their partners' lives and create empathic bonds. Both of them were fortunate not to have contracted hepatitis, which helped them to move away from the drug subculture.

The underlying factor leading to declining self-esteem, which does not surface in the above accounts, occurred when some of these men found out they were Hepatitis B or C positive. This became the major fear, as they were anxious about becoming too close to a woman in case they passed on the virus sexually. This was compounded further when one of the men discovered he had HIV. This fact hung over him like a Damoclean sword, thwarting efforts to reconnect for fear of being rebuffed and isolated.

When Wayne, Alex and Simon formed relationships, there was an expectation from their partners that they would shift away from the drug subculture. Tensions arose when their partners had children and the relationship dynamics changed. The focus of the partner is centred on her child and, as Alex revealed, many of the men became jealous as a consequence. This important revelation points to a form of domestic violence erupting as the men try to wrestle with these emotions when their children are born. Recalling Gary's memory of his father, his marriage may have been the only time that he had received love, but then he found himself having to share it with his children. This involves connecting emotionally with someone outside oneself, despite the fact that no one may have connected with these men when they were younger. This produces an emotional turmoil around how to express connection, yet not having the ability to show it. This is clear in the way Damien talks about *"what fucking idiot trades in a family for a bit of gear?"* There is a desire, but also dread and, ultimately, self-shame. The residual emotions become subsumed through the drug use and then discharged through violence.

VII. VIOLENCE

To understand the relationship between violence and drug use, I will analyse the link between the institutional 'culture of violence' and Billy's anger and substance use. This will provide the context, drawing on Deleuze and Guattari (1972), for understanding how 'flows' of violence existing outside the family impacted upon Billy. This chapter concentrates on this relationship, drawing principally on Foucault's "Discipline and Punish" (1977) to understand how power operates.

Billy explains his anger in terms of resistance to disciplinarian regimes. This is created by his 'front' of violence, formed as a protection against receiving pain, and sustained by 'masking' his feelings. He holds feelings of anger, creating a resistance to being hurt, enabling him to clash with authority structures, thereby getting revenge.

Truancy, Billy's Emotional Connection with his Mother

I started working with Billy on issues concerning his drug use, eventually exploring further as he developed enough trust to talk to me. This process took four years. Billy, along with Simon, Gary, John and many other men I have worked with, either truanted from school (excluding themselves) or were expelled.

In listening to Billy describe his life, I reflected on how institutions had classified and controlled him through the infliction of punishment. I will show how the power of officialdom impacted upon Billy, linking to the previous chapter's critique of the Freudian Oedipal complex, where behaviour is understood within a predetermined framework, rather than from asking the participants for their accounts.

The emerging themes were associated with the discipline meted out to him by the school for his truancy, the taunts produced by the punishment and the emotional connection he had with his Mother becoming a catalyst for pain.

Billy's 'resistance' took place at the critical juncture of his physical growth from boyhood into adolescence. This is a crucial time, as the body is undergoing chemical and hormonal changes, making the individual more physically powerful through the development of musculature. At the same time, he is still considered a boy within his family and is subject to the disciplines of boyhood. I will explore how Billy coped with these tensions, drawing on his emotional insights. Billy had to contend with his father's rages and his mother's pain, creating a constant process of connection and disconnection. I began by asking him about his experiences at school.

Dean: 'Cos you started truanting at school quite early?
Billy: Yeah.
Dean: Was that affected...was that caused by your Mum's disappearance?
Billy: Yeah. I mean I was at...I mean I didn't like used to like ermmmm...I didn't like to leave my Mum, you know what I mean? Sometimes I got to think if I go to school and I come back home that she might not be there, you know? So I used to get thoughts like that. If I go to school, I think that if I go back home my Mum ain't gonna be there, you know what I mean?

When I originally asked Billy about his truanting, I was thinking about the lack of structure in his family:

his father's drinking and his mother's absence when she was incarcerated. At this time, I was drawing initially on an unconscious Freudian conception of children. I felt Billy would have had the freedom to do as he pleased, with all social controls non-existent. He would be out of control, needing to have boundaries enforced to help him back into the school environment. However, Billy revealed something else: a hidden history. When he begins to talk, he finds it difficult and his speech begins to waver.

He truants because he wants to protect his mother, illuminating his hidden emotional secret connection. Because it was hidden, it has created a great deal of internal pain for him. He had never told anyone why he was truanting before.

Correction - the Appliance of the Disciplines

In the following section, Billy relates a chain of events intended to correct his unruly behaviour through the imposition of an authority structure, implying a top-down solution, resulting in the negation of his emotional world. This form of correction failed spectacularly, only intensifying his 'resistance' to the external pressures placed upon him as the stakes became higher.

Billy: *When they finally took me to court for not going to school, they took me away from my family. That really done something to me inside, that really traumatised me. That hurt me something chronically, mate.*

The discipline applied to Billy *"traumatised"* and *"hurt"* him instead of cowing him, creating a determination to fight back. Even though his family, in particular his father, were causing him emotional pain, the way in which he was taken away compounded his sense of humiliation. This provides an insight into the pain Gary's father may also have felt.

Through Billy's words, I began to try and piece together the rationale for such punitive actions undertaken against a child. I began to see the splits occurring in the institutional disciplinarian regimes resting upon a split between correction and empathy. The force applied on Billy was used to humiliate him and to force him into the school system. The state institutions were showing him they were stronger (Parker, in Stanko and Newburn 1994). This use of strength and force rests upon a particular notion of how people are formed. It seemingly rests upon a denial of emotional connection and the objectification of the miscreants, creating an understanding through the appliance of labels.

The Severance of Empathy

In taking him to court and placing him in an institution, the reality Billy fought against engulfed him: the severing of his relationship with his mother, his prime empathic bond.

I want to define the term 'empathy', as previously I have looked at the development of the 'protective cocoon' through the formation of 'basic trust', created by the nurturing and self-value developed through the 'flows' of love that parents provide. In the chapter "Mother and Son" I developed this concept further by drawing on Carol Gilligan (1990) and Chodorow (1978). Empathy is sustained through these bonds, creating a feeling of being loved and valued flowing between parents and child. Through this connection, an emotional language develops. This can be seen in Billy's bond with his mother, as Billy returns each day to make sure she was still there.

The principle of empathy is rooted in the recognition of mutual relationship and interdependency alongside the capacity to perceive others as autonomous human beings rather than as objects to manipulate and control. It is not merely an awareness of one's own feelings and emotions, but also the ability to be touched inside by another. (Woolf-Light, in Wild (ed.) 1999, p. 148)

Correctional power, in the form of being taken to court, is wielded "objectively", thereby denying the mother-son bond, Correctional power exists beyond the world of emotion. It is linked to abstract notions of justice defined by the state. This use of power, resting upon certain presumptions, acts upon Billy's developing 'front'. Billy was the recipient of 'stings' of humiliation in his family, marked by his mother being taken away, his father's drinking and verbal and physical attacks. All of these created emotional wounds and internal anger. Within Billy's family, his father had already used correctional discipline.

I began to see a link between how masculinity operated in Deptford and the systems of power based upon male values, which rested upon the divorce between emotions and force that Woolf-Light (1999) pinpoints. Whether children or mothers, the victims within the family are taught to bend to the will of the more powerful through emotional violence based upon a negation of empathy.

Woolf-Light (1999) led me to think about how decisions are made within institutions, where decision-making rests upon an apparent unwillingness to try to understand why boys such as Billy are truanting. Instead, the 'solution' is to punish him, thereby enacting a form of state revenge, 'for his own good'. The applied 'disciplines' in this case ignored Billy's emotional connections; instead, a corrective framework was imposed, manipulating him into the system. The state takes over the role of the father in correcting his aberrant behaviour through punishment, consequently compounding his feelings of humiliation.

Ideally, Billy has to attend school for his own best interests: to learn and then get a job. The decision to punish Billy as a miscreant involves the correction of his transgression by taking him away from his family, who are deemed unable to control him. The family had already been seen as an unsafe environment because of his mother's criminal acts.

However, if someone had sat down and built up trust with Billy, they would have found out he wanted to make sure his mother was there when he returned from school. He could not communicate this because there was no one to talk to. This shows how the culture of silence became imposed on Billy. There were no avenues for him to communicate his childhood and adolescent fears. The agencies active in Deptford at this time were either diversionary (the youth club) or impositional (the social services or the police). Billy also had insufficient trust in other members of his family to talk to them. It was through the process of holding secrets, I believe, that Billy learned to create his 'mask' of silence, burying his emotional world.

Being labelled a truant and sent away for correction created a sense of anger in him stemming from the 'stings' inflicted upon him. His experience of state institutions led to the creation of his own internal emotional blocks, and his 'masking' of his feelings because he was on the receiving end of power.

In transcribing the above account, I was struck by the similarities of parts of the passage to Foucault's "Discipline and Punish" (1977). 'Disciplines', according to Foucault, develop from the need to create individuals able to fit into certain roles in society. This becomes their rationale, creating boundaries around aberrant forms of behaviour, producing notions of good and bad forms.

> The disciplines function increasingly as techniques for making useful individuals. Hence their emergence from a marginal position on the confines of society, and detachment from forms of exclusion or expiation, confinement or retreat... They become attached to some of the great essential functions; factory production, the transmission of knowledge, the diffusion of aptitudes and skills, the war machine. (Foucault 1977, p. 211)

However, drawing upon Billy's account, I see another role for the disciplines. They are not merely abstract 'techniques': I see the individuals involved in administering the 'disciplines' as being engaged in their own emotional 'strategies of revenge'. The 'disciplines' become a way of legitimising these forms. The disciplined are often seen as being punished to uphold the common good in order to create a harmonious society. How they are enacted links to an enmeshing of 'strategies of revenge' based upon the suppression of empathic connection and the need to externalise 'stings' onto weaker bodies. Institutions of discipline within this paradigm develop through individuals releasing their 'stings' within a crowd (Cannetti 1960).

A reversal crowd comes into existence for the joint liberation of a large number of stings of command they cannot hope to get rid of alone. They unite to turn on some group of other people whom they see as the originators of all the commands they have borne for so long. (Cannetti 1960, p. 382)

Cannetti describes how angry crowds emerge to overthrow oppression. However, I want to think of the situation as also creating oppressive apparatuses, groups as well as gangs that are formed based upon the need to discharge 'stings' onto those perceived as weaker, a concept that appears consistently in this research: the link between differing masculinities and institutional power.

Within Foucault's (1977) analysis of the disciplines, Billy's behaviour is sanctioned, not for his own good but for the good of society as "the great essential functions". Foucault (1977) explains using a genealogical method how these 'disciplines' have been transmitted into the school curriculum, showing how the use of power becomes enmeshed within the pedagogy of the school system. There are resonance's for the present pedagogy in the school system of the last century:.

Thus the Christian School must not simply train docile children; it must also make it possible to supervise the parents, to gain information as to their way of life, their resources, their piety, their morals. The school tends to constitute minute social observatories that penetrate even to the adults and exercise regular supervision of them: the bad behaviour of the child, or his absence, is a legitimate pretext according to Demia, for one to go and question the neighbours, especially if there is any reason to believe that the family will not tell the truth, one can then go and question the parents themselves, to find out whether they know the catechism or the prayers, whether they are determined to root out the vices of their children, how many beds there are in the house and what the sleeping arrangements are... (Foucault 1977, p. 211)

The school authorities sanctioned by the state can police family morality "whether they are determined to root out the vices of their children". In taking Billy away from his family, they were also punished. The state showed its superiority to the family through exercising its power, as the state "must also make it possible to supervise the parents". Power operates within a hierarchy, the family being the recipient. This is encoded in statutes, resting upon the micro-actions of the workers for its application. These statutes formed in parliament become handed down as the will of the people. The need to uphold the 'disciplines' for the greater good becomes more important than the emotional effect on Billy, the recipient. This divorce, the split between emotional empathy and vengeance, also appears in the families of these men. I detected a link between this splitting process, which Chodorow (1978) describes and how Billy is treated. Chodorow (1978) describes this emotional split in gender terms as the denial of the feminine emotional world, supplanted by a rational masculine world based upon this denial. This may have provided the initial impetus for the split, but does not preclude women involved in the appliance of power from being as ruthless as men in the appliance of institutional discipline.

However, the non-emotional manner in which the rules are applied inflicts emotional violence upon him. This explains his process of correction. One of the hypotheses I arrive at in this chapter is that the men and women who make decisions in institutions are not sensitive to Billy's needs. They do not have the conceptual tools to understand him, so they unwittingly or intentionally discharge their 'stings' onto him. As they have become a part of disciplinarian regimes, they too have learnt to split themselves.

This leads me to speculate on how institutions are constructed. The 'masks' exhibited in Billy's family, the divorce between emotions and anger, appear to be worn by men and women who work in institutions administering discipline. This resonates with the findings of Alice Miller in "For Your Own Good" (1987) and Klaus Thewelait in "Male Fantasies" (1977,1978). Institutions operating the 'disciplines' described by Foucault (1977) subsume empathy for the individual into the greater cause. This is a short-term strategy with longer-term consequences for Billy.

Through listening and talking to people outside of work and this study, I have often heard 'ordinary' men talk about the beatings they received – whether from their families, the school or the police – making them into men. They say prepares them for the world that they are going to inhabit, leading me to question the role of masculinities within institutions.

What becomes clearer in the following extract is that masculine values based upon empathic divorce do not just exist within the families of these men, they also permeate social institutions. The form of emotional violence inflicted upon Billy is undertaken through bureaucratic procedure. However, institutions are created through the micro-actions of the people within them.

The creation of disciplinarian regimes relies upon the administration of corrective procedures that create 'stings', whether emotional or physical. This rests upon the split in feelings of empathy, with limited self-reflection or acknowledgement of the pain being administered, as the pedagogy of discipline has become intrinsic and taken for granted. This results in a reification of the common good, placing it over individual needs, with the following of rules becoming an end in itself. The legitimacy of an action becomes mediated through having access to power and being able to define a legitimate action. In these extracts, Billy shows how he externalises the pain he holds through the flow of violence, to avenge the 'stings' he receives. This provides another framework for understanding this masculinity as a dialectical process, intertwining with institutions as a form of discipline and resistance based upon an "emotional strategy of dialectical revenge".

Humiliation and Resistance

Billy creates a psychological site of 'resistance', masking his internal pain, channelling it into the creation of a 'front', thereby externalising anger – a transmutation of humiliation into anger and violence.

Billy narrates how being singled out for this type of treatment creates another form of punishment – ridicule – as the taunts of peers has its psychological effect. Billy's strategy for stopping these taunts is to attack the perpetrators, silencing them by firing his own arrows of pain. He learns to fight violence with violence, creating and sustaining a 'front' of 'resistance' (Willis 1978).

The secret of his truancy is hermetically sealed within Billy's memory. Again, the patterns of violence serve a rationale – the protection of his self-esteem. In this extract, the pattern of "tit for tat" – the 'strategies of revenge' – are exemplified, and their emotional basis is made apparent.

Billy: *I didn't know what to do when that happened. It was only for six weeks, you know? I was "in bits", mate. I didn't know what to do, about thirteen, thirteen yeah, twelve or thirteen.*

Dean: *So you were deeply hurt in that period?*

Billy: *Definitely, well I used to come... When I was in that Home, they used to take me to school, and they used to want to pick me up in a bus, outside the school. And the kids used to go: What's the bus there waiting to pick you up for? And I used to go "Oh that drops me home". And they used to go "Oh you liar, you're in a Home", and all that. You know what I mean, Dean? That really hurt me.* **That really hurt me.** *They'd go, "You're in a Home. Well, don't your Mum care about you?" And I used to steam into them and say: "Nothing to do with my Mum caring for me. My Mum does care for me". My Mum's gone to prison for me, you know what I mean? Imagine how humiliated I felt when I got a van to come and pick me up at school. People, kids, and you know what kids are like when you're at school: "Oh your Mum don't care for you, you're in a Home and all that". I think that played a lot, you know what I mean?*

Billy describes for me his emotional 'fragmentation' in the 'Home'. He was *"in bits"*. His desire never to be placed in this position again becomes pivotal for understanding his later actions. This was his nadir. His 'fragmentation' became more marked with the disruption of his family life.

This was due to his mother's incarceration after she was caught shoplifting. This compounded his shame. Billy's father was left in charge, but he was unable to care for the family as he was drinking continuously. The result was his family's public humiliation, and his father's problem became transferred onto him as a result of being taken away. The result, far from creating a "docile body", was that Billy became regulated by micro-disciplines of the state and generated hatred through being *"hurt"*, encapsulated in this quote: *"Imagine how humiliated I felt when I got a van to come and pick me up at school"*. Taunted that his mother didn't care for him exacerbated his humiliation, as he was unable to communicate how she tried to show her love for her family. Billy was caught within a number of competing 'flows', trapping him in a 'double bind'. His solution was to create 'resistance', which went further than just silencing his peers; it became a 'psychological resistance'.

Billy: So I vowed to be anti-authority.

Dean: Yeah, yeah, so it was like you were being continuously injured by, like you say, people who had authority: teachers, police or whatever, other kids. You've never been able to work it out have you?

Billy: No.

Dean: It's just one thing after another.

Billy: One after the other.

Dean: Which gives you more hatred for authority, it grows inside you, you get into more trouble and then pushed more and more into institutions.

Billy: Mmmmm, see when they used to come and pick me up, like, from school. That's when I really started getting violent. That's when I started getting violent, then. Once the policeman happened, I think that was the last straw.

Billy describes how his violence escalated as he faced violence within the family and more violence outside it, having to fight other children, being taken into care, being taunted and bullied. He describes how he began to see that he could use his own display of power in retaliation for the wrongs inflicted upon him. This again demonstrates the alchemy of sadness turning into violence, when Billy's self-integrity comes under attack.

Dean: That triggered off what was there?
Billy: Yeah.
Dean: Since that period?
Billy: I remember when I was in that Home. I used to lay there of a night and just cry, cry for me Mum, you know what I mean? I used to have these people saying to me: "You might not be going home to your Mum, for you could be here until you're eighteen" and all that, you know what I mean? I used to think I'm only twelve, telling me I'm gonna be staying away from my Mum for six years. I think I used to lay there some nights and cry all night to myself, you know what I mean? And to think, all I wanted was my Mum, you know what I mean? Couldn't ask for a better Mum, you know? I couldn't ask for a better Mum...it wasn't my Mum's fault like I was, like truanting, I mean I ermmm. I mean she had it hard, mate. She had seven kids and my Dad used to drink a lot. And at that time he wasn't much help, that's why she had to go out and shoplift.
Dean: He was drinking all the money?
Billy : Yeah.

Billy's treatment in the 'Home' 'stings' and wounds him. Firstly, there is the uncertainty of how long he is going to be there, coupled with the public humiliation of being taken to school in a bus. Billy's first response is to sink into a form of depression, trying to cope with his fragmenting world: *"I think I used to lay there some nights and cry all night to myself, you know what I mean?"* Billy's crying externalises his pain, but it does not help to resolve the problems he is facing; it only makes him more vulnerable by showing that he is hurt. The strategy he employs to halt the jeers, stop his 'fragmentation' and create some self-esteem is violence. After crying himself to sleep, Billy 'masks' his tears by creating a 'front' to protect himself from future situations: *"I vowed to be anti-authority"*, fighting violence with violence. Similarly, Foucault (1977) explains how prison operates its disciplines:

> The prison also produces delinquents by imposing violent constraints on its inmates; it is supposed to apply the law, and to teach respect for it; but all its functioning operates in the form of an abuse of power. The arbitrary power of administration: "The feeling of injustice that a prisoner has is one of the causes that may make his character untameable. When he sees himself exposed in this way to suffering, which the law has neither ordered or envisaged, he becomes habitually angry against everything around him; he sees every agency of authority as executioner; he no longer thinks that he was guilty: he accuses justice itself (Bigot Preameneu) (Foucault 1977, p. 266).

Foucault (1977) has an understanding of how the appliance of the disciplines creates a site for revenge. Billy's experience fails to teach him respect for the law; instead, he experiences the "arbitrary power of its administration". Already experiencing the force of power

243

within his family, the constraints imposed upon him reinforce his sense of injustice. He "becomes habitually angry against everything around him", creating a subsequent desire for revenge. I explore Billy's desire for revenge as he begins to define himself as a man through enacting violence, as someone who cannot be controlled by others. This desire for autonomy produces strategies of anger, as 'connection', the firing of his own 'stings' onto others becomes bound up with notions of control.

The discharge of emotions through the flow of anger is deemed acceptable in the social world Billy inhabits. As Nancy Chodorow (1978) observed, what emerges is masculinity built upon the sublimation of what is deemed feminine and therefore effeminate. This sublimation is not in Billy's case a rational decision to try to gain power. Billy learns to sublimate emotions because they leave him vulnerable to being hurt. It is through being hurt that he is being controlled. In talking with Billy, I can see how the construction of his 'front' based on the ability to inflict 'stings' reverses his humiliations.

The masculinities existing amongst these white men in Deptford emerge not as a rational lifestyle choice based upon access to economic resources and power. Billy's example shows how it is forced upon him and develops as a survival mechanism stopping him from being hurt. While developing this 'front' of toughness, Billy also has a corresponding desire to emotionally connect with his mother. He feels her pain, and, correspondingly, has little empathy with his father's pain. Billy describes how he developed his 'front' and provides an insight into the sacrifices this entails.

The Reversal of 'Stings'

In the above extract, Billy talks of being on the receiving end of violence. Here, he talks about his externalisation of it. Billy describes a series of events that shaped his perception of the world he lived in. On one level, his reflections exemplify a type of adolescent 'risk taking' that I explore through the work of Giddens (1991). However, as many of these boys moved on to criminal lifestyles where they began to accuse "justice itself", it also shows how the formation of gangs allows a discharge of violence directed at other males – the release of 'stings' within a "reversal crowd" (Cannetti 1960).

The basis of the incident Billy describes is in a group of adolescent girls and boys being taken camping by the Youth Club, as most of the families in the area were too poor to have family holidays. This event took place in the late 1970s. The gang was of mixed gender and race (White and Afro-Caribbean).

Deptford was one of the areas where Afro-Caribbean people settled in the 1960s and 1970s. Initially there was a great deal of antagonism, culminating in a battle in New Cross between NF marchers and demonstrators. As I have observed through my work and as noted by Hewitt (1986), one of the defining features of integration between black and white youths in areas such as Deptford is how the institutional pressures acted upon all families in Deptford, particularly in relation to housing (Back 1996). As people developed 'resistances' to these pressures, one of the defining features of the school system was the development of friendship networks (Willis 1978). The local white culture was already in existence before black families settled in Deptford. One of the tests of these new communities was to see how they coped within this environment, which meant, especially for the men, challenging the micro power structures (schools and police) to gain status.

One of the local trends I have noted in working in Deptford is how the people in this area more than in neighbouring working class areas mix more easily with other incoming racial groups. There are tensions, but not the same type of tensions that exist in nearby areas such as Rotherhithe and Bermondsey, which has the reputation of defining itself as white working class in opposition to other communities.

The gang Billy joined was formed through school, neighbourhood and kinship groups, and the focal point was the Youth Club. Of the twelve people mentioned as part of this Youth Club trip, four of them are part of this study. Here, Billy reflects on travelling to other areas for gang fights at the age of 13.

Billy: *Yeah, we had a little gang. In them times there used to be a gang of us and we even used to travel to different areas to fight with other gangs, and we done a lot of them, and got a sort of reputation.*
Dean: *How would you fight, with your fists or anything?*
Billy: *We would fight them with anything. If they had fists or if we had wood, or if they had knives, then we'd have to pull out a knife or wood. We even went to the_____, and we took about ten or twelve of us boys, and twelve girls. It was the Cavern it was, the Youth Club then, and we met two girls out there, and we were like getting hold of them yeah? And a couple of us got hold of these two girls. And the ones who come with us, we were going out with some of them girls, and they found out. Anyway, they bashed these two girls up, and then what the girls done to get us back, they*

*went out with these two boys from_____. And
the place we were staying in, the girls have come round
with all these big skinheads and that, on their arms,
to make us jealous. And then there was a fight there.
We had a fight with them, bust a couple of them up,
they run, and next day they come back. The girls were,
we were in this place, where we were staying, the girls
come in and said: "You boys are in trouble". They said
we should go and look at these boys round the back.
So we walked out and there was a wall, and a line
of about thirty of them on this wall, all flicking out
these lock knives and saying... "We hate you cockney
bastards" I can't pronounce how they talk and they
were saying, flicking these knives "We's gonna do you
cockney bastards" And there was about twelve of us and
some of them was big cunts compared to us, you know
what I mean? We thought corrr, and they done it for
a second day, and they done it for a third day, and in
the end we just thought shit. So we just went round
there, and one of my mates went: "Right, come on then,
I'll fight the best fighter out of yeh". It was some big
tall geezer. And anyway, my mate started fighting, it
went off, three of us stabbed three of them. Once they
realised they'd been stabbed, you should have seen him,
he was a giant. Him and two others got stabbed by me
and two of my mates. When he see it, he realised: "Oh
I've been stabbed" And he fainted, and the other two
nearly fainted, and the other twenty-seven of them
fucking ran. Got nicked for that, but they couldn't
prove which one of us done it. And we threw the knives
in the river, and there was about ten who had knives.
They found a couple of knives, but they didn't actually
find the three that caused the stab wounds. So what
they done is, they just... we were only there four days
but we was meant to stay there for two weeks. They*

told us to wrap up our stuff, escorted us to the van
and banned us from_____ and said we was not
allowed to come back there again. So it was things like
that. I'm not saying that it's clever, Dean, but after
that thing with the police that's how I sorta turned.
Dean: *So you became involved in a culture of violence.*
Billy: *Yeah, all the time.*

This incident has the status of myth. It contains a number of features such as the ability to attack a larger gang of older boys from another area. It demonstrates the local girls emotionally manipulating the boys. It also shows how these boys were able to keep silent when faced with the police, thereby outwitting the authorities.

The trouble begins when the Deptford girls see "their boys" with girls from another area. As an act of revenge, they attack these girls, then choose some older males as a form of emotional revenge on the Deptford boys. The Deptford boys then revenge themselves by attacking these boys. The latter return as a bigger and more powerful gang, seeking their revenge for their humiliation. The extract shows how tit for tat violence escalates, with the need to maintain a 'front' being paramount, sustaining it through displays of violence.

The violence spirals out from display into a physical attack, as the desire to retain honour intensifies. When the police intervene, the camaraderie of the Deptford boys sustains the silence. 'Grassing' brings sanctions applied by the community, who exact their own form of punishment on collaborators. The role of silence becomes important in understanding how these male identities are sustained through the ability to absorb physical and emotional pain without flinching. The whole incident becomes pivotal in creating local identities, showing how these boys became men through projecting a 'front' based upon violence and silence.

I see the Deptford boys as winning because they were more willing to move from a parade of violence into a reality, taking a risk that they may kill someone in order to win. Through violence, they are able to shift their humiliations onto others. Their targets become a substitute for the people who have discharged violence onto them, thereby becoming a "reversal crowd" (Cannetti 1960).

Risk-Taking?

I want to think about Billy's description and its relationship to risk, drawing on Anthony Giddens (1991). In Billy's description of the camping trip, the violence becomes part of a rite of passage for adolescent boys, asserting male values of toughness, virility and the ability to inflict violence and take on authority.

In "Modernity and Self Identity" (1991), Giddens describes "risk-taking" through the eyes of a man, although the gender is not specified, as testing the limits of what is possible – defining the self through self-affirmation. Giddens (1991) describes it as a "form of mastery" that contrasts with routine, whereas I began to understand it not as a contrast, but as an expectation.

> Mastery of such dangers is an act of self-vindication and a demonstration, to the self and others, that under difficult circumstances one can come through. Fear produces the thrill, but it is fear redirected in the form of mastery. The thrill of cultivated risk taking feeds on the 'courage

to be' which is generic to early socialisation. Courage is demonstrated in cultivated risk taking precisely as a quality which is placed on trial: the individual submits to a test of integrity by showing the capacity to envisage the 'down side' of the risks being run, and press ahead regardless, even though there is no constraint to do so. The search for thrills, or more soberly the sense of mastery that comes from the deliberate confrontation of dangers, no doubt derives in some part from its contrast with routine. (Giddens 1991, p. 133)

When Billy describes the fight, I see a dynamic other than a "test of integrity" operating. Risk becomes bound up with a flow of energy utilised in revenge for a slur on Billy's masculinity. This flow is encapsulated in the construction of his male identity; his 'front' avenging his past humiliations. The continuous process of risk-taking becomes a way for Billy to externalise his inner rage and win applause from his peers. This marks a shift away from the ridicule he experienced when he was taken to school in the "blue bus". The fear produced is not part of a "courage to be" but part of a "reversal crowd" (Cannetti 1960), constituting the externalisation of past humiliations.

Risks and exposure to physical danger is part of a problem Billy has to navigate continuously in this environment. The ability to inflict and receive violence becomes integral to the creation of his male identity, involving shifting away from the world of 'connection'. This idea is encapsulated by Paul Willis (1978), where he depicts the working class "lads" he was studying preparing for a fight, as "... the moment when you are fully tested; and disastrous for your informal standing and masculine reputation when you refuse to fight or perform very amateurishly." (Willis 1978, p. 35)

The processes impacting on Billy caused him to construct his own defences against possible threats to his integrity and existence, his 'fear' being that he may be humiliated once again. Therefore, he does everything possible to stop this by being prepared to kill if necessary, thereby creating his "masculine reputation", with the 'front' as a by-product. These are the conditions under which he acts, and he does this by strengthening his inner resolve, keeping silences and secrets, becoming more aggressive and violent, and avenging the various humiliations in his life on a substitute – other men.

As shown in Paul Willis's "Learning to Labour" (1978), fighting becomes a preparation for the adult world, primarily the world of men. For Billy, risk is not a "contrast with routine", but part of a backdrop to attaining a masculinity based upon revenge.

If these Deptford boys had backed down, their self-esteem would have been wounded; they would be known as the boys that ran away. This would entail ridicule, striking at the core of their male identities and creating a need to enact more violence in order to revenge the slur. As Gary and Billy have related to me regarding their experiences in young offender institutions, people leave you alone if you fight back, even if you do not win. Self-esteem and the need to display violence is as important as winning.

Drawing on Paul Willis (1978), in the working class culture of Deptford, school was perceived as largely unimportant and not a real preparation for manhood, which is measured primarily by manual skills rather than the development of intellectual prowess. Scrap metal, boxing, football and crime are more highly prized than academic skills for these boys/men.

Fighting is a preparation for entry into their fathers' male world. All their fathers were fighters, either in the pub, street or home. Billy's risk-taking is not a holiday from a sedate normality but is embedded within his everyday life.

Billy moved on to depict how his *"vow"* led to clashes with the police, fuelling his internal rage. This passage also explores the relationship between cultures of violence, showing how strategies of revenge are enmeshed through the institutions in Deptford and wider.

Fighting State Violence with Violence: An Escalation

Listening to Billy, I began to see a series of connections between the violence he received and the violence he inflicted. It appeared to be part of a continuation of a dialectical emotional flow. It shows how 'fronts', based upon the ability to inflict and receive violence, are not just creations of the men in this study. They can also be found in the agencies disciplining them. Violence is more than just 'risk-taking' but is embedded within the social actions of institutional patriarchy. The use of physical, sexual and psychological force by social agencies is directed through the thinking, planning and execution of various micro-actions, the reversal of 'stings' undertaken by institutional "reversal crowds" (Cannetti 1960).

Billy: Yeah I just keep getting harassed. I mean in 1987, when I was younger, I used to get a lot of grief, but in 1987 I was hanging about with a certain person, pals, and a police officer got stabbed yeah, and this friend of mine got arrested for it. The two people with him got away. Automatically they put two and two together and thought that I was one of the people that got away, and I got arrested for that. For three days they beat the fuck... they beat three different kinds of shit out of me. They kept moving me from police station to police station. I couldn't see a solicitor for two days and they was trying to get me to clean meself up, patch me up, but I wouldn't do it. After that I went to the Old Bailey on a trial and I got, obviously, I got it thrown out again. I was found not guilty because it wasn't me there. Since then I've had nothing but grief of them.

Dean: *It wasn't you then?*

Billy: *No it wasn't me, it was the other Billy. And when I got arrested now after being in the cell, the police would come up and open up the flap and there'd be five of them and go: "This is the bastard that goes about stabbing police officers. See, he's still on it now". What it is, the police have got their own computer and they can write what they want about you on the computer, and there ain't fuck all you can do about it, not even your own solicitor can do anything about it. It's their own little Internet, you know, they write what they want about you on it, see, and that was 1987. These years later I'm still getting grief about that, when it wasn't me and I was tried by judge and jury and found not guilty. The one who actually done it, he got sentenced for it. But they like forgot about him. Good luck to him, you know what I mean? What I'm saying is that they still think it's me who actually stabbed him, and I wasn't even with him that day. I know the two people who was with him that day, a black person and a white person. As things goes, that day I happened to* be with a black person, a black friend of mine, and we both got arrested.

Dean: Did he get beaten up as well?

Billy: Yeah he got beaten. They let him go after five hours, I think. They kept me for three days. For two days no one could find me. And two girls see them arrest me, and see me bashed up and get in the van. A dog bit me; they had a police dog there. The dog bit me and obviously my mother and sister rang up the solicitor straightaway. When they was ringing up, they took me to X. When they rang up they was saying that "They conveyed him to Y". And when they was ringing up they would say that "They've conveyed him to Z, too late". They done that for two days. I've gone form there, to there, to there, to there. When all the time they had me in the same place. And they stripped me naked, threw a wet blanket over me and just beat the fuck out of me. And then on the third day they knew they'd either have to charge me or let me go. So they got my solicitor, my solicitor come, they was trying to say to him, "Billy please have a wash and clean yourself up". And I fuck. I told them to piss off. And my solicitor come and he went mad. And he went mad, he said, "Who's the officer in charge?" The solicitor said, "You've taken a blatant fucking liberty here". He said, "You know it wasn't him, you either charge him or let him go". They did charge me but where they bashed me up so bad, they just let me walk without charge, there and then. I would've been able to do something about it, the way they treated me.

Dean: How did you cope with that emotionally, because you were shut off from your mum and solicitor?

Billy: It was, I went like a bit...bit like an animal, expecting any minute they was gonna come through the door and bash me again. At first I was really scared, for the first *day. They kept coming, but the second day I got them to take the cuffs off.*

The issues arising from Billy's account concern how the police used violence to extract a confession about his involvement in the stabbing. What can be derived from the extract is that Billy was not there that day, as was later proved in court. What is important is that he was part of 'them'. Billy had become a vehicle for the discharge of rage, a revenge attack, a reversal of 'stings' by an institutional crowd. During this time, Billy maintained his silence, taking the beatings.

Billy narrates how the acts of violence from the police officers were organised. There appears to have been a considerable degree of collusion, as his mother and solicitor were told he had been moved, necessitating considerable organisation in holding him for three days and beating him.

This incident portrays how male identity and the creation of 'fronts' are not just cultivated by 'out' groups such as drug users, but also by various groups of 'socially included' men. This idea of acting upon men to bend their will is undertaken through regimes where power is administered. This highlights how 'disciplines' exact revenge, not just for the notion of greater good, but also for psychological release.

In the previous extract, we can see how the school impacted upon Billy through its punishments and his subsequent desire for retaliation. The police officers, based upon Billy's words, appear to be engaged in the same process. His description highlights the degree of force used by social institutions at a micro-level. The debate shifts from 'risk-taking', testing the limits, to how violence becomes a strategy for survival.

Billy's male identity has so far been formulated through pain and the need to avenge it. The risks he takes are based upon his desire for revenge. This desire for revenge also permeates the micro-actions of men in various occupations, not just the labelled drug users within this study. This is also analysed in Klaus Thewelait's "Male Fantasies" (1977, 1978) and Alice Miller's "For Your Own Good" (1987).

The need to enact revenge attacks for previous pain and humiliation becomes intertwined, from their viewpoint, within the fabric of society and how men interact with each other. Revenge attacks become sanctioned as a method of marking power relationships through the application of force.

The police officers in Billy's account inflict violence not to extract a confession. They strip him naked, tie his hands, place a wet blanket over him and beat him. This type of violence creates a spiralling escalation, a 'tit for tat' based upon the need to uphold masculine fronts and discharge anger. Ryder (1991) draws parallels between the culture of offenders, especially youths, and that of the police: "Perhaps it is no coincidence that urban disorder has developed a strongly 'tit for tat' quality" (Spalding, in Newburn and Stanko (eds.) 1994, p. 48).

As described in the gang fight, emerging male identities come to be built on the need to discharge hurt and anger, creating enmeshing strategies of revenge – the dialectics of revenge. The violence had little effect in disciplining Billy and making him conform; instead, Billy discharges his humiliation, turning into an "animal". This 'tit for tat' culture sets the template for continual confrontations between the police and Billy.

Billy: A sergeant came to the door and I said: "Come on, take the cuffs off". I mean I was stark bollocked naked. He said: "Come to the flap". So I went to the flap and he took the cuffs off. (Billy shows me the scars on his wrist) And a couple of hours later they come back in and bashed me up again. But the next day I was ready for them. After that, I got over the phase where I was scared.

Dean: How did you manage to get over it?

Billy: I just got over it and thought fuck it, if they're gonna go for me, I'm gonna at least get one of them. And when they came in again, the first one that got me. I just grabbed him and I bit. I bit...I bit his cheek. They was beating me but I was holding his head, and I had his cheek in my mouth and I was biting it. And in the end he was going, "Aghhhhhh, stop hitting him". As they was punching me, it was ripping his face. After that, that was the second day, they stopped coming in for me. They left me alone.

Dean: So it was only after you were forced to retaliate?

Billy: Yeah they stopped. I mean for the first two days, I was really scared. Cos when they kept coming I thought I was gonna die. They kept throwing a wet towel over me and having me on the floor, beating me and standing on my neck and that, cutting off my breathing, where I was panicking also. Imaging if you're cuffed up behind your back, and you've got people doing that, standing on your throat and all that and know what I mean? I was seeing white flashes and that, thinking I was gonna die. That's how I was thinking. I didn't know I was gonna come out of there alive. I thought I was gonna come out of there in a body bag. "So you think you can go about stabbing police officers do you?" bla bla bla. As I say, they kicked the shit out of me for two days. It's a good job I got the sergeant to take those cuffs

off. I just grabbed the first one as I say, and bit into his
cheek, and I didn't even get charged. They knew they
took such a liberty, that they daren't even mention it.
Dean: *Looking back on it now, how do you feel about that*
period, Billy? Does it make you angry?
Billy: *Yeah.*
Dean: *Anger that you still carry around with you?*
Billy: *Especially for the police, you know, definitely...*

Billy stops the violence through being violent himself – biting into an officer's face. This is the same lesson he learned when stopping both his father's violence and the taunts at school: halting violence by inflicting it on the perpetrator. This portrays how the institutions perpetuate the violence they are trying to control.

The 'Front' of a Hard Man

In "Life after Life" (Parker 1994), another 'hard man' narrates his experiences of violence. This account portrays institutional violence weaving itself throughout social structures, creating strategies of revenge – the 'tit for tat' violence. The level of violence necessitates the creation of a strong 'mask' and well-protected 'fronts' in order to cope. This 'mask' acts as a dam, requiring the creation of a 'front' to allow violence to be discharged from continuous perceived threats to the mind and body as a form of self-defence.

Violence. I was thinking about it afterwards the other night. Either you understand it or you don't. If you understand it, you find it hard to explain to somebody who doesn't. You've never questioned it, you've always taken it for granted, part and parcel of everyday life. It's normal: what would be abnormal would be if violence wasn't your life.... Before I stopped at the DC (Detention Centre). Now that is real violence, real violence a detention centre is. They do things to you at a Detention Centre, mentally and physically, as bad or worse than anything you could have got sent there for in the first place. Beatings, kickings, humiliations: they heap them on you on top of another. The idea's to break your spirit, to show you violence doesn't pay, that if you give it out you'll get it back ten times over. So what do you learn? If you haven't got it already, you learn hatred of authority and determination you're not going to let it break you spirit. You're not going to let it win, you're going to show them that you're stronger and tougher than they are. If you don't you go under. You come out looking back on it with pride. They didn't break me. I won, I won. It's like graduating from an academy, it's a great feeling. Stay violent you say to yourself, stay violent and you'll win in the end. You come out bitter at them and what they tried to do, but proud because you didn't let them. You could really call yourself a fully fledged hard man. (Parker in Newburn and Stanko (eds.) 1994, p. 86-87)

This extract resonates eerily with Billy's experiences of institutions. It shows how the 'mask' and the hardened 'front' are created, based on the same issues arising in this counselling session. For Parker (1994), violence has haunted him throughout his life until he reflects upon it here. The 'disciplines' ("Beatings, kickings, humiliations: they heap them on you on top of another") have been enforced to "break your spirit, to show you violence doesn't pay, that if you give it out you'll get it back ten times over". That is why this disciplinarian method is seemingly taken for granted – it also illuminates how violence has become so embedded that it is almost invisible, except for the resonant effects creating further 'flows' of violence. Therefore, I perceive violence as not concerned so much with "mastery" (Giddens 1991) as with being "part and parcel of everyday life" (Parker in Newburn and Stanko (eds.) 1994).

What Parker (1994) describes as the desire to create a site of resistance resonates with Billy's experiences: "You're not going to let it win, you're going to show them that you're stronger and tougher than they are". Billy: *"But the next day I was ready for them. After that, I got over the phase where I was scared"*, showing how his psychological mask is kept intact as he learns to subsume his feelings and project his anger, ready for violence.

The message Billy learned in silencing his persecutors echoes with Parker's (1994) "Stay violent, you say to yourself, stay violent and you'll win in the end" The later statement, "You learn hatred of authority", resonates directly with Billy's statement, *"I vowed to be anti-authority"*. It is the process of needing to keep self-integrity intact, and using violence to beat the violence, that becomes the key defining force. If this is lost, then they, the oppressor, have won and the spirit becomes broken and 'fragmented'. This is seen as a psychological break, entailing a sense of personal failure.

Within this process of developing a masculine 'front', the more violence you are willing to inflict, the likelier you are to win. Having other emotions in these situations, apart from anger, creates vulnerability. Concentration of anger leads to action, in turn creating a positive outcome.

However, Billy the 'hard man' was originally a 'soft man', becoming hard through being the recipient of violence. Being beaten reinforced Billy's childhood experiences, so he was already emotionally and physically prepared for it.

Drug Use: An Alternative to the Culture of Violence

I started to understand the role drug use played in Billy's emotional life. I had a feeling heroin controlled his burning anger, within the framework of his *"vow"*. I asked Billy about his drug use. Billy states why he uses them, outlining the stepping-stone approach to drug use that reflects the commonly held view: his use is part of a risk-taking strategy that goes wrong. He started off on cannabis and eventually gravitated to heroin. Along the way, he used Tuinal and cocaine. This pattern can be explained in terms of the needs of adolescents engaging in risk-taking and experimentation behaviour, so often the basis for drug education in schools. To me, it marked how he had learned to separate off his emotions from his actions; he described himself to me as a thrill seeker.

I perceived his chronic, dependent usage embodying another dynamic: a defusion of his anxiety. This linked to his desire to halt his 'fragmentation' through the emergence of sublimated memories. He spoke of his heroin use as *"mellowing him out"*, the same description Phil provided. This provided me with a connection between his anger and his drug use: they could help him subsume his anger but not eradicate it.

Dean: Where do the drugs come in then? Did they come in after the _____(Youth Club trip)?
Billy: Mmmmmm, I was smoking cannabis then, but that was it, coming at, I started taking ermmm, pills like Black

Bombers, and then I started taking Tuinal, and some other tablets called Lemantal (Nembutal), me and with my mates. Then we started taking cocaine.

Dean: *Is this with the gang you were going with?*

Billy: *It was with my mates who I was with all the time. It went from Tuinal to cocaine, and then basically on to heroin, and then it used to be heroin, pills and coke. It kinda went on from there. I stopped using coke really, and pills, just started taking heroin, and that started mellowing me out, sort of.*

Dean: *Right, so you weren't becoming violent?*

Billy: *No, I mean I took heroin, and when I had a confrontation, where I wasn't taking heroin, that confrontation might have happened. If I hadn't been taking heroin at the time I would've had a fight there and then. Where I've taken heroin I've let it ride. I've let it go, you know? A lot of things, Dean, I'm not just saying because I've been on heroin, if I wouldn't've been on heroin at the time, someone would've got hurt. I'm not saying that it could've been them – it could've been me. I'm not saying that I'm invincible or nothing. I've been stabbed and that. What I'm saying is that, in times I've been on heroin, and really after, I've thought, I've thought I was a bit glad on it, so that I let it ride, or I woulda been hurt over it, you know?*

Dean: *So in some ways heroin has helped to calm you down?*

Billy: *Calm me down, sorta let things ride.*

Dean: *But to keep that calmness you had to support this habit continuously?*

Billy: *Yeah, that's how I got into crime.*

Dean: *Yeah, so it's costly to keep it going?*

Billy: *Yeah, yeah.*

Billy speaks of his drug use being related to his violence, as heroin helps him to find serenity while keeping his anger at bay. This anger has led Billy into some near-death experiences, as he has moved from being a person who discharges anger through violence into a man who seeks the solace of drug-induced bliss to cocoon him from the outside world. It helps him to *"let things ride"*, allowing him to 'mask' his anger.

I perceived a shift in his anger from direct confrontation, instead being directed into crime. He sustains his heroin use through crime, but psychologically needs to take something from someone else as an act of revenge displacing his actions onto substitutes (Miller 1987). Through crime, Billy can participate in consuming, as he takes items from shops and people's homes then sells them within a local economy partially sustained by these acts. Far from being socially excluded, Billy, as with many men I have worked with, has earned hundreds of thousands of pounds through crime.

The discharge of his 'stings' is temporarily satiated through his drug use. Billy has found a way of not caring about direct confrontations; he has found a strategy to directly control his anger. On reflection, I noted how he had diverted his anger – Billy has a lack of empathy for his victims, as they are perceived by him to be objects for him to plunder, reflecting his own objectification. Ironically, this objectification, a break in the flow of empathy, also constitutes a 'flow' between institutions, Billy and his victims.

Violence as an Expression of Love

Billy's anger becomes sublimated as his moods alter through his drug use. However, his anger is never far away, and he only needs to be provoked for it to emerge. In this part of the counselling session, Billy speaks of his use of violence to resolve a situation where he felt hurt by his niece's behaviour. In re-reading this session, it became clear Billy's violence becomes a one-dimensional strategy he applies in every situation where he is faced with overwhelming emotions. He has developed such expert strategies to camouflage his feelings of connection that he is constrained in showing them to others. Here, he applies his anger in an effort to show his care.

Dean: How will you deal with all this anger inside you though? I mean, if you come off heroin, I presume it's still there somewhere? Those feelings aren't just gonna go away are they?

Billy: Yeah, it is there a bit, but it takes... it takes a lot to bring it out now, it's truly got to be something. Like, I mean, I know, I'll tell you something that happened last week, it's ermm you know of these. Jane is on heroin yeah? Well her boyfriend, his name is Rick. Well, he drives a car. What he does is take her out, he drives her out and she goes shoplifting. But she does it for him, he gets her to do it. Last week, outside my sister's house, he was holding a bag. She gave him a bag to hold and then he had the front, he got nicked with the bag, and he had the front, to, where he got nicked, he had the front to put it down to my niece. Anyway, she got arrested, she had it. We let it go.

Billy explains how Rick 'grassed' on Jane, Billy's niece, to the police, breaking one of the major taboos. Billy shows how he and his family "let it go", meaning no retribution was taken.

What happened last week, last week is... I've got the hump about what's happened and anyway I've seen 'im, and I try to tell him to fuck him off, because he ain't no good. He's using her, you know what I mean? We sorta had a little argument,

264

and I said to her: "Jane, listen, all he wants you for, is for his habit, because without you, he'd be fucked, 'cos he ain't got no arsehole to go out there thieving. All he does, girl, is drive you about, he sits in the car, he don't do fuck all. He sits in the motor, sends you into the shops and lets you do the thieving". He's got out the motor and gone, "Why should I go in the shop thieving, when I got her to do it for me?"

And I back...if you ask my sister Zoe, Dean, I just lost it. I mean I bashed the, I mean I really bashed him up, until I gave him such a head butt, I knocked him spark out. I done all this with one head butt like, I was bashing him up first. I grabbed him by the ears and had such force that I hit his eyes and his ears and knocked him out. I wanted to kill him, but my sister and my brother-in-law came out, and they dragged me off him, and that was left at that. Yeah so I still know it's there, but it took a lot to bring it out, you know what I mean? It really hurt me, mate, to do that, and the way he got out of the car: "Why should I go thieving when I got her to do it for me?" You know, that's my niece, know what I mean? And I love her, and I'm trying to say to her: "Look, look that's what I'm saying about yeh, he's taking the piss out of you, what sort of man is he? If he loved you, it would be the other way round, he would be doing it for you, yeah. He don't have sex with you or nothing".

Billy's notions of masculinity revolve around the belief that the man should support the woman at all times. What becomes degrading for Billy is his niece having to support Rick and his lack of empathy for her suffering. He reveals his care and love for his niece but he finds it difficult to express it to her directly and cannot ask her what is wrong. He is blocked, as he does not know how to use this language. I detected a connection to his own experiences, since no one ever asked him how he felt when he was growing up. This highlights how strategies of silence become embedded with the denial of emotional worlds.

Instead, Billy uses a strategy he has developed over the years to try and solve problems – the application of violence. The aim is to warn Ricky about his behaviour, but a flashpoint arises when Ricky acts almost suicidally in his nonchalant description of his use of Jane. This makes her appear disposable, which is a slur on the family, a deliberate 'sting'. Billy's explosion is an inevitable result of being confronted by Ricky in this manner. Ricky knew that he was not just disrespecting Jane, but also her family, where respect is a key commodity. The 'front' Billy has in the community comes about because of his violence, and through this has emerged fear and awe.

The subsequent violence provided a release for Billy, but left him shocked at his anger and potential for violence. He has a 'recoil'; it "hurt him" to beat up Ricky. He shows feelings of empathy, even when engaged in violence that nearly kills Ricky.

Billy speaks of his role in protecting his family, and shows how his feelings of empathy are directed through violence as a form of care for his niece.

Billy: I'm just trying to explain to her. Listen, no he doesn't want you, yeah he don't love you gal, he's just taking the piss out of you, mate. It hurts me, please, for my sake, not just for my sake, but for your Mum's sake, because it is killing her Mum, my older sister. It's literally killing her, mate. I mean she's got the pox (angry at her frustration) ..."

Billy wants to support his older sister but he can only express this through violence. As a strategy, this has failed, as Billy's use of violence has driven his niece away from him. Its one-dimensional application was futile. Another dimension to our session canvassed his feelings on being split. He does not apply his own learning in this situation – that violence does not resolve a situation – it makes the desire for revenge paramount. He also feels his niece should reflect on what has happened to him, and not emulate his mistakes. She has a 'teacher' in Billy, but clearly she does not take any notice of him. I sensed Billy had not reflected on Jane's underlying reasons for engaging in this behaviour, just as he has not reflected upon his own reasons. However, what emerges as a positive is Billy's ability to reflect on his own behaviour within a moral framework. He does not try to justify his drug use, knowing the personal cost to himself.

Billy: But it hurts me, 'cos I try to explain to her: " Look at me, you know? Fucking couldn't have had a better teacher, me, you know, to show you what's gonna happen if you carry on, taking heroin, and taking crack, and things like this and going out shoplifting". You couldn't have a better teacher than me, Dean, to show you what's gonna happen. I said to her: "Look girl, you're gonna wind up in and out of prison all your life, you know it ain't no good, just drop it, and drop him, 'cos it ain't no good, he's just using you".
Dean: Maybe you appear glamorous to her?
Billy: I hope I don't. I mean, as I say, I've sat her down many times, Dean, and you know what I mean? and explained to her that it ain't clever, and, Dean, it ain't glamorous. When you're away a year and a half here, and a year and a half there, missing your family, well, you hurt inside, really, you know what I mean? But she goes, "Yeah but you done it". And I go: "Yeah but

I'm a boy, but I'm not ashamed to admit it that it's hurt me, you know it has hurt me, being away from my family".

The split emerges in his connection to his family causing him bodily pain: *"well, you hurt inside really"*, showing the tear between his 'mask' and his hard man 'front', his vow. He sees Jane taking on the role of a man through her drug use and crime. He believes Jane does not have the 'front' to survive, as she is soft and vulnerable and would not be able to withstand prison life as he has, as a man.

Underneath Billy's 'front' lie emotional connections he is able to show to his niece, revealing his softness, his feelings of loss at being away from his family, the loss he initially wanted to avenge. His vow has caused further isolation from them. However, he hides this when he is on the street because this emotional expression becomes a weakness others may exploit. He is known locally as a 'hard man' and this is the image he inhabits. He reveals to me the 'hard man' is an act, but it is not easily shed. Nevertheless, underlying this 'front' is another Billy, who tries to protect his family, but to no avail.

Billy's words illuminate how strategies of revenge become formulated. They materialize from his need to hide his emotional connections due to the pressure he is placed under within his family and in his wider social life. There is no one to communicate his adolescent pain to, so he shuts it off, 'masks' it, and then projects a 'front' of violence to ward of further attacks. As he comes into contact with school, courts, social services and the police, this 'front' is further sustained as a 'resistance'. The disciplinarian regimes are engaged in trying to break him, but they unwittingly having the opposite effect, as he simply resolves to strengthen his 'front'. The strategies they use in trying to get him to conform are the same as the ones he employs in his emotional and physical violence. The result is that the violence escalates.

Even when he is fully engaged in being a 'hard man', Billy is still able to show his empathy for members of his family and their suffering. He discloses his empathy for his mother, which eventually leads to him being taken away. It is Billy's lack of understanding of his emotional world that fuels the continuous battle. One of Billy's defining problems is that he had no one to speak to because he had to uphold his code of silence. Instead, he stores up these 'stings', waiting to discharge them in his battle with the state.

Billy disclosed to me his love for his niece, but this came to be projected as an extreme distaste for her boyfriend's lack of manhood: *"what sort of man is he? If he loved you, it would be the other way round, he would be doing it for you, yeah. He don't have sex with you or nothing"*. Billy cares for her, but he cannot say so, and it emerges as a put down of her boyfriend for his lack of masculinity. Unable to express himself emotionally, he launches into a physical attack, after provocation, demonstrating to his niece how weak Ricky is by beating him. Billy's love and concern transforms into violence, emerging through the prism of his 'mask'.

In the next chapter I will look at how heroin is used to block out reality through the process of 'shrinking' from the world. Rod describes how he was not physically capable of fighting back, and developed a strategy of shutting himself off.

VIII. BODY UNDER THREAT – 'SHRINKING'

In the previous chapter, Billy spoke of the violence shaping his life and how he revenged his 'stings' through explosions of violence, showing how the 'strategies of revenge' enmesh with other men and institutions, creating a "tit for tat" quality (Ryder, in Stanko and Newburn (eds) 1994).

In this chapter, Rod relates the impact of a series of accidents that transformed his body. The connection to Billy's experience is in being subject to the 'disciplines' of the school: taunting, bullying and later, detention centres and prison. Rod does not have the same physical power as Billy to avenge the 'stings' fired into him and is very much at the mercy of institutions and his peer group due to the effects of his accidents on his self-esteem and body.

Rod recollects a series of events, related to me in a low monotone, describing the decimation of his body. I reflected on how these memories haunted him both physically and emotionally. He was reminded of them every day, inhibiting his ability to act as he wished within the world. They also caused him an emotional pain, which he found difficult to articulate because he appeared to have 'masked' the after-effects.

It took three years before he spoke about his memories in depth for the first time. When I first asked him why he used heroin he told me, *"because I was bored"*. As we began to build trust, his 'masking' of the past began to dissolve. It was that then it became apparent to me he was traumatised, and I reflected on the issue of the after-effects of this "Post-traumatic Stress Disorder" (1993 De Zulueta).

As a child, Rod received support from his mother, his sisters and his brother. He spoke very little of his father. Latterly, Rod cares for his mother, who is ill, a return of the flow of love, although he expresses it here as a form of duty. This bond is the one major support relationship Rod has sustained throughout his life, which he reveals to me as care he has also resented. Another issue that arose was his silence and his inability to verbalise his traumas.

As an adult, Rod's 'mask' has sustained the silence but his strategy involves more than just forgetting. This entailed a desire to disassociate himself from his experiences, constructing an outward 'front' of nonchalance: *"I just get on with it"*. This phrase also arises with Gary and Pete as they describe aspects of their lives.

PTSD is a current psychiatric diagnosis for the after-effects of traumatic events (Zulueta 1993). I use it to describe the 'masking' of events, not as a distinct category in itself requiring medical intervention. This concept has never been applied to Rod by anyone else who has worked with him. Referring back, I used this term in the chapter on "Fathers and Strategies of Coping" to understand and analyse how men returning from war had to readjust from battle conditions to civilian life. I make this connection with Rod's use of heroin. His silence is bounded by not having the emotional space to explore the emotional after-effects with his family or the authority structures enforcing discipline upon him.

Consequently, Rod's feelings have never been allowed to 'flow' because he has never been deemed to have any by other people outside of his family. His emotions have become sealed up to this point, as no one has asked him how he has been feeling. This raises the issue of how illnesses are institutionally defined seemingly divorced from the emotional lives of the subject. This is explored by Seidler (1994), describing how some of the care professions have "too often rendered people as passive through a process of 'objectification'. It becomes important to enlist the understanding and willingness of people as active subjects and participants in their own recovery" (Seidler 1994, p. 144).

In "Unreasonable Men", Seidler has traced this process of 'objectification', drawing on Foucault's "The Birth of the Clinic" (1976), to the introduction of medicine, which eradicated the feelings of the body, leading to a separation of the emotions from technique. This lack of theoretical conceptualisation has a significant impact on Rod's self-concept. The process Seidler describes reifies objectivity and rationality over feelings and emotions, drowning the emotional needs of the subject within a technical language.

In this session, Rod describes how his reactions to his injuries were never explored; subsequently I realised he had become emotionally alienated from his physical recovery. His body seemingly exists independently from him, as experts have diagnosed and cured his physical conditions. This paradigm seemingly institutionalises a form of disassociation. Seidler, drawing on Carol Gilligan (1988), highlights how other forms of masculinity are embedded in institutional practices where the emotional context of the patients' lives is deemed to be of little relevance.

I can understand why Rod's emotional experiences have not been validated, since they have not been conceptualised, thereby creating an inner turmoil. One of the reasons why he has hardly ever sought help previously is in his perception of what defines strength and his need maintain his self-esteem. When I picture Rod, I see a man who has been buried by the incidents, pain, and trauma of his past, both physically and psychologically.

The layers of 'stings' Rod has received have denigrating his self-esteem and confidence to act within the world, sealing this burial. The wounds of the past have lodged these 'stings' in his mind, where they are held as traumatic memories, resonating in the present as he reflects on his self-image. These 'stings' have defined both psychologically and psychically the parameters of Rod's ability to connect with the world.

Rod's self-reflection is also bounded by the scars criss-crossing his torso. His ability to engage in the social world is constrained by his deafness and blindness. These were his immediate limitations, linked to emotional after-effects. Therefore Rod's trauma is also embodied, as he is reminded daily of the after-effects, creating a sense of shame at not being the same as other men.

Embodied Pain

When Rod began to talk about his early years, I could not fully comprehend the effects of these experiences. I thought perhaps he was exaggerating, as all of this could not have happened to one person. I could see his eyesight was poor as he wore thick-lensed glasses. He also wore a hearing aid. I began to explore with him his ability to engage in the world and how he felt about this.

Dean: What, your burn? Is it pretty bad still then?

Rod: (Gets up and pulls shirt and shows me) Up there to down there, you know what I mean? It goes round there, you know what I mean? And it ain't far from my three-piece (pointing to groin). It's not just a burn, I got that there, (Pointing to operation scar on chest) and up here I've got big stretch marks. (Pointing)

Dean: What's that one for, is that a stabbing?

Rod: No, that's where I 'ad me kidney taken out. See what I mean?

Dean: What are the stretch marks from then?

Rod: Birth, I think. That's from where I had a kidney taken out.

Dean: So you've got quite a bit of scar tissue on your chest. Err, Is that another reason why you feel depressed about yourself?

Rod: (Coughs)

I felt startled when he pulled up his shirt. How could I have had any doubts? There was layer upon layer of molten flesh. It looked horrific. I began to reflect on how he may have coped with the pain as a child, enduring the operations and the disfigurement, which had left deep scars on his body. It was only through the relationship we had developed that I felt comfortable in asking him how these scars had formed, aware at all times that my comments could lead to further wounding. Although we had a bond, this had to be carefully nurtured for him to explore his painful memories.

I learnt the scars were not only physical, but had left 'wounds' in his memory. Rod revealed he had been labelled as backward and this had led him to search for an explanation for his pain. He believed he had found an answer after watching a TV program.

Rod: I see a programme once on the telly about ten years ago I think it was. You know, like babies that are born err... like born early, what are they called?

Dean: Premature.

Rod: Yes, it says that them people are always slow. That's always been in my head. You know what I mean... where I was born premature and that as well.

Dean: Right.

Rod: Plus where I think where I banged me head, it's stopped me learning to read and write. 'Cos at primary school, my teachers...you know, like, when you leave and go to secondary school and the parents go and they tell you how their kids got on and that, don't they?

Dean: Yeah.

Rod: She said there was no reason why I should not be able to read and write. I had a good memory and that.

Dean: Right.

Rod: You also have a medical thing before you leave and they said I had a mental blockage.

Dean: Do you think that?

Rod: I think it's something where I've hit me head. 'Cos sometimes I get right bad headaches.

Dean: What, even now?

Rod: Mmm. When I done it and I had the pain there then... yes? It tends to come back, you know what I mean?

As an adult, Rod is searching for an explanation for his problems, but having no one to communicate his sense of shame about his inability to learn, he finds a meaning from a TV program, which has *"always been in my head"*. I reflected on why Rod chose this explanation. It appears plausible, but there is also an element of pre-destination.

Within this meaning, Rod does not question the teaching methods used in his education. All of his problems stem from how he was delivered into the world. The impact of what he is about to describe is a continuation of his 'bad luck', a type of predestined curse. However another contradictory explanation is revealed in the extract. Drawing from Carol Gilligan (1990), I term this an "emotional wall", which creates a 'mask' of disassociation.

Rod is caught within two competing theories; I felt he would have preferred to believe in the scientific explanation shown in the TV program, but he knew the other explanation was more accurate, even if it was also more problematic. The clue lies in his words: *"there was no reason why I should not be able to read and write. I had a good memory and that"*. As a teacher related, he had *"a mental blockage"*.

Therefore, there are two accounts: being born *"slow"*, and the after-affects of trauma, where Rod has created a *"mental blockage"*. In talking to Rod over the years and through getting to know him, his ability to sustain a drug habit (despite his obvious physical drawbacks) highlighted for me that he was not 'slow' in terms of being 'stupid'. So I began to explore the basis of his mental blockage with him. As Rod began to talk about himself, his blockage immediately became apparent to me, but because Rod had lived with the trauma and had never spoken of it, it was a journey into a foreign land for him.

I noticed a disconnection between Rod's use of language and his view of himself. This split first appears in his description of himself. He describes the TV program on premature birth about *"them people"*, when talking about himself. His description implies distance and downgrading when depicting himself. Implicit in his description is that he is also one of *"them people"*.

This split in his descriptive language reveals one of Rod's coping strategies, as he has learned to disassociate himself from his traumas, thereby viewing himself from the outside. He 'masks' his pain and projects a 'front' by becoming someone else and distancing himself from the pain he has endured. Although he sees himself as part of a labelled group, he also looks at this group from the outside.

In exploring the term 'disassociation' I was drawn to the work of De Zulueta (1993), who drew from Pierre Janet, a contemporary of Freud.

> He described it as a process whereby feelings or memories relating to frightening experiences are split off from conscious awareness and voluntary control to show up later as 'pathological automatisms'. These intrusive images, somatic experiences or anxiety reactions are reactivated by conditions similar to those experienced at the time of the original trauma. (De Zulueta 1993, p. 163)

For me, this relates to the Nietzschean idea of forgetting one's experiences. In the chapter "Fathers and Sons", John described how under a certain set of conditions (when staying in his bed-sit) his feelings of trauma arose, and these memories contained as visualisations in his head reoccurred. John then spoke of how drugs used to *"block things out"*, become one form of disassociation. Another connection between Rod and John is not just the mental images, but the scars on their bodies. Rod is reminded everyday about how he is perceived by others. These are historical resonances, which he carries mentally as well as physiologically.

Post-traumatic Stress Disorder

In reading Felicity de Zulueta's "From Pain to Violence" (1993), I gained an insight into how Rod's defences against traumatic memories had formed, and why he developed this disassociative language. I am interested in Rod's ability to cope, and the reactions of the people around him to his coping strategies. Rod appears deformed compared with the norm; people also speak about him differently, as if he is subnormal. These comments reinforce his lack of self-esteem, entrapping him in a negative image. Another issue is the lack of care and the lack of empathic connection he experiences from 'care institutions'. These also fail to validate his internal emotional feelings, trapping him in this frozen image where he gains a sense of who he is only from the derogatory comments of others, where he has been 'objectified'.

Rod's internal self-image is primarily negative, creating minimal self-esteem. There are resonances with all of the men in this study regarding formation of negative self-image. However, Rod's image is reinforced by his inability to fight back physically, so he has had to find other strategies to sustain himself including heroin use and crime. Another strategy is discussed at the end of this chapter –Rod's ability to care for his family. He cares for others so as not to care for himself.

For most of his life Rod, has felt trapped within his horrific memories. A consistent pattern emerges of men being trapped within historical silences surrounding their pain. Deleuze and Guattari (1972) have analysed how the resonant effects of historical events, in that case coping after being demobbed from the war, created difficulties in readjustment. Pete's father's silence became sealed within an institutional denial of the events. PTSD, the holding of psychic pain, is an analytical concept I use to describe the ripples of these historical resonances and here I will use it to explain Rod's behaviour.

> A person has experienced an event that is outside the range of usual human experience and that would be markedly distressing to almost anyone such as; a serious threat or harm to one's life or physical integrity; serious threat or harm to one's children, spouse or other close relatives, sudden destruction of one's home or community; or seeing another person who has recently been or is being injured or killed as a result of an accident or physical violence. Diagnostic and Statistical Manual of Mental Disorders (DSM-III) (De Zulueta 1993, p. 169)

PTSD is increasingly being studied in order to ascertain how children cope with the after-effects of trauma, particularly after war (Heinl 2001). Rod describes his life in these extracts as a series of events "outside the range of usual human experience". The issue of children's emotional lives not being conceptualised by caring institutions becomes a key theme in this chapter, highlighted through Rod's labelling and subsequent treatment. It also illuminates a wider problem concerning how the emotional world of children is conceptualised.

> The links between psychological trauma and violence are often denied and minimised, particularly in relation to childhood abuse. In some circles children are still believed to be exempt from the effects of psychological trauma. (De Zulueta 1993, p. 182)

Rod spoke about an incident at school, which through the school failing to conceptualise his pain, led to Rod having to deal with his emotional turmoil alone. At an early age Rod learnt to construct a 'mask' to sublimate his feelings of physical and emotional pain. This sublimation left him with residual feelings of psychological pain. Rod describes how he came under attack for being different and outlines his strategies for coping.

Felicity de Zulueta (1993) conceptualises this 'splitting' process that evolves when a person is threatened by a series of overwhelming events. These processes involve either denial (it did not happen) or splitting (it happened to someone else, not me) – differing forms of the 'mask'.

> Although denial and psychic numbing are often absent in children who suffer single shock trauma, these defences are usually very much in evidence in those who have been through longstanding and repeated horrific experiences such as have been described by childhood victims and/or sexual abuse. (De Zulueta 1993, p.188)

Rod's strategies are to retreat from the social world, enacting a form of psychic numbing and disengaging.

Dean: So you were quite shy at school then?
Rod: Yes.
Dean: Were you bullied as well?
Rod: At Primary School yes, at _____ I was.
Dean: Why was that then? Is it because of the accident with your eye?

Rod: I dunno, I was a loner weren't I? I didn't mix with people or that.
Dean: How come you were a loner then?
Rod: I dunno.

Rod becomes *"a loner"*, disengaging from other people; he feels *"shy"* – a code for feelings of shame. In becoming a *"loner"*, Rod develops a strategy of shutting off from contact with the outside world and retreating within himself, highlighting how he began to create a *"mental blockage"* – his inability to concentrate because of his inner turmoil. His shame is heightened by not being able to read and write because of the long periods he has spent in hospital and the consequent time off from school. This becomes compounded due to his sense of shame about his body and his trapped feelings. He cannot relate to his inner emotional world, but as this session shows, his traumas are forever present within him. They impact upon his hearing, vision and clothing, hiding his shame about his body, which inhibits him from having a relationship with a woman.

I had an intuition that Rod had developed a strategy of shutting off the outside world at an early age because it was too painful to deal with. With this shutting off strategy, Rod learned to disconnect from school because it was perpetuating his humiliation. This mental blockage is Rod's 'mask', the dam that stops him from being overwhelmed by the traumatic incidents he is about to describe. The 'mask' also blocks out all sources of perceived humiliation, as Rod would rather retreat from the world than face any more pain, thereby isolating himself.

However, this isolation creates the conditions for him to be bullied. He is an easy enough target, as he does hot have the physical power to fight back. Rod speaks little about support from the school: none was forthcoming and there was little expectation that it would be provided.

Rod's strategy of disengagement became reinforced and bounded by the taunts of his peers. This provided Rod with a 'social' mirror, reinforcing his feelings of shame. When he was physically attacked, he received further physical and emotional pain. This was another blockage imposed upon Rod, stopping him from communicating what he was experiencing internally. He not only had to contend with the trauma of his body, but also with the ridicule he received for his perceived ineptitude. When he does try to engage in the social world, he receives further pain. He relates how he tried to compete within the school environment, leading to disastrous consequences. I knew from talking to Gary and Simon how important football was to them. I asked Rod if he had ever participated.

Dean: Were you any good at football or anything like that then before your accident?
Rod: No, not really. That's how I lost my sight, playing football. I didn't play at all after that.
Dean: Yes. How did that come about, how you lost your sight?
Rod: I tripped over the ball and hit my head on the floor. Tarmac it was, the playground.
Dean: Yes.
Rod: I got a detached retina.
Dean: Were you running for the ball, or something?
Rod: No, you know where you, like, tackle someone?
Dean: Yes.
Rod: The ball's in between you so one of you falls over. I went in, and hit that bit of my head on the floor. What do they call it? Somersault sort of thing. (Getting up and demonstrating) Say like that's the ball there and I

tripped like that and went poooo, with this bit of my
head on the floor.
Dean: *How long were you in hospital for?*
Rod: *(Coughs) ...I went hospital next day because all me eye*
was puffed up, sort of thing, all red round there. Me
mum took me to the _____ Clinic down ____
_____and they sent me to _____ Hospital.
Then a week, or two weeks later they took me in for a
X-Ray...
Dean: *Right.*

When he related this incident I had a feeling of
being stuck. I had no idea playing football could have
caused further pain. He had an accident leading to a
catalogue of mistakes. The pain he describes is beyond
my comprehension. This accident led to the loss of
sight in one of his eyes, and badly damaging the other.

What is initially unclear for me is the school's
responsibility in making sure Rod attended a hospital after
the accident. His mother was not called in. It was not
until the next day, after his *"eye was puffed up"* that his
mother took him to the doctor, who referred him directly
to the Accident and Emergency Department. Two weeks
later, they took an X-Ray. This delay in sending Rod
for treatment compounded the problems that followed.
In transcribing and hearing his words, I was struck
by how lightly the incident was treated by the school.

In the previous chapter, Billy described how he was taken
to court and punished for not going to school. This was an
example of the use of discipline to enforce correction. Here,
the care from the school appears to be absent, and the divorce
of discipline from empathy arises once again. However, this
instance takes place within different parameters. With Billy,

there was a concern for him to learn the rules, regardless of what was happening within his home. Here, there appears to be a disregard for the physical welfare of Rod.

The school was seemingly slow to give him support, but what is clear is there was no after-care support when he returned. There was an expectation he would just fit in, again linking with how men such as Pete's Dad returned from the war and received no emotional support. This shows the link between institutional denial of Rod's emotional world and the development of his 'front', as he 'masks' his suffering in silence.

When he speaks to me in the present, I feel he is understating his pain, keeping control of his emotions. It is the one defining act of strength he can employ and this begins to explain his splitting. I felt his anger surfacing in the session at the same time he told me he was not bothered.

Rod is eventually admitted for an eye operation, creating further problems which evolve into a Kafkaesque nightmare.

Rod: I get an headache and I have that same pain, just there behind my ear. But I also remember waking up on the operating table, when they was going to take my eye out...I wouldn't 'ave a needle at first, they give me a drink. I drunk that, then I woke up and I saw they already had me eye out then. But then they just went and got a needle, PHHUU and knocked me out again.

Dean: What do you mean had your eye out, actually physically had it out?

Rod: Like I was laying on the operating table, yes. Before I went in to have the operation. Right. They took me in and instead of giving me a needle. Cos where I was

young they said I could have a drink or the needle. So
I said I'd 'ave the drink, yes. It knocked me out. They
took me in the operating theatre. I'm laying there,
what do they call the thing there? In the operating
theatre? The bench thing where they do it all, yes?

Dean: *It's just the table isn't it?*

Rod: *Well I woke up, I was out then, yes.*

Dean: *Yes?*

Rod: *Then they put another needle in and put me out.*

Dean: *That must have been traumatic then, wasn't it?*

Rod: *(Coughs)*

Dean: *Have you still got your original eye now then?*

Rod: *Yes. All they done was took the eye out and try to put the*
retina back on, but it ripped back off. Also remember
running around the front room alight when I was
three.

Following the initial incident of going for the ball,
the after effects are compounded by a series of blunders,
occurring even during the operation ***"then I woke up and***
I saw they already had me eye out then". Rod does not
blame the hospital for this mistake, instead it was his
fault for making the wrong choice: *"they said I could have*
a drink or the needle. So I said I'd 'ave the drink, yes. It
knocked me out". Within Rod's description, it was not the
fault of the anaesthetist, as Rod is clear he does not want
to make himself a victim. Again I detected this as his
form of exerting control over the situation: he made the
wrong choice, therefore he takes the blame on himself.

The mental and emotional pain he experienced is
excruciating for me in its narration, as I see the images
he is describing. I reflected on the reasons for this lack of
care. Initially, I explored this incident through the prism
of class dynamics. Rod did not receive care because of

his class position in relation to the forces operating upon him, not having the means to challenge decision-making processes. However, I distinguished another dynamic underlying this: the divorce of emotional empathy from technique (Seidler 1994). Implicit in Rod's conversation is his separation of himself from his emotions. Rod's isolation was compounded because any support he has been offered has been through the appliance of technique on his physique rather than through assisting him to emotionally recuperate. This would explain why he received no after-care. There was no conception that he would need it, as he was a young white working class male. This also recalls the challenges Billy faced being placed in the Home, this lack of conceptualisation of his emotional world.

Gary, Billy, Simon, John, Phil, Alan, Alex and Rob were excluded from school for their behaviour. In talking to them, it is clear that the impacts of their family lives had a significant impact on how they experienced school. Disciplinarian regimes (Foucault 1977) were enacted to try and force them to fit in. When these failed, further sanctions were applied, leading to exclusion. What is not analysed is why these men have failed the system. This in itself is never debated, as the problem has become individualised. The resonance of the many experiences of the men in this study point to a divorce between empathy and discipline in institutional practice.

Once he began to speak, a flood of memories flowed. I asked him about the molten flesh on his chest.

Dean: Mmm...Is that when you got behind the fireguard? How did that come about then?

Rod: I just pulled the fireguard out and got behind it. There wasn't a lot of coal in there. I got right near the coal and it then caught the dressing gown alight...

Dean: emmm... Were your mum and dad about then?

Rod: No, my dad was out working and me mum was out shopping, but me older sister and that were there. That's who put me out. It weren't none of their fault. It was my own fault for getting behind the fireguard.

Dean: Yes, how did you feel about that, thinking about it now ?...

Rod: (Pause... drums on table)

Dean: Does it make you feel angry ?

Rod: Mm. (Pause...Drums on table)

In relating this experience that left his body deeply scarred, Rod talks about it as *"my own fault for getting behind the fireguard"*. Rod does not direct any blame onto his family for what happened. His feelings about these incidents seemingly reflect back to the TV program – it was 'bad luck' for being born premature. I did not want to push him because so much had happened to him and his family appeared to be an anchor for the after-effects. I felt that if I took this away, what would Rod be left with? This highlighted a limit to our relationship.

This also shows how the recollection of events becomes shaped from the present to provide meaning in the past. I asked him how he felt and this created a silence between us; he began to drum his hand on the table as his emotions began to surface. I noticed he was marking and controlling his feelings on the edge of a precipice and I did not want to wound him. However, when I moved on he began to talk about another incident defining his overwhelming sense of inhabiting a body under constant threat – the partial loss of his hearing.

Dean: Because you have problems with your ears as well?
Rod: Yes, perforated eardrums. (Drums on table)
Dean: How did that happen?
Rod: I used to get ear infections when I was young, but all the doctor used to keep doing was give me silly eardrops instead of sending me to a proper ear specialist.
Dean: Yes, when you get angry, who do you get angry at?
Rod: No one in particular.
Dean: Is it directed at yourself?
Rod: Yu... I should've done this and done that...
Dean: Right. So your life is filled with a little bit of regret then?
Rod: Yes.
Dean: Regret you went behind the fireguard and regret you went for the ball?
Rod: Well, everything seems to have been against me, you know what I mean?
Dean: Yes.
Rod: Nothing's ever seem to go for me.
Dean: Yes.

Again, I use understatement in order not to wound him. It is at this point that he begins to shift from blaming himself to directing his blame onto how he has been treated. In this case, it is the GP whom Rod felt made a wrong diagnosis, leading to his hearing loss.

In the previous extracts, Rod showed how he was angry with himself for what had happened. This marked the first time Rod had expressed anger at how he had been treated, as he believed a misdiagnosis had been made. Again, the emotional after-effects of the loss of hearing are not explored. It is just another problem Rod is left to contend with. This is highlighted by the critique of Seidler (1994) concerning the divorce of medicine from emotions, which has repercussions for Rod's future strategies of pain negation.

I wanted to explore Rod's traumas and trace the possible connections to his heroin use. As he spoke, I understood how his drug use would allow him to shut off these continual traumas. I was also acutely aware we were edging towards the deep chasm of his depression, so I had to tread carefully.

When I asked him how he felt, Rod spoke of a feeling of constant dread: *"Well, everything seems to have been against me, you know what I mean?"* I did not know what to say to him as what he had told me was so overwhelming it was difficult to see any resolution, only to provide space for him to express what he had held tightly bound for the past twenty-five years.

Being Labelled

Rod's accidents left him with feelings of dread around his body. I believe this led to the construction of his 'mental block', a reaction to PTSD. This would explain why Rod fell far behind in reading and writing, and became unable to cope within the school environment. This would also explain why he was sent to a Special School for children with severe emotional needs, which he describes here.

Rod: Mm. Then they sent me to err..._____ School... really I don't think I should've went there, 'cos there were people like this, bad disabled, you know what I mean?
Dean: Yes.
Rod: Like, mongrel sort of people I call 'em. I used to go to school in a big blue bus, didn't I? So they used to...

know what I was...make up silly names and things like
that.
Dean: You were marked out as being special yet again?
Rod: Ehh...Like if you go school on a big blue bus, they count
it as a Mongrel School all the time, don't they?
Dean: Right. Is that what the local people use to say to you?
Rod: Yehh...(pause)

After the physical traumas, Rod was institutionally labelled due to his inability to concentrate. From listening to what had happened to him before starting school, the trauma of his birth, the burning, the loss of his sight and his hearing at primary school, Rod was clearly in a state of shock. No one had asked him what he was experiencing emotionally. Although he had the support of his mother and sisters, Rod was physically and emotionally isolated from the outside world.

However, in being sent to a special school, Rod experienced the further perceived degradation of being driven in the *"blue bus"* with people whom he felt he had minimal connection with: the severely disabled.

His splitting off became identified as difficult behaviour, requiring the use of the 'disciplines' as a form of care, which resonates with Billy's experiences. These 'disciplines' were applied without recognition of the emotional lives of Rod and Billy, marking their powerlessness and leading to taunts from other local children. This created anger in Billy and resignation in Rod, producing further isolation. Rod was caught in a 'double bind': whether to accept the definition or to fight against it. The outcome was a mixture of the two. A clue to this appears in the description of his fellow pupils in the above extract.

Initially he describes them as: *"there were people like this, bad disabled, you know what I mean?"* Rod is saying he was not the same as them; however, there was also conveyed a feeling of empathy with their pain rather than disgust. The disgust becomes pronounced in the following quote. *"Like mongrel sort of people, I call 'em".* Rod fights against this label by choosing to see himself as separate from the others. However, the taunts make him realise he is perceived as being the same. *I used to go to school in a big blue bus, didn't I? So they used to...know what I was...make up silly names and things like that".* This marks Rod's humiliation at being perceived as different.

The taunts led Rod to internalise his sense of difference. In order to reconnect with the people he grew up with, he distanced himself from these taunts by directing them onto the people who were more disfigured than him. Reconsidering his initial explanation for his *"slowness"* – from watching the TV program about premature births – I see a connection. Rod experiences himself through the eyes of others and defines himself within these concepts. In not having his own feelings validated, Rod searches for meaning outside of himself, here seeing himself through the eyes of his persecutors.

His strategy is to separate himself from his fellow pupils in his description. Rod felt he should never have been sent to this special school, a continual mark of shame. This failed as an education strategy anyway, as he still cannot read.

Being Bullied

Rod spoke of the effects of the taunts and bullying. There are three key themes: the first is how he defines himself through the taunts, showing the power of derision in creating this image, which is sustained through speech, the enactment of verbal 'stings' creating internalised wounds. In the second, Rod speaks of the effects of being emotionally bullied and how he "shuts off". In the third, Rod's brother uses violence, putting an end to the physical bullying.

Rod: What else has done me 'ead in, you know, like people read things in things like that. Like when you're in a crowd and they go look at that joke in the paper, that sort of thing, and I couldn't read it, and you get, and I know it's just people, going oh you Div, you know what I mean?

Dean: Right.

Rod: Then after a while you think that you are a div, dun't yer?

Dean: So they labelled you as somebody who they could pick on then, isn't it?

Rod: Yeah.

Dean: So you ended up believing what they were saying?

Rod shows the power of mocking speech, which saps his self-esteem. Having no other positive inputs, he defines himself through them: *"Then after a while you think that you are a div, dun't yer?"* Rod has already suffered tremendous pain, received little emotional support, and been labelled by the authorities as *"slow"*. He now suffers further pain targeted at his identity. This reflection is mirrored through the taunts of others, evaporating any self-esteem he may have: he defines himself as a *"div"*. Rod was also under siege because of his perceived weakness. This did not stop him from fighting back physically, but the name-calling had a big effect upon him.

Rod: I ain't got no calcium in me teeth. I've been called yellow teeth for years and all, you know what I mean? Look,

they are yellow. But that is where they pumped so many
drugs in me when I was just born.
Dean: Right...so you were quite an easy target at school then
for being picked on?
Rod: Not physically bullied.
Dean: More mental.
Rod: Ehh.
Dean: Just as bad though, isn't it?
Rod: Emm...Think it's worse in a lot of ways...
Dean: Mmm...How did you cope with that bullying then?
Rod: Just kept it to meself really, apart from the physical.
Right after I got hit and that.

This marked a breakthrough in our relationship, as Rod spoke for the first time about his emotional world and how he coped with the pain he was enduring; not the physical pain of the events, but the name calling that resulted from his disfigurement. His strategy was *"just kept it to meself really, apart from the physical".*

Each insult lodges itself, as a 'sting' inside him, wounding him further. He describes the emotional abuse being worse than the physical. It reminds him of who he is – a degraded body in the sight of others. His unsightliness becomes a source of amusement for others; he is seen as weak and is the recipient of physical bullying.

Dean: Were you hit as well?
Rod: My first year, like, a couple of geezers tried to bully
me.
Dean: What, at the school?
Rod: Yer...They were like the top kids, you know what I
mean?
Dean: Yer.
Rod: They just to think they were the hardest and that.

Dean: (Interjects) How did you cope with that then?

Rod: (sighs) I let it go on for a little while and then I set at 'em one day one week. My brother and a couple of his mates went up there. They was waiting round the corner. Three of us used to go the same way, and they use to try and dig us out all the time. So I told my brother and that to wait somewhere, and like, when they come round they started bullying us. My brother and his mates just beat 'em up.

Dean: Right.

Rod: They never done nothing after that...

Dean: So your brother seems quite supportive then, doesn't he?

Rod: Yes.

This passage illuminates a familiar theme threading through the sessions: the use of violence to halt the 'flows' of pain. Within Deptford's local white culture, Rod knows the only way of dealing with the violence being inflicted on him is to use more violence to bring it to a halt, so Rod calls on his brother and his friends. This shows how cultures of violence operate through sustaining the dialectics of revenge. The development of a 'front' becomes crucial for Rod's survival. It stops the 'flows' of received violence and Rod realises his power in being a perpetrator. If Rod had not had his brother to protect him, he may have endured years of bullying. The strain on his mental health would have been considerable, given the pain he had already endured as a child.

The Fear of Care

Rod went on to divulge how being looked after by his family was creating a problem for him. I felt this marked a tension between his independence as a man and his need for emotional connection. This care from his family was stopping him from realising his masculinity as he defined it, as he could not split away from the 'protective cocoon' they offered him. I was left in a quandary about this, feeling that the protection his family offered him was a way of staving off further attacks, but it also trapped him within a certain role in the family. Rod described his resentment at having to rely on his brother to stop the bullying, not being capable of stopping it himself.

Rod: He would look after me, you know what I mean?
Dean: Yes.
Rod: I think that was the trouble. I used to feel that I was petted too much as well.
Dean: At home?
Rod: Looked after too much.
Dean: By your mum, you mean?
Rod: Yer and like...she used to go to me brother all the time: "Look after him", an all that, and me sisters used to look out for me and that.
Dean: so you were petted too much you say?
Rod: Yes, well I feel like I was.
Dean: Right...How do you think that has affected you?
Rod: That I always think there's gonna be someone there to help me, but there ain't, is
there?
Dean: Yeah...so a kind of reliance to help you all the time...So what you're saying is that there's a lack of independence?
Rod: Mmm.
Dean: Are all these issues connected to your drug use then?
Rod: In the long run I think they are. (Pause)

Rod gained something positive from his family, who supported him through the crises he narrates above. This 'flows' primarily from his mother, who asks his brother and his sisters to look after him. His brother then fights off any tormentors, showing his care through 'flows of violence' transmitted through his 'mask' of masculine power, easing Rod's pain. This highlights the separation between the feminine and masculine worlds, as it is his brother who uses this power to avenge the 'stings' Rod receives. His mother and his sisters look after Rod in the home.

Despite everything that has happened to him, he feels *"petted too much"*, *"looked after too much"*. This appears paradoxical when taken at face value. However, Rod seemingly resents this care because he is not able to assert his own independence, his own power to avenge and take care of himself. Rod's words take on a different meaning when it is understood that he feels the connection with his family for emotional and physical support to be a weakness. Rod's solution to the dilemma of his need for connection whilst at the same time feeling negated by it is to seek isolation. He is then able to remould himself within a new identity through drug use. He sees the way he is *"petted"* as being linked to his drug use. Whilst using drugs, Rod is never able to wholly shed this connection between himself and his family.

Injecting Confidence

I asked Rod why he was using heroin and what role it played in his life. One of the key emerging themes was that it helped him with his confidence.

Rod: Oh, you know like something that'll make... eermm, like build my confidence up and things like that.

Dean: Yes. Is that the major problem you have at the moment?

Rod: Yes.

Dean: Confidence...

Rod: Yes but if I take like heroin, it makes me feel like I can put myself across better and things like that.

Dean: What does the drug actually do then? It helps to give you Dutch courage in some ways? Or does it make you into a person that you want to be?

Rod: I suppose so.

Dean: Mmm...How would you describe the effect of the drug then?

Rod: It makes me forward more, you know what I mean?

Dean: Why is that?

Rod: Where I've been I feel...I've been on it ten years roughly, yeah?

Dean: Yes.

Rod: Before I started taking gear, I'd hold right back, you know what I mean? When I took gear, I put meself across better and things like that.

Dean: Before you were taking gear you were what, back?

Rod: I'd hold meself back, you know what I mean?

Dean: Hold back in terms of what though?

Rod: Talking to people, things like that.

Dean: Talking.

Rod: Like doing things.

Dean: So you had trouble expressing yourself?

Rod: Yehh.

Dean: Right...How did you come across using it?

Rod: People I was mixing with really.

Dean: Was it the same time as everyone else who comes here?

Rod: Uhh..I started use, like, it was early eighties, the boom of it came then. That was when I first started using it, really.

Dean: Yes, can you remember the first time you took it?
Rod: Yes.
Dean: What happened?
Rod: Just had a line, like that line, and just sucked it up like this.
Dean: Yes, then what happened?
Rod: It buzzed me like nothing ever buzzed me before. But it scared me a bit as well. Where it was so strong... well, I just fell down and woke up. I was alright the next day.
Dean: Right...How often did you take it first of all?
Rod: Phh...Not often at all. I was fifteen the first time I took it.
Dean: Yes.
Rod: Then I didn't touch it again until I was eighteen.
Dean: Right. Did it give you any confidence the first time you took it?
Rod: No, not really...
Dean: So it just made you go to sleep? It was 18 then that you began to dabble?
Rod: Yes.
Dean: What brought that on then?
Rod: Dunno, just the people I started hanging about with then.
Dean: Yes.
Rod: Started going out more then.
Dean: This drug gave you the confidence then?
Rod: Yes.

Rod's drug use helped him to end his isolation through being a part of something – a gang – the same as other local Deptford men. When he initially took the drug it *"buzzed him like nothing ever did before"*. Heroin the painkiller provided Rod with access to a different world where he was free from pain and was no longer trapped within his body.

When he started again at eighteen he took the drug because it could help him express himself. I see his heroin use helping him to forget who he is. Therefore, through the process of forgetting the past, he is able to be the person he wants to be, someone *"more forward"* and more outgoing. His use of heroin ends his sense of self-isolation, being trapped within a deformed body that brought jeers from his childhood tormentors. In thinking about his sense of emotional blockage, one of the ideas that I would highlight, drawing on Nietzsche (1984), is that the energy he had previously used in the act of forgetting is now incorporated within his heroin use. He no longer has to suppress his secret emotional world by himself, a strategy that required isolation. Through his drug use, Rod is able to relate to his peers and break out of a previously self-imposed world. Through his drug use, he can act within the world and at the same time forget who he is. He does this with other Deptford men who are involved in their own forms of 'self-medication'.

Flows of Love and Care

Despite everything that has happened to him, Rod is still able to show empathy. In this extract, he describes how he looks after his seriously ill mother. It marks the strong bond of their relationship, where the roles have been reversed. Unlike Phil, Rod can express his care, as he does not have to prove to others he is a 'hard man'.

I was exploring with Rod why he did not go into an Inpatient Detox unit.

Rod: *Plus, me mum's ill at the moment, so I've had to look after her... Got worse than what she usually is...been up since 4 o'clock this morning with her.*

Dean: *Really...you must be really tired, aren't you? How do feel looking after her?*

Rod: *I don't mind looking after her.*

Dean: *No, I mean emotionally.*

Rod: *I feel like, she could go anytime, know what I mean?*

Dean: *Yes...*

Rod: *Like die...'Cos like her breathing is what it is, know what I mean?*

Dean: *Yes.*

Rod: *There ain't a lot I can really do, if she really went into hospital, well, she's got asthma now. She had an attack and that.*

Dean: *Yes. It must be a bit upsetting for you though, isn't it?*

Rod: *Yes...*

Dean: *How are you coping with that?*

Rod: *mmmph...I keep it to myself though, don't I?*

Dean: *Yes. What kind of state is your mum in? Is she panicking?*

Rod: *(Exhales)...Well, she can't go out the house, and like, I have to help her up and down the stairs, know what I mean?*

Dean: *Yes.*

Rod: *But she only does that once, I mean, she wakes up well, bring her down and that's it.*

Dean: *Yes...*

Rod: *Till, like, nighttime and then I take her back up*

Dean: *Is your Dad visiting every day as well?*

Rod: *Yergh. But he's got the flu as well.*

Dean: *Right, so you're scared at the moment your mum's getting worse?*

Rod: *Ehhh.*

Dean: *Right...So you've become a carer?*

Rod: I'm the only who lives at home now.
Dean: Yeah.
Rod: Like my sisters come round in the day but they've got
their own families to look after.
Dean: Yes.
Rod: (Coughs)

I worked with Rod to try and understand the emotional impact of being a carer. He evades the question but I push him to answer. His reply, *"I keep it to myself"*, is part of a familiar strategy. He has learned to hide his feelings, as he has no one to speak to, since his emotional world has never been validated. His feelings are now subsumed within his heroin and methadone use, blocking out his thoughts, particularly those concerning his mother's illness, where *"she may go at any time"*. He speaks about this with a type of numbed detachment.

However, his care is shown through his expression of love and empathy with his mother. Whilst he is expressing his empathy, Rod is also feeling pain at seeing his mother, who was once physically and emotionally strong, disintegrating before him. This pain has haunted him since his childhood, through all of the incidents he has suffered. This time he is faced with the loss of the one emotional bond that has sustained him though his childhood, adolescence and adulthood. He has been able to disassociate himself from this pain by injecting heroin.

The bond between mother and son has developed over the years and he feels safe in expressing his love for his mother by caring for her. This highlights the emotional flow, described in the chapter on "Mother and Son", which Carol Gilligan (1990) analysed as the expression of love and empathy. This expressed feeling of being nurtured provides an insight into the development of Rod's emotional language. This becomes an important part of his ability to show care for his mother when she is ill. I can only speculate, but this bond of empathy may be one of the few golden moments of childhood Rod can recall; it seems part of his 'protective cocoon' that sustains him into the present.

Rod has also become the carer because he is deemed by himself and his family to be too weak to sustain himself in the masculine world of Deptford. Rod has negotiated another role for himself in response to this. He is also lonely, feeling that no woman would want him because of his deformities. He cannot make other bonds because he does not have any confidence in himself. He is able to project confidence through his heroin use, by *"putting himself across easier"*, but this is a façade made necessary through his loss of self-integrity from traumas and bullying.

I also began to see Rod's caring for his mother as another form of disassociation, another strategy that marks his particular form of masculinity: as long as he is caring for her, he does not have to care for himself. He can project outwardly onto his mother what he cannot do for himself. This has seemingly become a self-sacrifice that requires no introspection on his part, a "transference" (Yalom 1989) of feelings of empathy that he can find for significant others but not for himself. I did not want to challenge him about his actions at this point, seeing it as a way that he had managed to find a role for himself that provided a sense of value and worth.

Another strategy he utilised whilst caring for his mother was involvement in crime. This created another tension in his life, as he did not want to go to prison whilst his mother was terminally ill. His involvement in the local criminal subculture allowed him to discharge his anger. Previously, when I had asked him about his victims, he told me *"They're insured aren't they?"* This denoted the limits of his empathy for the 'other', who were seen merely as having objects to be taken. Within this context, the 'flows' Deleuze and Guattari (1972) describe become 'flows of stings' – the objectification of the other – reflecting Rod's own sense of objectification.

This chapter shows how the after-effects of Rod's accidents have had both a physical and an emotional cost where he has tried to keep the latter hidden. These are resonant memories that damage his self-esteem. Rod has seemingly split himself off from these memories by creating his own strategy of distancing himself from the after-effects of trauma.

Through working with Rod, I began to see how his experiences had resonances with those of Sassoon (1972), especially the lack of acknowledgement of experiences and the stifling of a conceptual language to explore pain and experiences. Within Rod's description of his experiences there appears to be no institutional acknowledgement of any emotional after-effects. This connects to Sassoon (1972) and to the other men in this research in not having had their feelings validated, thereby creating a fear in them of self-expression.

Rod's childhood experiences of institutional power resonate with Billy's. They both experienced a top-down approach, the appliance of techniques. Whilst Rod was physically healed, he was emotionally wounded. Billy was emotionally wounded through being taken away from his family. The voices of the children were buried. In Billy's case he wanted to revenge his 'stings' by directly confronting the state. Rod unable to physically compete with other men retreated into heroin use, shrinking away from human contact because he had been continuously hurt for much of his life. He would then seek revenge through acquisitive crime as his form of revenge.

Rod's early adolescent strategy had been to eradicate his feelings and memories through heroin use. However, Rod is able to express his care for a loved on openly, unlike the other men in this study. It is a role where he can dissolve his 'stings', through a return 'flow' of care. He speaks of his feelings of being burdened and his need to fulfil his duty, but I understood that he also loved his mother. He recognised a number of emotions through talking to me; however, recognition was only the beginning because the difficulty was in integrating emotional recognition into behaviour.

The difficulty Rod faces is that he occupies a certain masculine role in the local Deptford culture where consumer goods are swapped, deals undertaken and heroin consumed. Apart from the economic rewards gained from crime, there also arose in the sessions other connections, particularly between crime and a man's emotional state, particularly in the need to discharge 'stings'. Crime within this context operates as a form of revenge for Rod, intertwining with his drug use as another emotional strategy, thereby creating an explosion of emotion followed by a feeling of obliteration.

IX. STRATEGIES OF REVENGE

In this chapter, I will explore how the 'strategies of revenge' – the externalisation of anger – sustain a 'front', and its relationship to crime. All of the men in this study engaged in criminal acts, including Rod. Although all the men claimed that crime was an economic necessity to pay for their heroin and crack, I became aware of another dimension to their criminal acts within an emotional revenge framework.

Drawing on Pete's session, I will look at some key themes; firstly, his inability to dissolve his anger following his humiliation after his marital break-up. In the chapter "Relationships" I outlined how drug use became an emotional insurance policy when relationships dissolved. Here, Pete reveals a connection between his marital breakdown and an attempted armed robbery. Pete relates how his confidence dissolved after this disintegration and revealed a connection between his lack of confidence and his feelings of internal shame. Pete had a choice between holding these feelings in or externalising them. In the session he revealed three strategies: the injection of amphetamines, armed robbery and an addiction to shoplifting.

Cannetti's (1960) 'stings' of humiliation, discharged through vengeance, helped me to understand Pete's emotional turmoil as he coped with the after-effects of the break-up. I became aware how he externalised his anger in various 'strategies of revenge'. This involved a redirection of his humiliation in his desire to externalise his anger, stemming from his shame. The subsequent 'recoil' and the formation of a 'front' are two products of his anger. The formation of the 'front', upheld through wielding power, creates both respect for the acts undertaken as well as awe and fear in the onlooker. The use of drugs such as amphetamines, alcohol and Valium helped him to keep his 'front' intact through subsuming his memories and creating a silence.

I will explore these themes drawing extensively upon Elias Cannetti (1960) and Jim Gilligan (2000), showing how strategies of revenge became so predominant for two particular men, Pete and Rob. Rob's account, in the second section of this chapter, shows how his thinking is colonised by images of violence. It raises a number of themes connected to respect and power, and the creation of awe, both central to these masculine images based on violence.

The Treasure of Silence

Silence, in the context of the work of Deleuze and Guattari (1972) is a break in the flow of emotions, a dam, a holding within. Within this research it also marks the watershed between receiving pain and the externalisation of violence, the transmutation of sadness into anger (Seidler 1991).

This helped me to understand how 'resistances' are formed and then sustained at great personal cost as well as its relationship to the masculinities I am dealing with at Orexis. Cannetti (1960) defines the power of silence and I draw on this to understand how Pete perceives keeping quiet as an internal strength, based upon his suppression of an inner secret. This type of secret was also analysed in the chapter "Violence", discussing Billy returning home to make sure his mother was safe. Here, I want to look at Pete's secret and understand his pain following his relationship collapse, which was compounded by the way she left him.

The secret concealed in silence should never be forgotten. Its possessor is respected for not surrendering it, even though it grows in him and burns him more and more fiercely. Silence isolates. A man who remains silent is more alone than those who talk. Thus the power of self-sufficiency is attributed to him. He is the guardian of a treasure and the treasure is within himself.

Silence inhibits self-transformation. A man who will not speak can dissemble, but only in a rigid way; he can wear a mask, but he has to keep a firm hold of it. The fluidity of transformation is denied him; its result is to be uncertain; he cannot know where it would take him if he surrendered to it. People become silent when they fear transformation. Silence prevents them from responding to occasions for transformation. All men's movements are played out in speech; silence is motionless. (Cannetti 1960, p. 343)

Pete's "secret" is shrouded in silence. Up until the point he, like the others, agreed to be taped as part of this research, he has remained silent. This quote, relating to numerous strands of this research, illuminates why this has occurred. Firstly, it shows how silence creates an aura around it, creating an impression of an internal strength, the use of the will to keep it intact, his "masking process" inhibiting his transformation. However, this does not mean the feelings of shame and humiliation have been eradicated, merely sealed off through the use of substances that help to suppress his memories.

"Silence isolates". Pete defines his masculinity through restricting his emotional expression as an act of strength. The repercussions result in his isolation and inability to express himself. Cannetti (1960) portrays how status and respect is conferred by silence, with status being sustained through the awe of the onlooker. Within a white working class community such as Deptford, respect becomes a defining concept for these men, elevating silence into a positive attribute: "the power of self-sufficiency is attributed to him". Keeping silence is the opposite of 'grassing', a sign of weakness. Billy and his gang uphold the camaraderie of silence in a trial of strength with the authorities. Their impenetrable silence keeps the authorities from impacting upon them as the 'disciplines' are played out through speech. Keeping up a 'front' sustains this silence as a form of strength, the opposite being the creation of flows of communication, the effeminacy of talking.

There is great uncertainty for Pete in dissolving his 'mask' when played out in the realm of speech with me. Whilst the mask is intact, he has a feeling of being in control; shedding the mask entails a descent into the unknown, a dissolving of his 'front'. Within his 'mask' he feels comfortable, he knows the contours and the limitations; a shift means a move into uncertainty. I see Pete sustaining a silence around his feelings of humiliation, propelling him into chronic amphetamine use and armed robbery to sustain his 'front'. The power of silence therefore lies in the background of this extract.

I had been working with Pete for over a year before he began to talk about his experiences. The background to this extract consisted of Pete talking about his marital break-up as he discovered his wife having an affair with another woman. She eventually left him, taking his son and leaving him isolated. This was Pete's secret he felt so ashamed to talk about to anyone else.

Dean: Do you think that's partly what you've been lacking in, self-esteem?
Pete: Oh a hundred per cent, hundred per cent, mmmmm.
Dean: And that was knocked out of you when you split up with your wife, first wife, yeah, just before the affair happened?
Pete: Just before yeah, and that's why I started to WHUMP, right downhill, yeah.
Dean: And from there on in, you got involved in drugs and then you did that robbery?
Pete: Mmmmmm.

This secret burns inside him, and with it he went "downhill", leading to his increased drug use and violence. After he discovered his wife having an affair, his life disintegrated. He left his job and began to watch her, creating a further spiral of distrust.

Pete: Because I found this letter that'd come from the FREAK that Miriam had had the "do-da" with, and I just went "garrottey" about that and I just chucked in me job. Sort of kept dog eye on her all the time and that was it.
Dean: Did your relationship with her finish at that point then?
Pete: No, I kicked her out and she come back. We were back together two weeks, she went again, we come back together and she come... she stayed with me until the robbery happened, yeah?

Pete *"went garrottey"*, as what he had taken for granted began to unwind. In order to create some stability he began to use amphetamines to gain some control and block out his pain by enhancing his feelings of self-confidence and self-belief.

In the chapter "Fathers and Strategies of Coping", Pete's father coped with his secrets through drinking to 'mask' his memories. There are similarities in the keeping of secrets between father and son. The after-effects, the resonance of keeping secrets, the behaviour and substance misuse, results in isolation. The lack of avenues to communicate his sorrow necessitates his need to control his emotions: the anger, shame, distrust and betrayal. He becomes the "the guardian of a treasure" poisoning his external relationships, as he cannot communicate his pain for fear of being seen as weak.

The Descent into Shame

Shame surfaces in many forms in these sessions. I visualise it here as a kind of toxin developed through holding back feelings of humiliation that floods the body; it is a 'bitterness', a deep lack of self-worth based on the dread of being unmasked as worthless. Here, Pete's wife has torn off his 'mask', the 'mask of self-sufficiency', leaving him with residual feelings of not being good enough to sustain a relationship. James Gilligan (2000), describing his experiences working in American prisons, provides the connection between silence, secrets, shame and the 'front' of masculinity of violent men.

> This is a secret that many of them would rather die than reveal; I put it that extremely because many of them, in fact, do die in order not to reveal it. They try so hard to conceal this secret precisely because it is so deeply shameful to them, and of course shame motivates the need

to conceal. The secret is that they feel ashamed, deeply ashamed, over matters so trivial that their triviality makes it even more shameful to feel ashamed about them, so that they are ashamed to reveal even what ashames them. And why are they so ashamed of feeling ashamed? Often violent men will hide this secret behind a defensive mask of bravado, arrogance, "machismo", self-satisfaction, insouciance or studied indifference. Many violent men would rather die than let you know what is distressing them or even that anything is distressing them. Behind the "mask" of the cool or self-assurance that many violent men clamp on their faces with a desperation born of the certain knowledge that they would "lose face" if they ever let it slip, a person feels vulnerable not just to "loss of face" but to the total loss of honour, prestige, respect and status - the disintegration of identity, especially their adult, masculine, heterosexual identity, their self-hood, person hood, rationality and sanity. (James Gilligan 2000, p. 111-112)

Gilligan (2000) does not use the concept of 'fronts', but I feel this is implicit in his use of "machismo". His reference to the 'mask' is related to concealing a secret, as "shame motivates the need to conceal". This halts the complete 'fragmentation' of a "machismo" identity. Pete's use of drugs allows him to cope with his feelings of shame by actively forgetting his past and creating a new identity in the present. However, for Pete, as his session illustrates, these feelings are never completely eradicated, they are merely kept under control. His descent into shame entails creating more shameful acts to seal his 'mask'. Moral value systems based upon empathic relationships become torn as he tries to stop himself from disintegrating. As the process continues, his 'front' is all that he has left.

The creation of 'shame about shame' is a dialectical process pinpointed by Jim Gilligan (2000). This also becomes part of the secret. Each descent into shame creates another 'recoil', another 'shame' which needs to be obliterated. It becomes an endless procession threatening to engulf the man.

In the chapter "Mother and Son", Phil speaks of his shame when he abuses his mother. In that chapter, I showed how this created a 'recoil' allayed by his discharge of violence or becoming *"mellowed out"* through drug use. Pete describes how his sense of inner shame leads to amphetamine use as he tries to forget.

Dean: So your drug use got worse then?
Pete: Tenfold worse, easily, easily.
Dean: So you were trying to cope with the rejection?
Pete: Yeah, but there again that false crutch was there immediately, immediately.
Dean: Did it take away all your hurt?
Pete: Yeah very much so at the time, yeah very much so, but there again when it stopped it was back again worse. When I started again it would go and when I stopped it would come back again. I suppose it took me oooohhh...four or five years before I started to come to terms with it, you know?
Dean: How did you manage to come to terms with it?
Pete: I'm still coming to terms with it now, you know? I DUNNO, I kept going into nick, out of nick, in the nick, out of nick. In the end I lost it all...this SHIT MAN. Why am I doing this? It's only me that's getting hurt and the people that love me, and I started to calm down a bit.

Dean: So it really turned your brain upside down?
Pete: Yeah, completely destroyed it yeah.
Dean: What was the speed doing again?
Pete: Giving me that false hope.
Dean: Giving you confidence?
Pete: Yeahhhh, mmm.
Dean: So it's almost like injecting confidence into yourself?
Pete: MMM, 'cos that's when I started injecting, 'cos I never injected nothing until I was twenty-seven.

Pete reveals what had been hidden and the strategies he used to heal his 'fragmenting' world. Each time he injects, it eradicates his shame until the drugs wear off, and then it reappears. Then there was the crime, which was undertaken not just for money, but as a discharge of anger and humiliation onto a 'substitute'.

Three Strategies of Reversal

1) Drugs

The use of drugs has a dual effect. Pete injects himself, eliminating his shame until it becomes embedded in this eradication. The drugs also have another purpose – they provide him with the confidence to sustain his 'front'. This is only a temporary solution, as when the drugs wear off, his reality begins to flood in once again: the loss of his family, his job and his home. Pete's solution is to take more drugs to make this disappear. This strategy lasted for four years, a form of self-inflicted violence that took his pain within.

This solution to emotional problems is one I analysed in the chapter "Relationships". Simon, Alan and Alex all spoke of how their drug use increased when their relationships disintegrated. Their solution was to block out feelings.

These feelings of loss impact upon Pete's self-esteem and sap his confidence. He is no longer the family man; his wife and son no longer need him. This loss of status and the severing of the emotional connection creates turmoil: *"it turns [his] brain upside down"* as his world has 'fragmented'. I explored with him how his drug use helped to heal this rift, halting his 'fragmentation'.

Dean: Is that one of the problems you've been having then, getting sort of, like, tense. Does that trigger off your drug use?

Pete: Yeah, yeah, I didn't realise that but yeah.

Dean: So instead of punching the wall, you would rather go out and buy some amphetamines.

Pete: As a false crutch, yeah.

Dean: Did the actual injection represent anything to you? Did you have any ideas around your drug use?

Pete: Sorry?

Dean: You know the actual injection at times can be quite painful can't it?

Pete: Yeah, mmmm.

Dean: Did you see that as part of the process of working out your anger, the inflicting of pain on yourself?

Pete: Yeahhh, yeah, yeah, self-inflicted. It all boils down to self-destruction, yeah, yeah but you put up with that, don't you? Because it gets rid of that anger or whatever you've got inside you, ermmm, that might be painful, but the anger you are holding inside you is worse, and more painful than that.

Dean: What happens if you let your anger out? Were you scared of letting that anger out?

Pete: Yeahhh, yeah, mmmm

Dean: Who for, yourself or for others?

Pete: Mainly for others.

Dean: Have you ever been in situations where you've unleashed your anger then?

Pete: ie

Dean: Well, I just can't be bothered to bottle it up by taking drugs, I'm just gonna take it out on someone?

Pete: Oh yeah a few times, yeah, but then I've realised that's not really the way because it's not whoever faults it is who's getting that anger, yeah. And then you turn back to drugs again. You know that helps the anger, doesn't it?

Dean: So it's like a big circular process then?

Pete: Yeah.

Dean: So you don't even feel better when you've let the anger out?

Pete: Oh, you feel good when it's happening, but sometimes you do it to the wrong people, don't you? And that's when it's not really on, but the anger who it should be directed to, it's a much better way, like directing it at the person, you know or whatever the situation, in the end should be. But not people that are innocent, you know. You tend to hurt the ones you love and care for most, don't you?

At this point I prodded Pete to look at why he was injecting, hearing from other users such as Ross that drug use created an "S and M" relationship, with the drug occupying the place of the master and the user the servant. This marks a surrender of control to a 'thing', an object lying outside him, becoming controlled through this surrender, and at the same time feeling the power of being able to make the choice.

This extract provides the link between Pete's anger and his amphetamine use. He knows he is engaged in a process of *"self destruction"*, but he would rather do this than unleash his simmering anger. His drug use helps him to contain this anger through sublimating it, *"because it gets rid of that anger or whatever you've got inside you."* Behind his 'front', Pete makes continual choices and has considerable insight into his usage when he describes it as *"painful, but the anger you are holding inside you is worse, and more painful than that"*.

This simmering anger is not directed at his former wife. Unleashing the anger at her would create a further slip of his "mask of cool self-assurance" (J. Gilligan 2000). It would show he cared for her and was hurt by what she had done. Previously, he had spoken about being *"dog eyed"* watching her every move, looking for signs of betrayal. He also spoke of his desire to have her back, despite everything that had happened between them. However, he also felt hurt by her behaviour – he was caught in a 'double bind'. So instead he turned the anger onto himself, marking his body through his poor injecting practice, seemingly recreating the sites of pain. However, this time he is in control of the infliction of pain. He chooses when to do it and how to do it. It is leading to his self-destruction, but he does not care because his self-esteem is so low.

2) Shoplifting

Another strategy Pete used to externalise his 'stings of shame' was shoplifting, a form of explosion sustaining his 'front' and simultaneously providing the means to buy the drugs. He became an adept kleptomaniac. He had recently been on a Therapeutic Day Program, providing him with the space to reflect on his behaviour with other men. He had tentatively moved to stop his thieving.

Pete: I hope that when I say this, right, gone is that fool which has been going out nicking things, because I haven't been doing that. I hope that's for good, touch wood. I am learning to cope with Lady Temptation, yeah. I can't say it's never tempted me because it has, but I've just ignored and walked on.

Dean: It was almost compulsive behaviour before, wasn't it?

Peter: MMMM, mmm very addictive, yeah, and very much so.

Dean: What was making you do it? I know there was need...

Peter: Er, I think it was an inside cry for help perhaps, Dean, yeah, you know, subconsciously, you know. Wanting to be, I dunno, wanting to be needed, loved, I don't know, I don't know how to put it.

Dean: By Miriam or what, society?

Peter: Everyone, society mainly, yeah, yeah.

Dean: Were you getting a buzz from nicking then?

Peter: Oh yeah, oh yeah, definitely, but it's the wrong sort, isn't it?

Dean: Planning it, you mean, planning or doing it?

Peter: No, the actual doing it more than planning it.

Dean: What about when you got the stuff home? Did you still get the same buzz or did you think, oh, I've got it now?

Peter: You still get a buzz, but it's not as good as going in doing it, getting it and getting out. That was the right good buzz, the actual getting away with it, yeah.

Dean: I suppose that became addictive though, didn't it?

Peter: Yeah, mmm, but it's been er....three months. It's quite a long time really, for me.

Dean: Mind you, there's nothing much anyone can say to help you in the future.

Peter: I know that, I know that.

Dean: The courts get a bit tired after a while.

Pete: I've had every sentence possible, to deter me from it, you know.

Dean: Is that the only time you've been to prison then, when you've been on remand?

Pete: No, no, no, I've had three sentences, and four lots of remand, yeah.

Dean: Does prison frighten you then, going in there?

Pete: It doesn't scare me, Dean, because I make the most of it. I don't like it at all, you know. But when you're there you've just got to do it haven't you? There's no use just sitting there going uuuu, that's life isn't it?

In asking Pete why he stole, two answers emerge: he receives *"a buzz"*, and he wants to be loved by society. In reflecting on the connection between the two answers, I was initially struck by a puzzle. I could understand his need to shoplift to feed his drug habit, which was the solution to an economic problem. I could also comprehend the 'risk-taking' (Giddens 1991) involved, a notion I explored in the chapter "Violence". The *"buzz"* may have evolved from undertaking this 'risk-taking strategy', which would explain the basis for the punishment in stopping him. The euphoria of creating a "buzz" connects with his initial use of amphetamines and to his description of his father's *"buzz"* from being the *"life and soul of the party"* as he became progressively inebriated. Pete' s father portrays a 'front' of "puissance", an expression of his joy of life but he is also destroying himself as he 'masks' his painful memories.

To have no one show interest in, pay attention to, or admire one's distinctive assets can deprive one of pride, as strongly as others look too closely at one's personal liabilities can expose one to shame, but the net result in the economy of self-

320

esteem is the same…The poor man tends to be ignored and disdained when he would like to be noticed, and exposed or attacked when he would like to have his privacy respected. Both constitute forms of slighting. (James Gilligan 2000, p. 198)

This marks one of the shameful effects of poverty – to wander around unnoticed. Pete's shoplifting marks his existence and his need to be loved, existing within a tension of revenge aimed at the State. The emotions arising from his shoplifting exploits are complex. They involve more than just mastery or a method of upholding masculinity but, surprisingly, also include a hidden cry for help: *"Er, I think it was an inside cry for help perhaps, Dean. Yeah, you know, subconsciously, you know."* Pete would not seek out external help for fear of being labelled as mad or bad. He found his own means of rescuing himself from his depression whereby he could uphold his 'front' and hide his feelings. This 'cry' is undertaken through an act of revenge, providing him with a sense of euphoria in taking items from shops. However, like the drugs, this euphoria quickly wears off. He needs a constant fix to overcome the sense of dread at his actions. The shoplifting becomes addictive, as does his amphetamine use. They both appear to sustain his 'mask' of self-sufficiency, halting his 'fragmentation' by giving him the appearance of being in control.

He becomes engaged in an escalation of wills: Pete versus the State. Prison does little to reform his actions, as he sees it as occupational hazard. The applied disciplinarian force does not cause Pete to reflect on his behaviour. Instead, it strengthens his resolve to continue by creating a 'resistance'. Seemingly, this form of behaviour is the only way he can reclaim his self-esteem and escape the obscurity of poverty by making himself noticed.

3) Armed Robbery

Another strategy Pete pursued during the break-up of his relationship marked a different form of revenge. Pete's drug use began to escalate as he tried to cope with his 'fragmenting' world. He began to sell amphetamines and cannabis to sustain his habit. It was whilst doing this that he met an acquaintance who had just come out of prison.

Dean: *From there on in you got involved in drugs and then you did that robbery.*
Peter: *MMM.*
Dean: *How did the robbery come about?*
Peter: *Well I was knockin' out gear and then ermm, this guy who used to come round and score off me, he's a smackhead, but he used to come round and get bits of puff off me right, and er, he's in and out of nick all his life, Mr, ermm what's the word, when you go in and out of nick all the time you become?*
Dean: *Institutionalised.*
Peter: *Mr. Institutionalised, that's it. He come round and he's always telling me how he's done this, done that and how he's got this bit of money, and like, I was on a right low ebb one day 'cos me money, I was just spunking me money, it was all going, yeah, and he come round with this idea that there was loads of dough round at this garage, blah blah, and I didn't have any money. I owed out some money. I want all of it, bang bang, bang, that was it. I was gullible.*
Dean: *So you went up there with a gun.*
Peter: *Imitation, yeah...*
Dean: *How did they catch you, were you on video?*

Peter: No, through his girlfriend. They asked her and she just told them like where Pete had been, who Pete had been with. That was it.

Dean: So you got the money then?

Peter: Yeah, not much though. We was about eight minutes too late to get the big lot. It was £89.

Dean: Eighteen hundred?

Peter: Eighty-nine pounds.

Dean: Eighty-nine pounds?

Peter: Eighty-nine, yeah, we just missed out on seven grand. Sent us on depositions, me mate being a junky had to have his fix before he done it, yeah uhhm. That kept us a little bit late. When we got there all there was was the till money.

Pete describes the robbery stemming from a *"low ebb"*. At this juncture his friend suggested they work together to rob a garage. Pete could have refused, however he was using all his money to buy drugs and he owed someone money. This meant he had to take some form of action for his own safety and self-esteem. This represented another crisis point for Pete, and marked an escalation in his coping strategy when he decided to go along with the robbery suggestion.

Pete says he did it for practical reasons – money – and because he was vulnerable. It was not really something that he wanted to do; it was his friend's suggestion. Pete is trying not to present an image of a 'hard man' to me, but of someone who was easily led – in his words, *"gullible"*. This can be explained by the fact he was caught at his first attempt. This was also his defence when he went to court and, I suspect, a notion he had internalised in describing his actions.

Thinking why he chose to do this at this particular time, I see another dynamic operating. The major underlying event is his disintegrating relationship. He does not tell me he went to rob the garage because his wife was having an affair with a woman and was on the verge of leaving him. What he does narrate is a series of incidents, a narration similar to Rod's, illustrating a divorce between emotion and events. To some extent he is presenting another type of 'front' in keeping hold of his dignity while talking to me. I work with him to see if there is a connection between the collapse of his relationship, his inner rage and his drug use. Pete speaks through inferences. While he wants to talk about his actions, at the same time he does not want to tell me too much about his emotions for fear I may hurt him, or perhaps laugh or ridicule him for his 'sentimentality' towards and care for his wife.

This analysis of armed robbery as more than a desire to gain riches resonates with James Gilligan's "Violence" (2000). This provides a similar analysis of men who commit violent acts, linking the themes of revenge and respect.

> Some people think armed robbers commit crimes in order to get money. And of course sometimes, that is the way they rationalise their behaviour. But when you sit down and talk with people who repeatedly commit such crimes, what you hear is, "I never got so much respect before in my life as I did when I first pointed a gun at somebody" or, "You wouldn't believe how much respect you get when you have a gun pointed at some dude's face". For men who have lived for a lifetime on a diet of contempt and disdain, the temptation to gain instant respect in this way can be worth far more than the cost of going to prison, or even of dying. (James Gilligan 2000, p. 109)

Pete realises his drug use "*helps the anger, doesn't it*"? In his narration, other reasons for the armed robbery materialise. It was not just because he needed money; he was selling cannabis and using the proceeds to buy amphetamines but he was using so much and had fallen into debt. His confidence had drained away and the security of his world was shattered. I could see he was emotionally 'fragmenting', supported only by his "*false crutch*". I could see his reasons for undertaking the robbery, as a need for him to compensate for his failure and to obliterate what had happened to him. I also felt there was a need for him to re-establish pride and respect, two concepts intertwined with his masculinity to such an extent that they overrode all other courses of action at this point.

Within this framework, drawn from James Gilligan (2000), Pete takes part in the robbery as an act of self-assertion. He rises above the hidden poor, becoming a man of self-esteem by having the 'bottle' to go and rob a garage with a gun. He has received the 'stings' of humiliation from his wife (his care is not enough for her) and now he discharges the humiliations onto a substitute. Within this extract from Cannetti (1960), there is an explanation for the development of the systems of revenge based upon the creation of a silence, resonating with Winnicott (1965).

> It is very difficult to get rid of the sting. It must in fact dislodge itself and can only do so if and when it reacquires force equal to that with which it originally penetrated. For this to happen there must be an exact repetition of the original command-situation, but in reverse. This is what the sting waits for through months, years and decades. It

is though each sting had a memory of its own, but of one thing only: the situation in which it was implanted. When the situation occurs, the sting cannot fail to recognize it, for this is its sole content. Suddenly everything is as it was before; only the roles of the actors are reversed. When this moment comes, the sting seizes its opportunity and hastens to fall on its victim. The reversal has at last taken place. (Cannetti 1960, p. 380)

The above quote points to a clear case of revenge for a clearly defined act. However, the relationship between the attack on the garage and Pete's loss of his wife is not a reversal. It is a displacement of his anger onto a substitute. I was not able to work with Pete to discover whom he really blamed. I suspected it was partly himself, as he wanted his wife back. He spoke of how he carried memories of their relationship, reflecting on how it had sustained him in the past.

The act of armed robbery produces adrenaline, similar to an initial injection of amphetamines, creating a *"buzz"*. Taking amphetamines involves a soothing of anxiety though the injection of confidence. It also produces disorientation and a feeling of grandeur. Armed robbery, as described by J Gilligan (2000), is also about exercising physical and emotional power over another person, getting them to bend their will to that of the protagonist – an act of merging through fear. The 'stings' of command flow from the protagonist onto a victim, the cashier. The waving of the gun produces total control. Jim Gilligan (2000) shows how this act of power becomes intoxicating in itself, enhancing the feelings of omnipotence: "the temptation to gain instant respect in this way can be worth far more than the cost of going to prison, or even of dying" (J Gilligan 2000).

The act produces respect because of its direct confrontation with the State, breaking all the taboos concerning restraint and societal values. The fact that Pete's first attempt at armed robbery came after the breakdown of his relationship led me to think that Pete may be trying to reverse the accumulated stings, but this does not connect back to the original site of his pain. He has chosen to take part in an act where he feels he can reverse his crumbling self-esteem. In this case, he thinks he has found a reversal. The inherent problem is that the cashier has not harmed Pete. In being a recipient of his violence, she had to contend with receiving her 'stings': a gun being pointed at her and the fear that her life may be taken away at any moment. She did not know the gun was a fake. Subsequently she would have to deal with the after-effects of this incident, creating her own problems of PTSD. This shows how strategies of violence ripple and enmesh, due to the actions of Pete's 'front'. Each act entails a further resonance impacting upon other people's lives. The discharge of 'stings' entails the sublimation of feelings of empathy and an objectification of the victim, a negation of her right to exist. Pete at this point had lost his feelings of empathy for others, highlighting the split between his use of force and his lack of empathy.

The ongoing problem for Pete is twofold: his actions create a 'recoil' inside him, an internal shame; secondly, this substitute for the displacement of anger, where he is now the protagonist, is only a temporary fix for his emotional turmoil.

I want to show how the strategies of revenge develop and what role they play in the reversal of 'stings', where humiliation is built upon successive layers. It also points to how substitutes are chosen when

...the sting loses its clear outline and develops into a monster which endangers life. It grows until it forms the main substance of its host. He can never forget it and carries it around, seeking any opportunity to get rid of it. He finds innumerable situations which seem like the original one and thus suitable for reversal. But they are not. The command has been repeated so often and from so many angles that the original situation has been obscured and he can no longer find the key to it. One memory has overlaid another, as one sting on another sting. His burden can no longer be broken up into its elements. Whatever he attempts his general situation remains the same. Alone he is no longer capable of freeing himself from his burden. (Elias Cannetti 1960, p. 381)

This highlights how armed robbery can become an addiction in itself. For example, Pete would need to undertake this act continuously to achieve the same feeling, as it becomes a temporary displacement, highlighting how a psychological addiction forms. "Whatever he attempts, his general situation remains the same". The 'stings' have layered to the extent where they "have lost their clear outline." Revenge becomes an end in itself, a need for discharge, upon whom it does not matter.

The effect of the armed robbery was to deepen the rift between Pete and his wife. In an attempt to show her what type of man he was, he felt she would return. After the court case finished, Pete still had his amphetamine problem but he had lost his wife and son as well as his flat. He was deeply hurt by his wife's abandonment of him, as she had provided an anchor after having grown up in a family marked by "emotional fatherlessness" (Heinl 2001).

Images of Respect

I want to shift the analysis at this point to look at why images of crime, drawing on Rob's words, have become dominant in creating these masculinities. Gilligan (2000) illuminates the importance of the means by which wealth is acquired for these men. Whilst they have all been involved in crime to gain money for their drug use, they were also involved in crime prior to their drug use. Pete described prison as 'hard' emotionally, due to his having been torn away from his family, but also something he accepts and gets on with. It's part of his lifestyle.

Pete revealed his need to be loved, which I linked to his need to escape from the invisibility of poverty by becoming someone important, respected and feared. Pete's robbery was a failure, but I am left feeling that if it had succeeded he would have continued upon this path until he was caught. The importance of armed robbery is in the respect it engenders, a hushed awe, a fear created through having a reputation as a man of violence. This is also apparent with other men involved in armed robbery and murder, not part of this study, whom I have worked with.

Criminality as a form of revenge

Rob related how images of crime gripped his imagination. I have heard expressed a similar respect for armed robbers from many other men in the counselling sessions. Gary, for example, told me he was in awe of local men who flaunted their wealth, believing their stories of excitement. This glamour was something he wanted to emulate. Once he embarked upon his emulation he realised the hollowness of their 'fronts'. As he sat in prison cells, he spoke of how they had not mentioned the boredom of being locked away.

Thinking of the power of these initial images, I will draw together some of the themes emerging from this research. Initially, these men were recipients of emotional violence at home and then in institutions before they began to discharge their own violence. The local images are important for gaining a sense of the outside world and its expectations. The "Great Train Robbery", the Kray twins and the exploits of local hard men have become part of Deptford white working class mythology. These events and personalities seemingly mark a wider cultural 'resistance' to the invisibility and shame of poverty, producing a local respect for an ability to reverse 'stings'.

The alternative route of education is perceived as flimsy compared with the status real men have in the world (Willis 1978). The reversal of 'stings' begins in school, with its emphasis on 'discipline', particularly in secondary school, from where all of these men had been excluded or expelled. School is deemed not to be a real preparation for manhood (Willis 1978). That preparation exists in the male world outside.

I want to look at these images drawn from Rob's session, as they provide a way of understanding how his actions became channelled in one particular direction. In this extract, Rob is speaking about how he views the world around him, resonating with Parker in Newburn and Stanko (1994).

Rob's World

Rob has been in and out of prison continuously since adolescence. In previous sessions he had spoken briefly of his family dynamics: his father's alcohol use and his power within the family. He revealed that his mother had eventually asked his father to leave. He now feels sorry for his father, who lives alone with no one to care for him. This session marked the limits of our relationship and showed how much he trusted me. Subsequently, Rob revealed what occurred in his family, and the nature of the physical and sexual abuse he suffered from another counsellor.

Rob revealed he had been using heroin since he was eighteen. When he took part in this research he was twenty-nine. By the time he sat down to talk in this extract, he had spent seven out of eleven years of his adult life in prison for various violent offences. He was subsequently sentenced again for an act of violence – revenging a slight against a friend.

The session with Rob shows the contours of the criminal world he inhabits. His social world is wholly reflected through this prism formed through his recurrent spells of incarceration. Rob sees nothing beyond the world bounded by the prison system and his criminal lifestyle. As I worked with him to shift this perception, I became locked within it also, as he had little conception of life outside. Within this session, I thought I had made a breakthrough when he questioned the respect accorded to armed robbers. He saw it as a charade, realising the long prison sentences they received marked a failure rather than a victory over the State. However, instead of this putting him off, he replaced it with another more extreme image – that of the 'face', a man who directs events rather than engages in them. This marked the limit of how far we could work together in unravelling the 'front' he had created.

Rob was far from ready to analyse what sustains a 'front', as he was locked within his vision of crime, violence and drug misuse. His session shows the journey that other men in this research have made in revealing aspects of their personal histories. Rob provides an insight into the defences he has erected in fending off any reflection on his personal history.

Rob: I know at the end of the day when you pick up a gun, Dean, you go into a place, you gotta be prepared to use it. 'Cos if you're with your pal and you got to shoot that Gabba, right, you got to shoot him to get out of the way, or if you don't shoot him, you're gonna do some. And I would not like that responsibility left on my shoulders. Do you know what I mean?
Dean: Yeah.
Rob: That's a lot of responsibility to take. That's why that circles there is not for me. They all give it the biggun, but when they get their "birds", they get their "birds". You see them on remand. I know, I say to myself, look at them. I think to myself, "alright getting your visits everyday mate, you get your big parcel, you got your clobber or whatever", but at the end of the day that's not helping them while they are in there, Dean, ten years and all that. Who wants to be wrapped up in jail for ten, fifteen years? You have to do a full ten before you even think about coming out or parole. No, they can keep their gangster life. I prefer to be, that's what I say... in our little role, you're (meant to) look up to a geezer who's done a ten or a fifteen. I don't. I look at him and think he's a mug, and a really unlucky cunt, you know what I mean? That's how I look at him, really unlucky, because to me the

person that don't go to prison is the "face", you know what I mean? And the sensible one, the ones that are in prison doing ten, fifteen, sixes and sevens. They're not the "faces" because there are no "faces" in prison. They go about, they're "faces", but at the end of the day the "Screws" are the "faces", 'cos when they take you down the block and give you a hiding, you ain't got no one on that stair or landing or down that block. Alright a few riots have kicked off, but I'm sure that ain't just been down to one geezer, do you know what I mean? Everyone just helping just one man. It's loads of different things going on, and everyone just took that one day, and kicked off.

Dean *Yeah?*

Rob: *You know whereas if you're a "face" on the street, you can get other people to do your dirty work, but inside you're in prison and you're not coming out of that little thing there so it don't come to play to give it the "Chap". I mean at the end of the day, the "Screws" are the Governors, that's why we call them "Gov". They do run the show even though they do turn a blind eye. When they get pissed off with it, they come in for yer, you know what I mean? And it's just you and them and they always win. They'll always win you know what I mean?*

Dean :*Yeah.*

Rob: *That's why I'm not really into that, Dean. I'm not into that limelight. It pays a lot of money but it's too much "bird" and I don't think I've got it in me at the end of the day, to get a gun and shoot someone, and that takes a lotta…that takes a lotta hate, do you know what I mean, Dean? That takes a lot of hate.*

The link between Rob and Pete arises in Rob's perception of armed robbery not as an act of glamour, but as the expression of an emotional need. This relates back to robbery as an act of revenge. Although Pete did not express his need to revenge his humiliation explicitly, Rob provides an insight and a connection to the work of James Gilligan (2000) and Cannetti (1960). Rob speaks about needing to have a *"lot of hate"* to undertake a robbery. The question is hatred for whom? What occurs in the above text is a connection between the emotional state of the protagonist and his capability of carrying out the act. James Gilligan (2000) highlighted how the act is more than just a method of obtaining money. However, it is also something more than wanting to assert male dignity. Contained within the act is a need to discharge hatred, which illuminates how Cannetti's (1960) conceptual thinking helps to explain the systems of revenge.

This hatred is held as a form of anger, sustaining the 'front'. Rob talks of the 'front' these men show when *"they give it the biggun"*. This 'front' is kept intact through silence, holding back a smouldering secret wanting to burst forward. Although Rob does not specify where the anger stems from, it becomes directed at particular targets: cashiers behind desks, or security guards; people with mundane, unglamorous jobs.

When Pete went to the garage with his imitation gun, he asserted control, thereby allowing his hatred to find a focus. The passage from James Gilligan (2000) shows how the act creates a feeling of power, allowing the discharge of violence. Underlying this need to assert power is a feeling of deficit, emerging in Pete's session. This provides a way of understanding systems of revenge based upon the flow of emotions.

Rob has reflected upon the psychological rationale behind criminal lifestyles, having had considerable time to think and observe whilst in prison. Within the prison system, he understands how men have constructed 'fronts'. Rob spoke of the 'front' of the *"blagger"*, the armed robber, and how this creates respect through engendering awe. Within the prison system, everyone is subject to humiliations when incarcerated; everyone loses 'face' being subject to the prison regime. The prisoners can construct 'resistances' and bully other inmates, but they are all locked up each evening.

Another aspect to his description of life in prison are the resonances with Billy's 'Home', the 'police cells', and Rod's 'special school'. It conveys a feeling of being at the mercy of institutional forces. Within the prison, the use of violence by the institution is ever-present and, in Rob's account, taken for granted. *"When they get pissed off with it, they come in for yer, you know what I mean? And it's just you and them and they always win. They'll always win, you know what I mean?"* Rob describes how the 'resistances' that are put in place dissolve under the social reality of being bounded by the prison walls. The group 'resistance' dissolves when the prison officers move on an individual. He can expect little help when he is taken *"down the block"*. The force of the State can dissolve a carefully cultivated 'front' at any moment.

It is through this experience that Rob challenges the respect given to armed robbers, replacing them with another, more violent, figure. He is in awe of the respect given to the man who directs events – the 'face'. Prison has done little to change Rob's core beliefs concerning criminality as a way of life. He only wants to be more successful at it.

Upholding Respect

The 'face' is the man who garners respect, the man who directs the violence. After discharging his hatred, the 'face' creates respect by making other men bend to his will. This is achieved through fear, stemming from the notion that violence can be inflicted with no one there to protect you. The 'face' directs the violence but does not become involved himself, this creates and sustains the respect he commands. However the spectator only sees the 'face', as indicated, from the 'front'. What lays hidden is the terror of being unmasked. (Cannetti 1960) 'Fragmentation' seemingly occurs when he is slighted and fails to respond appropriately, thereby shattering the illusion. Therefore, in maintaining his 'front' the 'face' needs violence to feed it, thereby sustaining a reputation. This acts as a currency, creating another 'flow' of fear.

There is also a link between adolescent gang violence and criminality: both involve the avenging and discharging of 'stings'. Here, Billy talks of his adolescence before he moved into crime: *"In them times, there used to be a gang of us and we even used to travel to different areas and fight with other gangs, and done a lot of them, and got a sort of reputation".*

Gaining a reputation means having others respect you. Within this spectrum, respect is the direct opposite of shame. The gangs are where Rob learnt to create a 'front' through being able to engage in acts of revenge, testing the boundaries of the disciplines and enduring punishment. For Rob, however, being involved in the drug culture does not create respect. Pete speaks about his friend who is a "junky", someone who shoots up heroin. This is a derogatory title, emphasising uncleanliness and lack of control. Since he shoots up amphetamines, Pete sees himself as being above his friend, believing he has more control over his drug use. This is revealed to be an illusion, albeit one that comforts him. His behaviour is no different than many men I have worked with who use heroin except that his addiction is cheaper to sustain.

Rob wanted to stop his heroin use because he felt it demeaned him, as he wanted to be a more successful criminal. The drugs devalued his currency of awe. However, I saw how his drug use had become interwoven within his life as a coping strategy, allowing him to project the image of being a 'hard man'. Rob's shift from one violent image to another seemingly rests upon his acknowledgement of "hatred" being a catalyst. I felt Rob was projecting his desire to be in control, wanting to be the 'face'. He had a strong desire to be outside of the system. I want to show the link between the need to create respect and Rob's imagery. At this point I realised Rob was at a crossroads, wrestling with himself over how he was going to proceed. In illustrating this turmoil, I will draw again on James Gilligan (2000).

> I have yet to see an act of violence that was not provoked by the experience of feeling ashamed and humiliated, disrespected and ridiculed, and that did not represent the attempt to prevent or undo this "loss of face" - no matter how severe the punishment, even if it includes death. For we misunderstand these men, at our peril, if we do not realize they mean it literally when they say they would rather kill or mutilate others, be killed or mutilate themselves, than live without pride, dignity and self-respect. They literally prefer death to dishonour. (James Gilligan 2000, p. 110)

James Gilligan (2000) writes about the need to "undo the loss of face", providing a direct link to Cannetti's (1960) ideas concerning the need for "reversal of stings". This has a resonance with street slang: the powerful man who comes to prominence requires a cool exterior to present to the outside world – the 'face' needs a 'mask'.

In order to create this image, empathy has to be subsumed, along with the feelings of shame. The need to keep the 'front' intact becomes a way of understanding Pete and Rob's acts of violence. This helped me to understand criminality as a form of enacting violence. Underlying these 'fronts', keeping them rigidly in shape, are feelings of 'lack' and the need to deflect any possible attacks upon the 'front'. Therefore, shame and respect are at the opposite ends of a polarity. It is this polarity that becomes a defining feature of Rob's worldview. Respect entails the feeling of being valued by others, of acting powerfully upon the world and also an escape from invisibility. Pete tries to gain respect through asserting power within a public arena. Having as his goal an attempt to attain power and create awe becomes a way of understanding his actions. The 'front' becomes a 'face', constructed through admiration, awe and fear coming from other men. Although he denies it in the session, Rob is also engaged in this process. Power without attention is meaningless for these men's masculine identities, and this is why armed robbery is given so much status – it is because it is a direct confrontation between the man and the State, with the prize being an escape from the poverty of working class life. It is the reversal of the 'stings' of institutions, but as Pete shows in his extracts, it also can become located within specific dynamics of family life.

The world of violent crime provides a forum for men such as Rob and Pete to acquire status as they become locked in a battle of wills with institutional power structures. After acquiring power, other men will gaze upon them with awe and fear.

For Rob, the worldview he has constructed revolves around crime, where he can assert his own form of respect. Once Rob has moved into this world, his options for escape are increasingly foreclosed because of the cycles of revenge within which he is enmeshed. He does not have any work skills, but has plenty of contacts in the underworld. Once locked into this peer group, it is difficult to escape because he is known by his 'front'.

This links to an insight Damien provided into the power of 'fronts': *"I cultivated my self into being a fucking nutter and I became trapped into being one, then I wanted to be the biggest criminal"*. He cannot shed this 'front' without the loss of his creation, his reputation as a man of power. As an adolescent, Damien had asserted himself with his reputation, so he could gain respect. In Rob's world he has worked out how to get status within this environment. Pete is also trapped within this world, as his numerous criminal convictions for shoplifting testify.

Within the wider Deptford culture, drug use has become so widespread the stigma of Class A drug use has diminished. The drug user also plays a role in the community, providing cheap stolen goods to the wider community of 'non-drug users'.

Crime, in the form of violent acts, becomes more than just a reduction to economics, the need to earn money to sustain an addiction. It becomes integral to the addiction as a strategy of inflicting 'stings' onto the wider community through symbolic acts of violence

– shoplifting – or physical acts such as armed robbery, which Rob portrays explicitly as being linked to hatred

Acts of violence become externalised in many different forms, but they also contain the desire to be noticed and stand out from the invisible crowd, thereby creating awe in the onlooker. They are, however, acts that these men become trapped within, requiring numerous displays to sustain the 'front'. It is this continuous process which consumes them, creating a gulf between their feelings of empathy and their desire to become known and feared. This results in emotional isolation, in not wanting to connect with their victims, whilst at the same time enjoying the exertion of power created by engaging in the act, the *"buzz"*. These acts based upon the separation sustain masculinities, which would become the presentation by which they are known unless other avenues such as those displayed in these counselling sessions existed. It is through this process, even if only for an hour per week, that they can dissolve their 'front' and reveal what has been hidden – their emotional lives – and what drives them to sustain their act.

X. CONCLUSION

This research interweaves many of the themes emerging from the counselling of these white men in the latter part of the twentieth century. I am aware the parameters of the research meant issues relating to race (whiteness) were embedded and ideas on homosexuality were not part of the study and the class position was stated as a given rather than explored. I will draw together some of the findings in this chapter, then highlight the gaps this research illuminates and the process of verification, before looking at further research paradigms.

This study was centred upon these white men's emotional experiences and how these were articulated in the sessions. Within this context, these men's violence directed onto other men and women around them flowed through the prism of the 'masking' process, sublimating empathic emotions, with only anger emerging, creating an emotional distance and leading to isolation. The anger flowed onto other men and women, perceived as 'other', implying a lack of empathic connection. The effect of this individual violence, I contend, sustains a wider local culture.

I have shown how these men's worlds are bounded by the 'flows' of violence and care emanating from fathers and mothers and by the physical and emotional violence emanating from local institutions, creating a social nexus of submerged and overt anger where desire has become channelled through the bondage of masculinities. Within this context, these men's drug use is part of this 'flow', a desire for sublimation and euphoria within strict parameters of emotional expression these men feel they can show publicly and privately.

In terms of this research, I have shown how notions of white masculinities are deeply embedded and sustained in these men's everyday worlds, and how they were formed as coping strategies when they were children. This is primarily derived from the care these men received from their mothers and the violence they suffered from their fathers. I have located the issue of this violence within the nexus of historical events that have shaped life in twentieth century Deptford and South London: the world wars, the poverty, and the emphasis on regenerating buildings instead of people, along with the economic booms and recessions of the postwar period.

This research analyses the sublimation of emotional empathy derived from neglect, and the emotional and physical violence derived from a group of men revealing their childhood experiences. This violence was part of a flow of repressed emotions their fathers held, emerging through the prism of their masculinities. This appears in Gary and Pete's recollections of their fathers' experiences, where the past is kept as a silence, linked to stoicism and the inability to find the emotional space to describe their problems. These fathers' lacked emotional connections with their children, particularly their sons. This resonates with Pasolini's Oedipus Rex (1967) and Alex's revealing statement concerning his jealousy when his son was born. This led me to reflect on the fathers' jealousy of their sons due to the strong bonds these children had with their mothers. This meant the one person they had developed a bond with, their wife, had turned her attention onto her children, creating an emotional distance. The fathers could not communicate this sense of loss, as it meant exposing their vulnerability. Their use of alcohol also helped to suppress these feelings through a form of shrinking away from contact, creating distance, or exploding. Violence was used to reinstate their power. This had the effect of tearing apart this early mother/child bond, creating a 'double bind' for their sons, where feelings of love, terror and hatred emerged at the same time, leading to unresolved tensions that were stored within the body.

Their fathers' violence also became justified, as Bri narrated in a later session, as part of a toughening-up process for their sons, as they were expected to take their place in a social environment where men were hardened to pain. I see this as a self-justification for violence, a form of masculine 'care' in preparing their sons to exist in the social world through brutalising them.

The sons received this violence, enduring the 'stings', and tearing the empathic mother-son connection. Caught within this 'double bind' of empathy and hatred, as John, Simon, Gary and Billy describe, they learned to sublimate their pain through the process of 'masking'. Instead, they created their own 'fronts', and learned the ability to wield their own forms of violence. This began to become dominant after they had attacked their fathers. This flows from Billy's session, as he revealed the strong bond he had with his mother the concern he showed for her, whilst at the same time coping with the emotional violence wielded by his father.

The institutions these boys entered operated in a gulf between discipline and understanding. This is a separation needing further research, but it depends on notions of empathic understanding being secondary to the use of emotional/physical force. The institutions within this conceptual analysis are seemingly built upon the same emotional split as the men's families. Rod and Billy describe their experiences at a school that failed to acknowledge their traumas. Billy fought against the school disciplines, whilst Rod retreated from the social world because of the emotional pain he was enduring. It transpired whatever the school had to offer in terms of sanctions was nothing compared to what they had already undergone at home. Rod's strategy was one of 'shrinking', of shutting himself off, whilst Billy's behaviour was labelled as truancy, although he revealed to me that he was worried about his mother's safety. The resulting punishment entailed both of these boys being taken away from their families. This lack of understanding of their emotional worlds created a further humiliation, which these boys revenged through creating their 'resistances' by 'masking' these humiliations and projecting a 'front'.

This 'resistance' emerged through the coalescence of gangs, where these Deptford boys, the recipients of 'stings' in their families and institutions, created a "reversal crowd" (Cannetti 1960). It is in the gang that these boys attempted to reverse and discharge the 'stings' they had endured, initially onto other boys and then upon the men and women who wield institutional power. There was a shift from undertaking physical violence to symbolic violence through theft and burglary, which also becomes part of an emotional reversal, the firing of 'stings' onto others. This occurs consistently in many men I have worked with, preceding their drug use.

The stakes are then raised, entailing further confrontations with the police, judiciary and prison authorities, where further State violence is used to discipline these young men. However, all the Deptford men, as well as Alex and Damien, accepted juvenile detention and prison as a rite of passage. It was seen as the making of them into real men, like the men who surrounded them in Deptford that appeared hardened and economically successful. These men accepted giving and receiving pain, creating 'fronts' as defences and the toughening up process they had endured as helping them to operate in this culture.

It took a great deal of trust to shift beyond the 'front', and this can be seen in the session with Gary as he wrestles with himself in deciding how much to reveal to me. For example, Gary described his initial use of heroin as experimentation. In talking to him, he appeared disconnected from the emotional turmoil of his father's illness, drawing on peer pressure as an explanation for his drug use. Far from being turned off when he saw a group of men who had sold off all of their possessions, he was drawn to it. This raises important implications for drug education as a strategy in stopping drug use.

This same process of deciding how much to reveal to me also occurred with John and Simon, who, towards the end of their sessions, described how their heroin use helped to eradicate all of their emotional problems. Heroin in this context is described as a form of emotional release, a euphoria that shrinks the reality of their pain.

These men faced very clear challenges when they tried to form and sustain relationships. All of these men, apart from Rod, tried to sustain a relationship with a female partner. In all cases these relationships disintegrated due to their inability to cope with the emotional and monetary demands made upon them. This became particularly exacerbated when their children were born and they began to feel left out and useless. This led to arguments and a return by Wayne, Simon and Alex to heroin as an emotional insurance policy, creating further isolation as their relationships disintegrated. They self-medicated to cope with the emotional after-affects.

One of the key links between this 'emotional insurance policy' and crime became clear when Pete described how he tried to assert his self-esteem by committing an armed robbery. This led me to understand his actions as a way of discharging his 'stings' onto another body through pointing a "fake" gun at a cashier at the same time as regaining the power he felt had been stolen from him by his wife. At the same time, he tried to inject confidence into himself in an attempt to cope with his sense of loss.

Rob's comments show the parameters of these men's worlds, the respect accorded to men who have the 'bottle' to use a gun and how this local culture of respect resonates with James Gilligan's (2000) research in the USA. It is this culture of respect that creates the parameters of men's ability to express themselves in the Deptford environment. There is minimal space to explore empathic emotions, as these men have to uphold their 'fronts' at all times.

Coinciding with the findings of Vic Seidler (1994), this study highlights the importance of relationships and the emotions as being the crux of understanding these men's worlds. This study also highlights the particular problem masculinity poses for these men's enjoyment of living, as it entails the masking and camouflage of a whole range of men's emotions through sustaining the 'front'.

This relationship between masculinity and the holding back of emotions is also sustained in a different form in social institutions. Again Vic Seidler (1994) has analysed the reification of the 'rational', which also entails a systematic denial of the world of the emotions due to the influence of a scientific method that denigrates this emotional world.

> Part of this belief is reflected in traditions of social theory that are less tolerant of the "subjective" or the "personal". They see their task in discerning a rational order out of this emotional disorder. This is integral to the rationalist quest. It is for men to be the guardians of reason and objectivity and so to refuse to be drawn into the unbounded and the chaotic that, like the feminine, can so easily overwhelm. Social theory and philosophy has to stay within the limits of reason, learning to stay within the province of what clearly can be said. (Seidler 1994, p. 202)

This denigration had practical consequences for these men, specifically emerging in the way they were treated by institutions.

This lack of analysis of feelings and emotions and the belief in the rational also has real effects in current social planning. For example, these research findings raise important questions for the current health and educational strategies in Deptford concerning substance misuse. These strategies have been undertaken with minimal research into the emotional states of the subjects, framing the problem as a health issue with the emphasis on finding a cure, rather than seeing it as one of embedded local culture.

In education, the problem has been framed as one of instruction rather than looking at the feelings and emotions that lead to drug use. This leads me to conclude that many of the educational initiatives undertaken in schools which ignores the emotional worlds of the young people will fail. Drug misuse is not just a risk taking behaviour (Giddens 1991) but in its chronic form a method of 'self medication' for trauma. The local schools have neglected to provide the appropriate pastoral support for their pupils, instead relying on the various disciplinarian methods to provide correction. As I have been informed by clients *"nothing the school threw at me was as hard as what the old man would do"*. School punishment was never as severe as that which these men received at home.

This inability to conceptualise the role of drugs in young peoples lives and an understanding of the role of emotions leads to a form of discourse that emphasises the irrationality of drug use derived from a higher moral plane, the realm of an 'unemotional' parent patiently narrating what is right and wrong without asking why.

It is my conclusion that chronic drug misuse is intrinsically rooted and cannot be divorced and solved without understanding the underlying emotional issues discussed in this research. Merely to take the drug problem away, without reflecting on why it has occurred, will not solve the problems these men face. The whiplash of emotions accompanying the 'fragmentation' of identity implies a return, as Damien describes himself wrestling through exerting his willpower to cease his drug use. However, his 'unmasking' and 'fragmentation' leads to his terror at not being able to emotionally connect, the fear of being vulnerable. His remedy is to revisit what he knows will take away his hurt – drugs. They will suppress his emotional pain at his inability to shed his habit and connect with his family.

Therefore, the current paradigms concerning the conceptualisation of drug misuse find it challenging to penetrate beyond the 'fronts' of these men, as they have no notion of masculine 'front' or 'resistance'. As an example, the report "The Health of Lewisham 2001, Everybody's Business" stated, "Lewisham men are four times more likely to commit suicide than women are (14.8:3.0). Men are more likely to use violent methods to kill themselves; women have much higher rates for deliberate self harm, not resulting in death". (Holdsworth et al. 2002, p. 30). In terms of drug misuse, the same report detailed Lewisham had one of the highest episode rates in London, 715 per 100,000 people. (Holdsworth et al. 2002, p. 51). The report also highlights the percentage of people currently in treatment: "74 per cent of drug users being white" (Holdsworth et al. 2002, p. 51).The report also states: "the data showed a strong link between drug misuse and unemployment" (Holdsworth et al. 2002, p. 51).

Although there is significant data highlighting the problems for men, there has been little further analysis, with ideology playing a central role in the interpretation of the statistics. This inability to consider the issue of 'masculinity', 'fronts', 'masks' and 'fragmentation' reveals that the underlying factors driving the substance misuse and violence are lost. Two sets of statistics, unemployment and drug use, are placed together and conclusions are drawn. On a micro level, whilst the men in this study do not work, their fathers did, but the money they earned was spent on alcohol. The problems in the 2001 study become reduced to employment, with the intrinsic idea that white unemployed men turn to substances to cope with their lack of work. However, this study shows a deeper embedded problem: what these men esteem and value in their lives, their feelings of emotional lack, connect with their drug use. All of these men lost their jobs because they had no sense of confidence or permanence in their lives, which was caused by their sense of shame, leading them to devalue themselves and everyone around them.

The layers of statistical interpretation leave no room to analyse the micro acts and the cultural processes taking place in the community. It does not make connections to these men. With no notion of trust building, the silence around personal pain remains intact.

The fundamental problem is a lack of theoretical conceptualisation around the idea that these men have emotional worlds to begin with. This indicates a wider issue for social science research. As Vic Seidler (1994) illustrates, the intrinsic problem in the social sciences in wanting to understand the problems through rationality is that it precludes the study of the emotions, and the vital role they play within men's lives. Nietzsche first formulated this problem in 1872, recognising the inherent challenges in this form of analysis.

> It does not inquire after the motives of an action, as if these had been present in consciousness before the action: but it first breaks up the group into mechanistic phenomena and seeks the previous history of the mechanistic motion - but it does not seek it in feeling, sensation, thinking. It can never take the explanation from this quarter; sensation in precisely the material to be explained. It's problem is: to explain the world without taking sensations as causes: for that would mean; considering sensations as the cause of sensations. Its task is certainly not accomplished. (Nietzsche 1968, p. 352)

The difficulty for social research is in connecting to these sensations. One of the key issues emerging from this research has been how these local men have colluded with this process, as they do not wish to appear weak through exposing their inner worlds, thoughts, feelings and sensations. Consequently, they have been ignored. For these working class men, this 'front' is all they have to hold on to. This leads to their lives remaining largely invisible in local research studies, except as statistics for alcoholism, drug misuse, heart attacks and cancer.

> Men in Lewisham tend to die more frequently (compared to E&W males) from all cancers (particularly lung cancer), respiratory diseases, suicide or as a result of homicide or an injury of undetermined source (undetermined injuries). (Holdsworth et al. 2002, p. 11)

One of the unexplored avenues in this research is the relationship between the holding of stress and its relationship to illness, explored, for example, in Reich's "Cancer Biopathy" (1948) and Sharaf (1983). See also Gerda Boyesen (1976) in the "Methodology" chapter, describing the relationship between the body's internal processes and illness. Gary's father, for example, died of cancer. It was clear from Gary's account his 'masking' of memories created a chronic stress. The other Deptford fathers had unremitting anxieties, masked by their alcohol and tobacco consumption. This highlights the need for further research analysing the relationship between masculinity, emotions and illness.

As for the positive aspects of this study, I have shown how the counselling and relational research methods draw on similar positions in creating an emotional understanding of these men's lives. Within this process, Terkel's (1982) methodology of creating a "jazz work" also applies to my research method. I did not know what was going to emerge in the sessions before I taped them. I did not know whether the men would talk and be open. The use of the tape recorder shifted the dynamics of the counselling process significantly and allowed me to create a breakthrough in working with them, as they felt they were genuinely being heard. The key process was creating trust, and thereby calling forth the hidden worlds.

This process also had another key aim in trying to heal the past through the recollection of memories that had been masked. I t was necessary to try to understand the past by shifting the feelings of shame through the process of talking and being listened to without being judged. This was a new form of social interaction for these men; it entailed a flow of emotions. It was a subjective process taking place between the men who took part in the research as I followed their flows of emotions by using empathy. This is crucial for understanding this form of the relational method.

In terms of the verification of my findings, one of my key aims in writing up this study was to look for truth in the form of an emotional resonance with the reader, to unfold the layers of rationality, to connect, and also to provide an emotional meaning. This stems from my excitement at discovering Willis's "Learning to Labour" (1978) and Terkel's "American Dreams" (1982) and making my own emotional connections to the texts.

In working with other ethnic groups, my conclusions are that similar masculine strategies are embedded in other cultural frameworks, where painful memories that men and women hold inside as a silence, given the appropriate environment, can flow. The discussions we had in groups of White, Afro-Caribbean, Somali and Vietnamese men and women highlighted the fact that the holding of emotions by men is a transcultural phenomenon requiring further research into how these flows have been channelled.

It is clear that the forms of trauma differ significantly, due to the impact of migration, cultural clashes, the inability to communicate and understand the host culture, the impact of racism and the forms of Post-traumatic Stress Disorder these men and women carry within them, but there are also intersections concerning the need to sustain 'fronts' and 'mask' the past because of painful memories. The pre-existing white Deptford culture these men and women have moved into offers one form of solution to these problems that connects back to why our agency now finds over half of its clients come from these different groups. The task is to understand the forms of 'resistance' these men have created to sustain their 'fronts' and 'mask' the past as well as the problems associated with 'fragmentation'.

BIBLIOGRAPHY

Abdulrahmin, D., Annan, J., Cyster, R., Perera, A., Drummond, C., Hackland, F., Lavoie, D., Marsden, J., Porter, S., & Strang, J. 2002 *Models of Care* London: National Treatment Agency.

Arthur, M. 2002. *Forgotten Voices*. London: Ebury Press.

Back, L. 1996. *New Ethnicities and Urban Culture: racisms and multiculture in young lives.* London: UCL Press.

Ball & Ross 1991. *The effectiveness of Methadone Maintenance Treatment; Patients Programs Services and Outcome.* New York: Springer Verlag.

Banks & Waller, T. 1988. *Drug Misuse*; Oxford: Blackwell Scientific Publications.

Beal, A., & Sternberg, R. 1993. *The Psychology of Gender* New York: Guildford Press.

Bepko, C. (ed.) 1991. *Feminism and Addiction.* New York: Haworth Press.

Bettelheim, B. 1986, first published 1960. *The Informed Heart.* London: Penguin.

Boadella (ed.) 1991, first published 1976. *In the Wake of Reich.* Boston, MA: Coventure.

Bowlby, J. 1998, first pub 1973. *Attachment and Loss.* London: Pimlico.

Boyesen, G. in Boadella (ed.) 1991, first published 1976. *In The Wake of Reich* Boston MA: Coventure.

Brehm and Khantzian 1992. *A Psychodynamic Perspective in substance Abuse: A Comprehensive Textbook.* Williams and Wilkins.

Buford, B. 1991. *Among the Thugs.* London: Secker and Warburg.

Burkitt, I. 1991. *Social Selves.* London: Sage.

Calsyn, D.A., Saxon, A.J., Blaes, P., & Lee-Meyer, S. 1990. "Staffing Patterns of American Methadone Maintenance Programs", *Journal of Substance Abuse Treatment*, 4, 255-259.

Cannetti, E. 1973, first published 1960. *Crowds and Power.* London: Penguin.

Chodorow, N. 1984, first published 1978. *The Reproduction of Mothering.* California Press.

Clare, A. 2000. *On Men Masculinity in Crisis.* London: Random House.

Connell, R. 1995. *Masculinities.* Cambridge: Polity Press.

Coombs, R. 1988. *The Family Context of Adolescent Drug Use.* Binghamton, NY: Haworth Press.

Dawe, S., Griffiths, P., Gossop, M., and Strang, J.J. 1991. "Should opiate addicts be involved in controlling their own detoxification?" *British Journal of Addiction*, Vol. 86, p. 977.

De Zulueta 1996, first published 1993. *From Pain to Violence*. London: Whurr Publishers.

Deleuze and Guattari 1992, first published 1972, trans 1977. *Anti Oedipus*.Minneapolis: Minnesota Press.

Deleuze and Guattari 1999, first published 1980. *A Thousand Plateaus*. London: The Athlone Press.

Dole, V.P. and Nyswander, M. 1967. "Heroin Addiction - a metabolic disease", *Archives of internal Medicine,* 120, p. 19-24.

Dorn, N., & South, N. 1985. *Helping Drug Users*. Aldershot: Gower.

Finkelhor, D., and Yllo, K. 1985. *License to Rape. Sexual Abuse of Wives*. New York: Free Press.

Foucault, M. 1991, first published 1977. *Discipline and Punish*. London: Penguin.

Freud, S. 1984, first published 1910. *Two Short Accounts of Psychoanalysis*. London: Penguin.

Freud, S. 1979, first published 1926. *On Psychopathology*. London: Penguin.

Giddens, A. 1996, first published 1991. *Modernity and Self Identity*. Cambridge: Polity Press.

Giddens, A. 1992. *The Transformation of Intimacy, Sexuality, Love and Eroticism in Modern Societies.* Cambridge: Polity.

Gilligan, C., Lyons, P., Hanmer, T. 1990. *Making Connections.* Cambridge, MA: Harvard University Press.

Gilligan, C., Ward, J., Taylor, J. 1988. *Mapping the Moral Domain.* Cambridge, MA: Harvard University Press.

Gilligan, J. 2000. *Violence-Reflections on our Deadliest Epidemic.* London: JKP.

Goffman, E. 1990, first published 1959. *The Presentation of Self in everyday Life.* London: Penguin.

Hammersley, R., and Morrison, V. 1987. "Effects of polydrug use on the criminal activities of heroin users". *British Journal of Addiction,*Vol 82, p. 899.

Heinl, P. 2001. *Splintered Innocence.* East Sussex: Brunner Routledge.

Hewitt, R. 1986. *Comparative Ethnic and Race Relations Series. White Talk Black Talk: Inter racial friendship and communication amongst adolescents.* Cambridge: Cambridge University Press.

HMSO 1998. *Tackling Drugs to Build a Better Britain.* CM 3945, London: HMSO Stationers.

Hocquenghem, G. 1993, first published 1972. *Homosexual Desire*. Durham and London: Duke University Press.

Holdsworth, G., Lindo, J., Rowe, J., Hetherington, K. 2002. *Everybody's Business: The Health of Lewisham 2001*. LSL Health Authority.

Joe, G.W., Simpson, D.D., & Hubbard R.L. 1991. Treatment predictors of tenure in methadone maintenance. *Journal of Substance Abuse*, 3, 73-84.

Kaufman, E., and Blaine, G.B. 1974. "Full services in methadone treatment", *American Journal of Drug and Alcohol Abuse,* 1, 213-231.

Khantzian, E. 1974. "Opiate addiction: A critique of theory and some implications for treatment". *American Journal of Psychotherapy,* 28, pp. 59-74.

Khantzian, E. 1985. "The self medication hypothesis of addictive disorders", *American Journal of Psychotherapy*, 142, 1259-1264.

Khantzian "Psychotherapy and Substance Abuse" in Washton (ed.) 1995. New York: The Guildford Press.

Laing, R.D. 1990 first published 1960. *The Divided Self.* London: Penguin.

Laing, R.D. 1990 first published 1961. *Self and Others.* London: Penguin.

Lawrence, D.H. 1995 first published 1913. *Sons and Lovers*. London: Penguin.

Lockley, P. 1995. *Counselling Heroin and Other Drug Users*. London: Free Association.

Longwell, B., Miller, J. & Nicholls, A.W. 1978. "Counsellor effectiveness in a methadone maintenance program". *International Journal of Addictions*, 13, pp. 307-315.

Mac an Ghaill. 1994. *The Making of Men: Masculinities, Sexualities and Schooling*. Milton Keynes: Open University Press.

Macintyre. 1991. "Feminism and Addiction", in Bepko (ed) Binghamton, NY: Haworth Press.

Meth and Pasick 1990. *Men in Therapy*. New York: Guildford Press.

Miller, A. 1994, first published 1987. *For Your Own Good*. London: Virago.

Miller, A. 1999. *Paths of Life*. London: Virago.

Newburn, T., & Stanko, E. 1994. *Just Boys Doing Business*. London: Routledge.

Nietzsche, F. republished 1994. *Human, All Too Human*. London: Penguin.

Nietzsche, F. 1968. *The Will To Power*. Kaufman ed., New York: Vintage Press.

Nowell-Smith, G., 1999. Oedipus Rex. Dir. Pasolini, P. Tartan Video, Insert Notes.

Oldman, G., 1998. Nil By Mouth, VHS Video

Oppenheimer, E., Sheehan, M., and Taylor, C. 1988. Letting the clients speak: Drug misusers and the process of help seeking. *British Journal of Addiction*, Vol 83, p. 635.

Pearce, J., and Pezzot-Pearce, T. 1997. *Psychotherapy of Abused and Neglected Children.* New York: Guildford Press.

Pearson, G., & Gilman, M. 1987. *Young People and Heroin.* London: Gower publications and HEA.

Potter-Effron. 1991. *"Anger, Alcoholism and Addiction.* Norton.

Ramer, B.S., Zaslove, M.O., & Langan, J. 1971. "Is methadone enough? The use of ancillary treatment during methadone maintenance". *American Journal of Psychiatry,* 127, pp. 80-84.

Rawson, R. 1995. "Psychotherapy and Substance Abuse", in Washton (ed.) New York: The Guildford Press.

Reich ,W. 1991, first published 1946. *The Mass Psychology of Fascism.* Farrar Strauss and Giroux, USA.

Reich, W. 1993, first published 1942. *The Function of the Orgasm.* The Guernsey Press Co.

Reich, W. 1993, first published 1948. *The Cancer Biopathy.* The Guernsey Press Company.

Renner, J.A. 1984. "Methadone Maintenance: Past, Present and Future". *Addictive Behaviours*, 3, pp. 75-90.

Rogers, C.R. 1957. "The necessary and sufficient conditions of therapeutic personality change", *Journal of Counselling*, 21, pp. 95-103.

Rogers, C.R. 1967. *On Becoming a Person*. London: Constable.

Sassoon, S. 1972. *The Complete Memoirs of George Sherston*. London: Faber and Faber.

Seidler, V. 1991, first published 1989. *Rediscovering Masculinity*. London: Routledge.

Seidler, V. 1993. *Men Sex and Relationships*. London: Routledge.

Seidler, V. 1994. *Rediscovering the Self.* London: Routledge.

Seidler, V. 1994. *Unreasonable Men*. London: Routledge.

Sennet and Cobb. 1993. *The Hidden Injuries of Class*. London: Faber and Faber.

Sereny, G. *Into That Darkness* 1995, first published 1974. London: Pimlico.

Sereny, G. 1996, first published 1995. *Albert Speer: His Battle With Truth*. London: Picador.

Sereny, G. 1998. *Cries Unheard, The Story of Mary Bell.* London: Macmillan.

Sharaf, M. 1994. *Fury on Earth.* New York: Da Capo Press.

Sim, J. 1994. "Tougher than the Rest", In T. Newburn and E. Stanko (eds) *Just Boys Doing Business.* London: Routledge.

Spalding, N. 1994. "Cop Canteen Culture", In T. Newburn and E. Stanko (eds) *Boys Doing Business.* London: Routledge.

Steele, J. 1993. *Turning the Tide: Deptford.* London: Deptford Forum Publishing.

Steinglas, P., Bennet, L., Wohlin, S., & Reiss, D. 1987. *The Alcoholic Family.* New York: Basic Books.

Stimson, G.V. 1990. "Aids and HIV: The Challenge for British Drug Services", *British Journal of Addiction,* 85, pp. 1263-1277.

Thewelait, K. 1996, first published 1977. *Male Fantasies Volume 1.* Cambridge: Polity Press.

Thewelait K, 1996, first published 1978. *Male Fantasies Volume 2.* Cambridge: Polity Press.

Trondman, M. and Willis, P. 2001, *Ethnographic Manifesto.* Cambridge: Cambridge University Press

Van der Kolk, B.A, and Van der Hart, O. 1989. "Pierre Janet and the breakdown of adaptation in psychological trauma". *American Journal of Psychiatry,* 146, pp. 1530-1540.

Ward, Mattick and Hall. 1992. *Key Issues in Methadone Maintenance Treatment.* Kensington, NSW: New South Wales University Press Ltd.

Washton, A., (ed.) 1995. *Psychotherapy and Substance Abuse.* New York: Guildford Press.

Wicks, B. 1988. *Not Time to Wave Goodbye.* London: Bloomsbury.

Wieder, H., Kaplan, E. 1969. *Drug use in adolescents: Psychodynamic meaning and pharmacogenic effect.* Psychoanalysis Study of Children.

Wild, J. (ed.) 1999. *Working with Men for Change.* UCL Press.

Willis, P. 2000 first published 1978. *Learning to Labour: How working class kids get working class jobs.* Aldershot: Ashgate Publishing, Ltd.

Winnicott, D., 1995, first published 1965. *The Family and Individual Development.* London: Routledge.

Winnicott, D. 1957. *The Child, the Family and the Outside World.* London: Penguin.

Winnicott, D. 1971. *Playing and Reality.* London: Tavistock.

Wolfe-Light 1999. "Men, Violence and Love," In J. Wild (ed) *Working with men for Change*. UCL Press.

Woolfe and Dryden 1996. *Handbook of Counselling Psychology*. London: Sage.

Woody, G.E., Luborsky, L., McLellan, A.T., & O'Brien, C.P. 1986. "Psychotherapy as an adjunct to methadone treatment", In R.E. Meyer (ed) *Psychopathology and Addictive Disorders*. USA: Guildford Press.

Woody, G.E., Luborsky, L., McLellan, A.T., O'Brien, C.P., Beck, A.T., Blaine, J., Hermann, I., & Hole, A. 1983. "Psychotherapy for opiate addicts. Does it help?" *Archives of General Psychiatry*, 40, pp. 639-645.

Woody, G.E., McLellan, A.T., Luborsky, L., & O'Brien, C.P. 1987. "Twelve month follow up of psychotherapy for opiate dependence". *American Journal of Psychiatry*, 144, pp. 590-596.

Yalom, I. 1980. *Existential Psychotherapy*. USA: Basic Books.

Yalom, I. 1989. *Loves Executioner*. London: Bloomsbury.

Yancovitz, S.R., Des Jarlais, D.C., Peyser, N.P., Drew, E., Freidman, P., Trigg, H.L., & Robinson, J.W. 1991. "A randomised trial of an interim methadone maintenance clinic", *American Journal of Public Health*, 81, pp. 1185-1191.

Zweben, J.E. 1986. "Recovery orientated psychotherapy", *Journal of Substance Abuse Treatment*, 3, pp. 255-262.

Zweben, J.E. 1991. "Counselling issues in methadone maintenance treatment", *Journal of Psychoactive Drugs*, 23, pp. 171-190.

Printed in the United Kingdom
by Lightning Source UK Ltd.
126253UK00001B/64/A